I0459180

Dementia Caregiver's Toolkit

Trusted Guidance and Emotional Support for Families Facing the Challenge of Alzheimer's and Other Dementias

Ben Clardy

Contents

Dementia Caregiving Companion

Dear Caregiver

Dementia Caregiving Companion

How To Provide Comprehensive Care At Home For Alzheimer's Disease And Other Dementias - Includes The Caregiver Self-Care Guide

This book is dedicated to the countless caregivers who, with unwavering love and extraordinary courage, navigate the challenging journey of dementia care. May this book serve as a source of guidance, support, & reassurance, reminding you that your efforts are deeply valued — and that you are never alone on this journey.

Ben Clark

Introduction

"I'm afraid the tests confirm a diagnosis of dementia."

The doctor's words landed like a stone in still water. The future you had imagined—for yourself, for your loved one—suddenly seemed to evaporate.

It was at this moment that you became a caregiver.

It's a position you likely never anticipated or prepared for. The shock of the diagnosis may leave you reeling, grappling with a whirlwind of emotions: disbelief, anger, sorrow, and perhaps even a touch of relief at finally having an explanation for the changes you've noticed.

As the weight of this new reality settles on your shoulders, you may feel overwhelmed by the magnitude of what's to come. Are you ready for this? Can you handle the responsibilities that lie ahead?

Take a deep breath. You don't have to have all the answers right now. This book is your guide, starting from the aftermath of diagnosis, and leading you through the winding path of dementia care that lies ahead by providing you with:

Comprehensive Knowledge: From understanding the different types of dementia to managing daily care challenges, this book provides a thorough education on every aspect of at-home dementia caregiving.

Practical Strategies: Concrete, tested strategies for handling everything from communication difficulties to safety concerns, giving you the tools to tackle each day with confidence.

Introduction

Emotional Support: Through shared experiences and insights, this book validates your feelings and challenges, reminding you that you're not alone in this journey. It offers comfort during tough times and celebrates the small victories with you.

Self-Care Guidance: Caregiver burnout is a natural and serious concern. This book emphasizes the importance of your well-being, providing actionable advice on how to care for yourself while caring for others. It's not selfish—it's essential for sustainable caregiving.

Decision-Making Tools: You'll face countless decisions, some of them potentially heart-wrenching. This book equips you with frameworks and considerations to help you make choices that align with your loved one's wishes and values.

Hope and Inspiration: While acknowledging the challenges, this book also illuminates the profound moments of connection, growth, and love that caregiving can bring. It helps you find meaning and purpose in your role.

Anticipatory Guidance: By outlining the progression of dementia, this book helps you prepare for future challenges, reducing anxiety and allowing you to plan proactively.

Resource Navigation: The world of dementia care involves a complex network of medical, legal, and social services. This book helps you understand and access the resources available to you and your loved one.

Long-Term Perspective: While focusing on immediate needs, this book also helps you plan for the long term, including legal and financial considerations that are crucial for your loved one's security and care.

By turning to this book, you're equipping yourself with the knowledge, skills, and emotional resilience needed for this challenging yet profoundly meaningful role. As you face the daily trials and triumphs of caregiving, let this book be your reference, your source of strength, and a constant reminder that you can not only manage this journey but also find innumerable opportunities for joy and growth along the way.

Each chapter opens with a vignette from the lives of a caregiver named Maria and her mother, Evie. Together, they navigate the challenges and triumphs of living with dementia, much like you will with your loved one. These brief, intimate glimpses into their daily experiences serve as a touchstone, connecting the practical advice in each chapter to the real-world complexities of caregiving. Their narrative not only illustrates the concepts discussed in each chapter but also serves to ground the book's practical advice in the messy, complex, and bitter-sweet reality of caring for a loved one with dementia.

Remember, every experienced caregiver once stood where you stand now—perhaps feeling just as unprepared. With each passing day and each new challenge faced and overcome, you'll discover reserves of patience, love, and capability you never knew you possessed.

Let's begin.

Chapter 1
First Steps After Diagnosis

The clock on Dr. Patel's desk ticked loudly in the silence that followed his words.

Maria's eyes immediately welled with tears. She turned to her mother, Evangeline—known by her friends as Evie, expecting to see fear, shock, or sadness in her face. Instead, she found a wry smile.

"Well," Evie said, her voice steady, "I suppose that explains why I've been trying to unlock the front door with the TV remote."

"Mom," Maria whispered, her voice choked with emotion. "This isn't funny."

Evie reached over and grasped her daughter's trembling hand. "Oh, sweetie. If we can't laugh, we'll drown in tears. And you know how I hate the way my eyes get all puffy."

Dr. Patel leaned forward, his expression kind but serious. "Mrs. Thompson, do you understand the implications of this diagnosis?"

"I understand that my daughter is about to turn our house into Fort Knox and probably bubble-wrap me," Evie replied, throwing a fond glance at Maria.

Maria straightened in her chair, already making mental lists. "We need to discuss treatment options, lifestyle changes, legal matters, future care plans…"

As Maria's voice faded into a buzz of medical terms and planning, Evie gazed out the window. She understood the implications. Somehow, despite the world looking precisely the same as when she walked into the Doctor's office, everything was suddenly different.

A dementia diagnosis brings with it a whirlwind of emotions and questions. In these early days, it's normal to feel overwhelmed, scared, and uncertain about the future. This chapter is designed to guide you through the crucial first steps in your new role as a caregiver, providing a roadmap for the days and weeks following diagnosis.

Processing Emotions

The first and perhaps most crucial step is to allow yourself and your loved one time to process this life-changing news. It's normal to experience a range of feelings, including shock, denial, anger, and sadness. Permit yourself to feel these emotions without judgment. This is a significant life change, and it's okay to grieve for the future you had imagined.

You might find yourself cycling through these emotions rapidly, or lingering in one state for an extended period. There's no "right" way to feel. Some caregivers report feeling a sense of relief at finally having an explanation for the changes they've noticed in their loved one. Others describe feeling numb or disconnected from reality for a time. All of these reactions are valid and common.

During this time, don't isolate yourself. Reach out to trusted friends or family members for support. Their presence and understanding can be invaluable as you navigate these choppy emotional waters. Sometimes, just having someone to listen to you without trying to "fix" things can be incredibly comforting. If you're comfortable doing so, share your fears and concerns. Allow others to support you emotionally and practically.

If you find yourself struggling to cope, consider seeking help from a therapist or counselor experienced in grief counseling. They can provide strategies to help you manage the complex emotions you're experiencing. Many caregivers find that professional support helps them process their feelings more effectively and develop coping mechanisms for the journey ahead.

Remember to be patient with your loved one as well. They may react to the diagnosis with denial, anger, or depression. Offer reassurance and be prepared to have multiple conversations as they come to terms with the news. Everyone processes difficult information differently, and it may take time for both of you to fully accept this new reality. Your loved one might have days where they seem to have forgotten about the diagnosis, followed by periods of acute awareness and distress. This fluctuation is normal and can be challenging for caregivers to navigate.

Understanding the Diagnosis

As you begin to come to terms with the diagnosis, it's essential to arm yourself with knowledge. Understanding what you're facing can help reduce anxiety and prepare you for the journey ahead. Start by learning about the specific type of dementia your loved one has been diagnosed with. There's more information on this in the next chapter. Whether it's Alzheimer's disease, vascular dementia, Lewy body dementia, or another form, each type has its characteristics and progression.

While everyone's journey with dementia is unique, having a general idea of what the next few months might bring can help you prepare. Research the typical symptoms and challenges associated with your loved one's diagnosis. This knowledge can help you anticipate needs and make proactive decisions about care and support. For instance, if your loved one has been diagnosed with Lewy body dementia, which often includes visual hallucinations as a symptom, you can prepare strategies for managing these specific symptoms when they occur.

As questions arise, jot them down to discuss with your loved one's doctor at the next appointment. Key areas to cover include:

- The current stage of the disease
- Treatment options
- Lifestyle changes that could potentially slow progression
- The specific tests used to make the diagnosis and if any further testing is needed
- How quickly the disease is likely to progress
- Any clinical trials or research studies that might be appropriate
- Recommendations for local support services or memory clinics

Don't hesitate to ask for clarification on medical terms or treatment plans you don't understand. Your role as an advocate for your loved one begins now, and being well-informed is crucial.

NOTE: It's okay to seek a second opinion if you feel uncertain about the diagnosis or treatment plan. False diagnosis of dementia does happen, so many families find this helps them feel more confident moving forward.

Essential Communication

Clear, compassionate communication is crucial in these early days after diagnosis. When discussing the diagnosis with your loved one, be honest but compassionate. Follow their lead in terms of how much they want to discuss. Some days, they may want to talk about the future, while other days, they may prefer to focus on the present.

When talking about the diagnosis and its implications, choose your moments carefully. Pick times when your loved one is typically at their best. Use simple, clear language and be prepared to repeat information as needed. Validate their feelings and offer reassurance. It's okay to say "I don't know" if you're asked questions you can't answer - honesty builds trust.

Prepare yourself for a range of reactions when sharing the news with family members. Some may be in denial, while others may want to help immediately. Be patient and allow everyone time to process the information. You might need to educate family members about dementia and its progression. Share resources you've found helpful and encourage them to learn more.

When it comes to friends, let your loved one guide how widely they want to share the news. Some people may prefer to keep the diagnosis private initially, while others might want to inform their wider social circle. Respect their wishes, but also gently explain the potential benefits of letting close friends know, such as increased understanding and support.

As you navigate these conversations, remember that communication is a two-way street. Listen actively to your loved one's concerns and wishes. They may have specific fears about the future or preferences for their care that are important to acknowledge and address.

Essential Organizational Tools

As you embark on this caregiving journey, two tools will become invaluable: a *caregiver's journal* and a *patient care binder*. Each serves a distinct purpose, and together, they will help you stay organized and provide the best care possible.

The Caregiver's Journal

Your caregiver's journal is a personal tool, primarily for your own use as a caregiver. This humble companion will become an outlet for your thoughts and emotions, and a record of your caregiving journey.

Start by dedicating a notebook or setting up a digital document specifically for this purpose. Use your journal to:

1. Pour out your heart on difficult days
2. Celebrate personal victories, no matter how small
3. Explore your emotions about caregiving
4. Reflect on how this journey is changing you
5. Dream about your future and set personal goals
6. Record moments of joy or humor amidst the challenges
7. Write letters to yourself, your loved one, or others
8. Create lists of self-care ideas and gratitude

Journaling can be a powerful tool for self-discovery and stress relief. Over time, you may notice patterns in your emotions or identify areas where you need more support. Your journal can help you advocate for your own needs and maintain your identity beyond your caregiver role.

Make journaling a regular part of your self-care routine. Even five minutes a day can make a difference. Your journal is always there, ready to listen without judgment and help you process this complex, emotional journey. Beyond its practical uses, your journal can be a place for emotional release. Over time, it may become a testament to your journey, reflecting both the challenges you've faced and the strength you've discovered within yourself.

Remember, there's no "right" way to keep your caregiver's journal. Whether you prefer bullet points, narrative entries, or a combination of both, the most important thing is that it works for you. Make it a habit to update it regularly, and keep it easily accessible.

The Patient Care Binder

While your journal is for your personal use, the patient care binder is a comprehensive resource for managing your loved one's care. This binder should be easily accessible so that you or other caregivers can access it. A large, 3-ring binder that zips closed often works well for this purpose.

Create a binder with the following sections:

1. **_Medical Information_**: Include a list of current medications with dosages and schedules, allergies, and a summary of medical conditions.
2. **_Medical Passport_**: A one-page summary of your loved one's medical history, current conditions, medications, and emergency contacts.
3. **_Healthcare Providers_**: Contact information for all doctors, specialists, and other healthcare providers involved in your loved one's care.
4. **_Appointment Records_**: Notes from doctor visits, including instructions and follow-up appointments.
5. **_Test Results_**: Copies of recent lab work, scans, or other medical tests.
6. **_Legal Documents_**: Copies of important papers like Power of Attorney, advance directives, and insurance information.
7. **_Daily Care Plan_**: A schedule of daily routines, including medication times, meal preferences, and favorite activities.
8. **_Emergency Information_**: Clear instructions for what to do in case of an emergency, including important phone numbers and any specific medical needs.
9. **_Support Network Contacts_**: This will include the names and phone numbers of various people who may be able to assist or support your efforts when needed.

The patient care binder serves multiple purposes. It helps ensure continuity of care, especially if multiple caregivers are involved. It's an invaluable resource during medical appointments, allowing you to reference important information quickly. In emergencies, it provides critical information to healthcare providers.

Update the binder regularly, especially after medical appointments or when there are changes in medication or care plans. Consider creating both a physical binder and a digital version for backup and easy sharing with other caregivers or healthcare providers when necessary.

By utilizing both a personal caregiver's journal and a comprehensive patient care binder, you'll be well-equipped to manage the complex task of caregiving while also taking care of your own needs. These tools will help you stay organized, communicate effectively with healthcare providers, and navigate the caregiving journey with greater confidence.

Immediate Practical Steps

Taking action can help you feel more in control and ensure you're prepared for what lies ahead. One of the most productive tasks to complete is to assemble your patient care binder, as this will be an asset for you throughout this journey. Start by organizing all medical information. Keep a comprehensive list of all current medications, including dosages and schedules. Note down contact information for all healthcare providers involved in your loved one's care. Having this information readily accessible will prove invaluable as you coordinate care and communicate with medical professionals.

Ensure your loved one has designated someone to make decisions on their behalf when they're no longer able to through a *durable power of attorney*. This is the most critical and over-arching legal form that you will require at this point. We'll go into greater detail concerning other legal matters in a future chapter. As a priority for now, ensure that this one crucial document is produced, properly executed, and on hand.

Conduct a basic home safety assessment as soon as possible. Look for potential hazards like loose rugs, poor lighting, or bookcases that can be pulled over. These small changes can significantly reduce the risk of falls and accidents, helping your loved one maintain independence for as long as possible. While your loved one may not need extensive safety modifications now, planning ahead and becoming more aware of this need can make future transitions easier.

Building Your Support Network

Caring for someone with dementia is not a solo journey. Start building your support system now. Make a list of family members and friends who can assist with care, run errands, or simply provide emotional support. Be specific about ways they can help – many people want to offer support but may not know how. Perhaps a neighbor could mow the lawn, or a friend could sit with your loved one for an hour while you attend to personal errands.

Research local resources available to you. The Alzheimer's Association or similar organizations in your area can be a wealth of information and support. Look into local support groups for caregivers, adult day care centers, and respite care services. These resources can provide valuable assistance and give you much-needed breaks from caregiving duties.

Connecting with other caregivers, either through local support groups or online forums, can provide invaluable advice and emotional support. These individuals genuinely understand the challenges you're facing and can offer practical tips based on their own experiences. Many caregivers find that these connections become a lifeline, offering understanding and companionship in what can sometimes feel like an isolating journey.

Caregiver Self-Care

As you embark on this caregiving journey, remember that your well-being is equally important to that of your loved one – *if not more so*. You cannot provide effective care if you're depleted. If you're self-care suffers, so will the care of your loved one. While we'll dive deeper into specific strategies for caregiver self-care in later chapters, it's crucial to establish this mindset from the start.

The dangers of neglecting self-care are real and serious. Caregivers who overwork themselves face high risks of stress-related illnesses, depression, and burnout. These aren't just temporary discomforts; they can lead to long-term problems concerning your health and relationships.

Prioritize your physical and mental health. Keep up with your own medical appointments, maintain a healthy diet, and find ways to incorporate exercise into your routine. Practice stress management techniques like deep breathing or meditation, even if it's just for a few minutes each day.

Set realistic expectations and be kind to yourself. It's normal to make mistakes and feel frustrated at times. Take regular breaks, no matter how short, to prevent burnout. This might mean asking for help from family members or exploring respite care services.

Caregiver's Corner

Remember, your journey as a caregiver is an act of profound love. Every step you take, no matter how small, makes a difference in your loved one's life.

Key Takeaways:

1. Allow time for emotional processing after a dementia diagnosis
2. Educate yourself about the specific type of dementia diagnosed
3. Create essential organizational tools: a caregiver's journal and a patient care binder

4. Take immediate practical steps, including home safety assessment and legal preparations
5. Build a support network and prioritize caregiver self-care from the start

Quick Tip: Start your caregiver's journal today. Even jotting down a few thoughts or feelings can help you process this new chapter in your life.

Reflection Question: What is one small, achievable self-care activity you can commit to doing for yourself this week?

Resource Spotlight: Contact your local Alzheimer's Association chapter. They offer valuable resources, support groups, and information tailored to your area.

Chapter 2
The Many Forms Of Dementia

Maria spread a rainbow of sticky notes across the kitchen table, each inscribed in her neat handwriting. "Alzheimer's is blue, vascular is pink, Lewy body is green..." she quietly muttered to herself as she arranged them.

Evie wandered in, eyebrows raised at the colorful chaos. "Well, if we're color-coding our problems now, I'd like to request polka dots."

"Mom," Maria sighed, "I'm trying to understand the different types of dementia. It's important."

"Oh? And here I thought you were planning the world's most depressing art project," Evie quipped, settling into a chair.

Maria frowned, "Can you take this seriously for once? This affects both of us."

"Honey, I am taking it seriously. I'm seriously considering whether I'd prefer to be a pink sticky note or maybe that nice light blue one," Evie said with a smirk.

"Mom!"

"What? If I'm going to be labeled, I at least want a color that compliments my complexion."

Maria took a deep breath, "The doctor thinks it's likely Alzheimer's, but—"

"Ah, blue it is then," Evie interrupted, plucking the blue note from the table and sticking it to her shirt like a name tag. "You know, this color really brings out my eyes."

As Maria began to explain the intricacies of each type of dementia, Evie held up a hand. "Honey," she said softly, "I appreciate all this research. But right now, I don't need a medical expert. I need my daughter."

The words hung in the air for a moment before Maria pushed aside her notes and reached for her mother's hand. In that simple gesture, both women understood that while knowledge was power, love and understanding would play an equally important role on the path ahead.

Understanding the specific type of dementia your loved one has been diagnosed with can help you better prepare for what lies ahead. It can guide your expectations about symptoms and progression, and also help dictate the care strategies you employ.

In this chapter, we will explore the most common types of dementia, their characteristics, and what they might mean for your caregiving approach. As we explore these different types of dementia, keep in mind that regardless of the specific diagnosis, your love, care, and support remain the most important factors in maintaining your loved one's quality of life.

Alzheimer's Disease

Alzheimer's disease is likely a term you've heard before—and with good reason. It's the most prevalent form of dementia, accounting for 60-80% of all cases.

Alzheimer's disease is characterized by the buildup of two types of protein in the brain: beta-amyloid, which forms plaques between neurons, and tau, which forms tangles inside neurons. These accumulations disrupt the brain's communication pathways, leading to the death of brain cells.

The hallmark symptom of Alzheimer's is memory loss, particularly difficulty in remembering recently learned information. As the disease progresses, symptoms worsen and may include:

- Disorientation to time and place
- Mood and behavior changes
- Deepening confusion about events, time and place
- Unfounded suspicions about family, friends and caregivers
- Difficulty speaking, swallowing and walking

Alzheimer's is typically a slowly progressing disease. On average, people with Alzheimer's live 8 to 10 years after diagnosis but can live as long as 20 years, depending on other factors. This gradual progression allows time for adaptation, both for the person with Alzheimer's and for you as a caregiver.

Vascular Dementia

Vascular dementia is the second most common type of dementia. If your loved one has been diagnosed with this type, it means that conditions affecting their blood vessels are reducing or blocking blood flow to parts of their brain. This can occur due to stroke, chronic high blood pressure, or other conditions that affect blood vessels and circulation.

Unlike Alzheimer's disease, which typically begins with memory loss, the symptoms of vascular dementia can vary widely, depending on which part of the brain is affected. However, common signs include:

- Problems with planning, judgment, and decision-making
- Difficulty focusing and slowed thinking
- Problems with organization
- Decline in ability to analyze a situation, develop an effective plan, and communicate that plan to others
- Depression and apathy

The progression of vascular dementia can be unpredictable. Symptoms may worsen gradually, or they may progress in a step-wise pattern, with sudden declines followed by periods of stability. This unpredictability can be challenging, but understanding it can help you be prepared for changes and adapt your care strategies accordingly.

Mixed Dementia

Mixed dementia occurs when a person has more than one type of dementia. The most common combination is Alzheimer's disease with vascular dementia, but other combinations are possible. If your loved one has been diagnosed with mixed dementia, it means they're experiencing the effects of more than one disease process in their brain.

Research suggests that mixed dementia is more common than previously thought, especially in older adults. The symptoms of mixed dementia can vary greatly, depending on the types of brain changes involved and the areas of the brain affected. Often, symptoms may be similar to those of Alzheimer's or another type of dementia. However, the disease may progress more rapidly than with a single type of dementia.

Caring for someone with mixed dementia can be complex, as you're dealing with multiple disease processes. However, many care strategies are effective across different types of dementia. The key is to focus on your loved one's specific symptoms and needs, rather than trying to disentangle which symptoms might be caused by which type of dementia.

Lewy Body Dementia

Lewy body dementia (LBD) is characterized by the presence of abnormal deposits of a protein called alpha-synuclein in the brain. These deposits, called Lewy bodies, affect chemicals in the brain, leading to problems with thinking, movement, behavior, and mood.

If your loved one has been diagnosed with LBD, you might notice that it shares symptoms with both Alzheimer's and Parkinson's diseases. People with LBD may experience:

- Visual hallucinations
- Fluctuations in alertness and attention
- Movement problems similar to Parkinson's disease
- Difficulty with complex mental activities
- Sleep disturbances

One unique aspect of LBD is that symptoms can fluctuate significantly, even from hour to hour or day to day. This can be particularly challenging for caregivers, as your loved one's abilities and needs might change dramatically over short periods. Patience and flexibility are key when caring for someone with LBD.

Frontotemporal Dementia

Frontotemporal dementia (FTD) is a group of disorders caused by progressive nerve cell loss in the brain's frontal or temporal lobes. These areas of the brain are generally associated with personality, behavior, and language.

Unlike other forms of dementia, memory often remains relatively preserved in the early stages of FTD. Instead, the most prominent symptoms are changes in personality and behavior. A person with FTD might:

- Become socially inappropriate, impulsive, or emotionally indifferent
- Lose their ability to empathize with others
- Experience a decline in personal hygiene
- Engage in repetitive or compulsive behavior
- Have difficulty communicating (either expressing or understanding)

FTD often begins at a younger age than other types of dementia, with symptoms typically starting between the ages of 45 and 65. This earlier onset can bring unique challenges, as the person might still be working or have young children at home.

Caring for someone with FTD can be particularly challenging due to the significant personality changes. It's important to remember that the disease causes these changes and are not intentional. Seeking support from others who understand FTD can be incredibly helpful.

Parkinson's Disease Dementia

Many people are familiar with the motor symptoms of Parkinson's disease, such as tremors and stiffness. However, as Parkinson's progresses, it can also affect cognitive function, leading to Parkinson's disease dementia.

This type of dementia shares many symptoms with Lewy body dementia. People with Parkinson's disease dementia may have trouble with:

- Visual perception
- Planning and organization
- Multi-tasking
- Memory (although this is often less affected than in Alzheimer's disease, at least in the early stages)

They may also experience visual hallucinations and changes in sleep patterns. Parkinson's disease dementia typically develops at least a year after the onset of movement symptoms. The average time from the onset of movement symptoms to the development of dementia is about 10 years.

Caring for someone with Parkinson's disease dementia involves managing both cognitive and motor symptoms. Working closely with healthcare providers to balance treatments for both aspects of the disease is crucial.

Other Types of Dementia

While the types of dementia we've discussed are the most common, there are several other, rarer forms that you might encounter:

Huntington's Disease is a genetic disorder that causes certain nerve cells in the brain to waste away. People are born with the defective gene, but symptoms usually don't appear until middle age. Early symptoms can include depression, mood swings, and trouble learning new things. Later, it can cause severe dementia.

Wernicke-Korsakoff Syndrome is a chronic memory disorder caused by a severe deficiency of thiamine (vitamin B-1). It's most commonly caused by alcohol misuse but can also be associated with AIDS, chronic infections, poor nutrition, and certain other conditions. Symptoms include confusion, apathy, and problems with vision and muscle coordination.

Normal Pressure Hydrocephalus is caused by the buildup of fluid in the brain. Early signs include difficulty walking, memory loss, and inability to control urination. It can sometimes be corrected with the surgical installation of a shunt to drain excess fluid.

Creutzfeldt-Jakob Disease is a rare, degenerative, fatal brain disorder. It progresses rapidly, usually causing death within a year of onset. Early symptoms include memory problems, behavioral changes, and lack of coordination.

Moving Forward with Understanding

Understanding the specific type of dementia your loved one has been diagnosed with can help you better prepare for the journey ahead. It can guide your expectations about symptoms and progression, and inform the care strategies you employ.

However, it's equally important to remember that each person's experience with dementia is unique, regardless of the specific diagnosis. Your loved one may not experience all the typical symptoms of their type of dementia, or they may experience them in a different order or intensity than what's typically expected.

The key is to focus on your loved one as an individual, not just a collection of symptoms. Pay attention to their specific needs, preferences, and challenges. Use the knowledge you've gained about their type of dementia as a guide, but always be ready to adapt your approach based on what works best for your loved one.

Remember, while understanding the different types of dementia is essential, what matters most is the compassion, patience, and love you bring to your caregiving role. In the chapters that follow, we'll explore strategies for providing care that can be adapted to suit individual needs and circumstances, regardless of the specific type of dementia.

You're doing important work in learning about your loved one's condition. This knowledge, combined with your care and dedication, will be invaluable as you navigate this journey together. Keep moving forward, one step at a time, and don't hesitate to seek support when you need it. You're not alone in this journey.

Caregiver's Corner

Knowledge is power, but compassion is key. Your understanding of the specific dementia type, combined with your loving care, will make a world of difference in your loved one's life.

Key Takeaway: Each person's symptoms, experience, and progression with dementia are unique, regardless of the specific diagnosis.

Quick Tip: Create a simple symptom tracker in your patient care binder. Noting changes or new symptoms can help you communicate more effectively with healthcare providers.

Reflection Question: How can you adapt your caregiving approach based on the specific type of dementia your loved one has been diagnosed with?

Resource Spotlight: Explore the website of the specific dementia organization related to your loved one's diagnosis (e.g., Lewy Body Dementia Association, Association for Frontotemporal Degeneration). These organizations offer targeted resources and support.

Chapter 3
What It's Like To Live With Dementia

The aroma of freshly brewed coffee wafted through the kitchen, but I couldn't remember pouring myself a cup. I stood at the counter, staring at the mug in my hand. Its contents untouched. Cold.

"Mom?" Maria's voice cut through the fog. She appeared beside me. Her eyes were a mixture of love and worry that made my heart clench. "Everything alright?"

I smiled, hoping it looked more convincing than it felt. "Just enjoying the morning, dear." The lie tasted bitter on my tongue.

The kitchen, my sanctuary for decades, suddenly felt foreign. Was the fruit bowl always on that side of the counter? Why did the wall calendar show the month of May when it was undoubtedly July?

"Mom," Maria said softly, "remember we're going through Dad's old records today? You said you wanted to organize them."

Records? A spark of recognition flickered, then faded. "Yes, of course," I lied again, ashamed of how easily it came.

"Why don't you finish your coffee, and then we'll start?" Maria suggested.

I nodded, grateful for the reprieve. As I made my way to the living room, the hallway seemed longer than usual. The family photos were adorned with faces that seemed somewhat less familiar.

Sinking into my armchair, I felt a wave of disorientation. The records... what records? Where did we keep them? The memories I'd always relied on were turning to quicksand—shifting and unreliable.

I was sitting alone, my gaze wandering about the space that seemed both familiar and foreign, when a subtle movement caught my eye. It was my own reflection in the mirror across the room. I stared back at the woman. She wore my face, but her eyes held a fear I didn't want to acknowledge. Who was she becoming?

"Ready, Mom?" Maria called from the other room. I took a deep breath and stood. My legs felt unsteady, but I willed them to move. Each step was an act of defiance against the fog threatening to engulf me.

When I reached the bookshelf where the records had always lived, a feeling of familiarity filled me. My fingers traced the spines, and suddenly, a melody played in my mind. It was our song—the one we danced to at our wedding. The memory was so vivid. So real.

"Do you need help?"

I turned to Maria, clutching the record to my chest. "No, dear. I've got it." For that moment, I did. I had the beautiful music. The crystal-clear memory. I even relived the emotions of that wonderful day so long ago.

As we began sorting through the albums, each one sparked a story. Some were clear, others fragmented, but all were pieces of me. I might be changing, but these memories—they were the core of who I am.

"Tell me about this one, Mom," Maria said, holding up an album with a faded cover.

And so I did. The words came slowly at first, then faster. With each story, I felt more like myself. The confusion wasn't gone, but it had retreated, overwhelmed by the flood of powerful memories and sharing them openly with my wonderful daughter.

I am Evie Thompson. My memories might be changing, but my story isn't over.

Caring for someone with dementia is a journey that requires not only practical skills but also a deep well of empathy. As a caregiver, one of the most powerful tools at your disposal is the ability to see the world through the eyes of your loved one. This chapter aims to guide you through the experience of dementia, helping you understand the unique challenges, perceptions, and emotions that your loved one may be facing.

By developing this empathetic perspective, you'll be better equipped to provide compassionate care, communicate effectively, and navigate the complex terrain of dementia caregiving. Remember, while we can never fully know another person's experience, especially one altered by dementia, striving to understand can significantly improve the quality of care and life for both the caregiver and the person with dementia.

Shifting Emotions

Dementia doesn't just affect memory and cognitive function; it profoundly impacts emotional experiences. Understanding this emotional landscape is crucial for providing empathetic care.

Fear is often a dominant emotion for those with dementia. Imagine waking up in a world that seems increasingly unfamiliar. Faces you feel you should recognize appear strange. Tasks that were once simple now seem daunting. This constant encounter with the unknown can lead to a pervasive sense of fear and anxiety.

Confusion is another frequent companion. Your loved one might struggle to make sense of their surroundings, the passage of time, or even their thoughts and memories. This confusion can be deeply distressing, leading to frustration and agitation.

Frustration often stems from the awareness of declining abilities. Your loved one may know they used to be capable of certain tasks but now find them challenging or impossible. This loss of capability can be a significant blow to self-esteem and independence.

Sadness and depression are common as the person with dementia grapples with their changing reality. They may mourn the loss of their former self, their independence, and their future plans.

However, it's important to note that people with dementia also experience positive emotions. Moments of joy, love, and contentment are still very much possible and should be cherished and encouraged.

These emotions may manifest in various behaviors. Fear might present as reluctance to try new things or suspicion towards others. Confusion could lead to wandering or repetitive questions. Frustration might result in angry outbursts or withdrawal.

As a caregiver, recognizing these emotions and their potential sources can help you respond with patience and understanding. When you see agitation, consider what emotions might be driving it. Is it fear of the unknown? Frustration at inability? By addressing the underlying emotion, you can often more effectively soothe and support your loved one.

Perception and Reality

Dementia can significantly alter how a person perceives and interacts with the world around them. Understanding these perceptual changes is key to creating a supportive environment and avoiding unnecessary conflicts.

Visual perception often changes with dementia. Colors may appear less vibrant, and depth perception may be affected, making it harder to navigate spaces or judge distances. Patterns on floors or walls might be misinterpreted as obstacles or changes in elevation, causing confusion or hesitation when walking.

Auditory processing can also be impacted. Background noise might become overwhelming, making it difficult to focus on conversations or tasks. Your loved one might struggle to locate the source of sounds, leading to confusion or startled reactions.

Time perception often becomes distorted. Recent memories may fade quickly, while older memories remain vivid, leading to a sense of living in the past. Your loved one might insist on going to a job they retired from years ago or ask about relatives who have passed away.

These perceptual changes can make the world feel unpredictable and sometimes frightening. A shadow on the floor might look like a hole, causing your loved one to step carefully around it. A coat hanging on a door might be mistaken for a person, leading to confusion or alarm.

By understanding these perceptual changes, you can take steps to create a more comfortable environment. Ensuring good lighting, reducing clutter, and minimizing background noise can all help. When your loved one reacts to something you can't see or understand, remember that their perception of reality is different from yours. Instead of arguing or dismissing their concerns, offer reassurance and gently guide them toward safety and comfort.

Common Becomes Foreign

For someone with dementia, everyday tasks can become complex puzzles. Activities that once were automatic now require conscious effort and may cause significant stress.

Consider the act of getting dressed. What seems simple to us involves multiple steps: choosing appropriate clothes, putting them on in the proper order, managing buttons or zippers, and adjusting for comfort. For someone with dementia, each of these steps can be a challenge. They might put clothes on in the wrong order, struggle with fine motor tasks like buttoning a shirt, or be unable to choose weather-appropriate attire.

Meal times can be equally challenging. Using utensils, recognizing food items, understanding when to start or stop eating - all of these can become confusing. Your loved one might use a fork for soup or try to eat the flower centerpiece, not out of defiance, but because of genuine confusion.

Personal hygiene tasks like brushing teeth or bathing can become frightening or overwhelming. The sensation of water on the skin might be startling, or the person might forget the purpose of toothpaste.

Throughout all of these challenges, there's often an underlying struggle for independence. Your loved one likely remembers being capable of these tasks and may feel frustrated or embarrassed at needing help. They might insist on doing things themselves, even when it's no longer safe or practical.

As a caregiver, patience is key. Break tasks down into simple steps, offer gentle guidance, and provide assistance only when necessary. Celebrate small victories and always prioritize your loved one's dignity. Remember, the goal is not perfection, but maintaining as much independence and self-esteem as possible.

Identity and Dignity

One of the most challenging aspects of dementia, both for the individual and their caregivers, is the threat it poses to a person's sense of identity. As memories fade and abilities decline, your loved one may struggle to maintain their sense of self.

It's crucial to remember that despite the changes brought on by dementia, the core of the person - their personality, values, and essence - remains. Your role as a caregiver includes helping to preserve and honor this identity.

Respect is fundamental. Even when your loved one seems confused or is behaving in challenging ways, they deserve to be treated with dignity. Speak to them as an adult, not a child. Avoid talking about them as if they're not present. Include them in conversations and decisions whenever possible.

Validation of their feelings and experiences is equally important. If your loved one expresses fear, sadness, or anger, acknowledge these emotions. Avoid dismissing their concerns or trying to reason them out of their feelings. A simple "I can see this is upsetting for you" can go a long way in making them feel heard and understood.

Support their self-esteem by focusing on what they can still do rather than what they've lost. Encourage participation in activities they enjoy and can manage, even if they can't do them as well as before. This might mean simplifying a beloved hobby or finding new ways to engage in old interests.

Maintaining connections to their personal history can help anchor your loved one's sense of identity. Surround them with familiar objects, play music they love, or reminisce about past experiences (being mindful that some memories might be upsetting).

Remember, preserving dignity often means allowing for choice and control where possible. Even small decisions - what to wear, what to eat, when to go for a walk - can help maintain a sense of autonomy.

Simulating the Experience

While we can never fully replicate the experience of dementia, some exercises can help caregivers gain perspective. These simulations can increase empathy and understanding, leading to more patient and effective care.

Sensory Alteration: Wear glasses smeared with petroleum jelly to simulate visual difficulties. Try to complete a simple task like setting a table or sorting laundry. This can help you understand why your loved one might move slowly or seem hesitant in certain environments.

Multitasking Challenge: Try to complete a familiar task while someone gives you a series of unrelated instructions. This simulates the difficulty of focusing and following directions that many people with dementia experience.

Dexterity Impairment: Wear thick gloves and attempt to button a shirt or use utensils. This can provide insight into the frustration of struggling with once-simple tasks.

Memory Strain: Have someone give you a list of five unrelated items to remember. Then, engage in a distracting activity for a few minutes before trying to recall the items. This offers a glimpse into the challenge of short-term memory loss.

After each exercise, take time to reflect.

- How did you feel?
- Were you frustrated, anxious, or overwhelmed?
- How might these feelings impact behavior over time?
- How could a caregiver have made these experiences easier?

Applying Empathy in Care

Understanding the dementia experience is not just an intellectual exercise - it should inform and improve your caregiving approach.

Here are some ways to apply this empathetic perspective:

Communication: Speak clearly and slowly, but not condescendingly. Use simple sentences and give one instruction at a time. Be patient in waiting for responses, as processing information may take longer.

Environment: Create a space that's easy to navigate and feels safe. Good lighting, clear pathways, and familiar objects can all help reduce confusion and anxiety.

Routine: Establish consistent daily routines to provide a sense of structure and predictability. This can help reduce anxiety and confusion.

Choices: Offer simple choices to maintain a sense of control. Instead of asking, "What do you want for dinner?" try, "Would you like chicken or fish?"

Redirection: When your loved one is upset or fixated on something impossible, gently redirect their attention rather than arguing or dismissing their concerns.

Engagement: Find activities that are engaging but not overwhelming. This might be listening to music, looking at photos, or simple crafts.

Self-care: Remember that taking care of yourself is crucial. You can't provide empathetic care if you're exhausted or frustrated. Regular breaks and support are essential.

Seeing through the eyes of someone with dementia is a continuous process of learning and adaptation. It requires patience, creativity, and a willingness to step outside your own perspective. Caregiving is not just about managing symptoms or ensuring physical safety - it's about preserving dignity, fostering connection, and creating moments of joy even in the face of a challenging disease. By cultivating empathy and understanding, you're providing the most valuable care of all - the recognition of your loved one's inherent worth and humanity.

Caregiver's Corner

Your efforts to see through their eyes not only improve their quality of life but also deepen your connection. Remember, in the midst of change, the essence of your loved one remains. Your empathy is a steadfast beacon of comfort in their shifting world.

Key Takeaways:

- Dementia profoundly affects emotions and perception, not just memory
- Understanding your loved one's altered reality is crucial for empathetic care
- Everyday tasks can become complex challenges for someone with dementia
- Preserving dignity and identity is essential in dementia care
- Simulating dementia experiences can enhance caregiver empathy and understanding

Quick Tip:

Practice the "SLOW" method in your daily interactions: **S**peak clearly and slowly, **L**isten actively, **O**bserve body language, and **W**ait patiently for responses. This simple acronym can help you remember key elements of empathetic communication, especially during challenging moments.

Reflection Question:

Think about a recent challenging interaction with your loved one. How might that situation have felt from their perspective? How could understanding their point of view change your approach in similar future situations?

Resource Spotlight:

Explore the Virtual Dementia Tour® offered by Second Wind Dreams (secondwind.org). This evidence-based simulation provides valuable insight into the physical and mental challenges of those living with dementia.

Chapter 4

The Progression Of Dementia

Maria and Evie walked side by side along the tree-lined path in the local park, enjoying the warmth of the spring afternoon. The air was filled with the sweet scent of blooming flowers and the cheerful chirping of birds.

"Oh, look at that bench over there, Maria," Evie said, pointing to a weathered wooden seat beneath a large oak tree. "Your father and I used to bring you here for picnics."

Maria smiled warmly. "Close, Mom. That was actually in the park near our old house. But you're right—we did have lots of picnics when I was little."

Evie's brow furrowed slightly. "Oh, yes... of course."

As they continued their walk, Evie began humming a familiar tune. Maria recognized it as an old lullaby her mother used to sing to her.

"That's a lovely song, Mom," Maria said. "Do you remember the words?"

Evie's humming faltered and she fell silent as she searched for the words to the song. "I... I'm not sure. The melody is clear as a bell, but the words seem to have faded away."

Maria saw a flicker of frustration cross her mother's face. She squeezed Evie's hand reassuringly. "It's okay, Mom. The melody is beautiful on its own."

As they rounded a bend in the path, Maria spotted a small patch of blue flowers growing near a bench. She led her mother over, and they sat down.

"Look, Mom," Maria said, carefully plucking one of the tiny blue flowers. "Do you know what these are?"

Evie studied the delicate bloom. "They're so familiar, but the name... it's just out of reach."

"They're forget-me-nots," Maria said softly, twirling the flower between her fingers. She looked into her mother's eyes, her voice gentle but earnest. "These flowers have a special meaning. They're a symbol of remembrance. Of enduring love."

Maria tucked the flower gently behind her mother's ear, her hand lingering for a moment. " I hope you'll always remember how much I love you, no matter what happens."

Evie's eyes glistened with emotion. "Oh, Maria. It's such a pretty little thing. And don't you worry, dear. You're etched in my heart. I could never forget you."

Maria smiled, touched by her mother's words and hoping they would hold true. "I love you too, Mom. Always."

As a caregiver, understanding the progression of dementia is like having a map for an uncertain journey. It helps you anticipate changes, adapt your care strategies, and prepare for the future. In this chapter, we'll explore the typical stages of dementia, from early signs to late-stage care needs.

It's important to remember that this journey is unique for every individual. Your loved one may not experience all these stages in the same way or order. Think of this as a general guide – it gives you a good idea of what may lie ahead, but the exact route will almost certainly vary.

As we discuss these stages, it's natural to feel a mix of emotions. You might feel apprehensive about the changes to come, or sad about the abilities your loved one may lose. These feelings are entirely normal. Remember, knowledge is power. Understanding what might happen can help you feel more prepared and in control, even in the face of uncertainty.

Early Signs: The Subtle Beginnings

The journey of dementia often begins with changes so subtle they're easily overlooked or attributed to normal aging. You might have noticed some of these signs before the diagnosis was made. Perhaps your loved one started misplacing items more frequently, or struggled to find the right words in conversation. They might have shown difficulty with complex tasks or problem-solving, or experienced mood changes and increased anxiety.

At this stage, your loved one may still be largely independent in daily activities, but you might notice they require more time to complete tasks or make occasional errors. They may become more reliant on calendars, notes, or reminders.

For family members and caregivers, this stage often involves a growing awareness that something isn't quite right. It's a time of uncertainty and concern, often prompting the initial medical consultations that lead to a diagnosis.

During this early stage, your role as a caregiver might involve helping to keep track of appointments and important dates, assisting with complex tasks like managing finances, and providing emotional support as your loved one grapples with changes in their abilities.

Remember, even with these changes, your loved one is still the same person. They may need more support in some areas, but they can still enjoy many of the same activities and relationships they always have.

The Grey Area: Mild Cognitive Impairment

As we age, some degree of cognitive change is expected. The challenge lies in distinguishing between normal aging and the early stages of dementia. This is where the concept of Mild Cognitive Impairment (MCI) comes into play.

MCI represents a stage of cognitive decline that's more pronounced than normal aging but doesn't yet meet the criteria for dementia. People with MCI may experience noticeable memory problems, more than would be expected for their age. They might have difficulty with planning or organization, trouble following conversations or instructions, or show impaired judgment or decision-making.

Despite these challenges, individuals with MCI can typically manage their daily activities independently. However, they may take longer to complete tasks or rely more heavily on compensatory strategies like lists and reminders.

It's important to note that not everyone with MCI will develop dementia. Some people's cognitive function remains stable, and a small percentage may even improve. However, MCI does increase the risk of developing dementia, particularly Alzheimer's disease.

If your loved one has been diagnosed with MCI, your role as a caregiver might involve encouraging the use of memory aids, supporting them in maintaining a healthy lifestyle, monitoring for any significant changes in cognitive abilities, and ensuring regular follow-ups with healthcare providers.

Mild Dementia: When Symptoms Begin to Interfere

As dementia progresses to the mild stage, symptoms become more noticeable and begin to interfere with daily activities. This stage often marks the point where a formal diagnosis is made.

You might notice your loved one experiencing significant memory loss, especially for recent events. They may have difficulty with complex tasks like managing finances or planning meals. Confusion about time or place becomes more common, and they might get lost in familiar places. Personality changes, such as increased irritability or anxiety, may emerge. Language difficulties, such as struggling to find the right words, often become more apparent.

At this stage, your loved one may still be able to live independently, but they're likely to need some assistance with complex tasks. They may withdraw from social activities or hobbies they once enjoyed. Safety can become a concern, particularly regarding driving or using household appliances.

For caregivers, this stage often involves taking on more responsibilities and providing more frequent support. It's a time of adjustment, as roles within the family may begin to shift. You might find yourself taking over financial management, accompanying your loved one to medical appointments, helping with household tasks, monitoring medication use, and ensuring home safety.

This is also a crucial time to start discussions about future care preferences and legal matters while your loved one can still participate in decision-making. Consider consulting with an elder law attorney to discuss power of attorney and advance directives.

Moderate Dementia: Increasing Care Needs

In the moderate stage of dementia, cognitive decline becomes more pronounced, and the need for assistance with daily activities increases. Your loved one might experience severe memory loss, including forgetting significant life events or the names of close family members. They may have difficulty recognizing friends and family, and show increased confusion and disorientation, even in familiar environments.

At this stage, living independently becomes challenging and potentially unsafe. Your loved one will likely need constant supervision and help with many daily tasks. Communication can become increasingly difficult as language skills decline.

For caregivers, this stage often involves significant adjustments. The level of care required increases substantially, and many families begin to consider professional care options or move their loved one into their home for closer supervision. You might find yourself providing hands-on assistance with personal care, managing behavioral symptoms like agitation or wandering, adapting communication strategies as verbal skills decline, and making decisions about appropriate living arrangements.

Remember to implement a daily routine to provide structure and reduce anxiety. Include activities that your loved one enjoys and can still participate in, even if they need assistance.

Late-Stage Dementia: Full-Time Care and Comfort

In the final stages of dementia, individuals lose the ability to respond to their environment or communicate. They may still say words or phrases, but communication can be limited. Your loved one may be unable to recognize family members, lose awareness of their surroundings, and require full-time assistance with personal care.

Care at this stage focuses on preserving quality of life and dignity. Caregiving priorities shift to maintaining physical comfort, preventing infections, and managing pain. Your role might involve providing comfort through gentle touch, soothing music, or familiar scents. Ensuring proper nutrition and hydration becomes crucial, which may include working with healthcare providers on feeding strategies. Managing pain and other symptoms in collaboration with medical professionals becomes a key focus, as does making decisions about end-of-life care.

Navigating the Stages

As dementia progresses through these stages, caregivers need to adapt their approach continually. Educate yourself about dementia and its progression; knowledge can help you feel more in control. Prioritize safety by regularly reassessing the home environment for potential hazards. Maintain consistent daily routines to provide a sense of security and reduce anxiety.

Encourage independence by allowing your loved one to do as much as they safely can for themselves. This helps maintain dignity and can slow functional decline. Simplify tasks by breaking complex activities into smaller, manageable steps. Use clear communication by speaking slowly and clearly, using simple words and short sentences, and maintaining eye contact.

Above all, be patient. Tasks may take longer than they used to. Allow extra time and avoid rushing. Manage your own stress by making time for self-care, and don't hesitate to ask for help. While focusing on current needs, also think ahead to future care needs and preferences.

Remember to celebrate small victories. Find joy in small moments and celebrate what your loved one can still do, rather than focusing on losses. Every shared smile, every moment of connection, is a victory worth cherishing.

Understanding the progression of dementia can help you prepare for the challenges ahead and make informed decisions about care. However, it's equally important to stay present and focus on making each day as positive as possible for both you and your loved one.

In the following chapters, we'll explore specific strategies for providing care at different stages of dementia, helping you navigate this journey with confidence and compassion. Remember, you're not alone in this journey. There are resources and support available every step of the way.

Caregiver's Corner

Understanding the progression of dementia is like having a map for an uncertain journey. While the path may be challenging, your love and care make a profound difference at every stage.

Key Takeaways:

- Understanding the stages of dementia helps you anticipate needs and adapt your care strategies proactively
- Each stage requires different levels of support, from subtle assistance to full-time care
- While cognitive abilities decline, opportunities for meaningful connection remain throughout all stages

Quick Tip: Create a "memory box" with items from your loved one's past. As dementia progresses, this can be a valuable tool for helping to stimulate memories and encourage communication.

Reflection Question: How can you adapt your caregiving approach to support your loved one's current abilities while preparing for future changes?

Resource Spotlight: Check out the "Progression of Dementia" section on the Family Caregiver Alliance website (caregiver.org). They offer stage-specific advice and downloadable fact sheets to help you navigate each phase of the journey.

Chapter 5
Legal and Financial Planning

Maria fidgeted with her car keys as she and Evie sat in the waiting room of the law office. They had scheduled this appointment shortly after Evie's diagnosis, knowing the importance of sorting out legal matters early.

Evie patted Maria's hand. "Relax, dear. You look more nervous than I feel."

Maria managed a small smile. "I just want to make sure we get everything right, Mom."

"And we will," Evie reassured her. "I may be forgetful sometimes, but I still know how to take care of business."

The lawyer, Ms. Wilcox, welcomed them into her office. "Mrs. Thompson, I understand you're here to discuss some important legal planning?"

Evie nodded firmly. "That's right. I've got this pesky diagnosis, you see, and we want to make sure all our ducks are in a row while I can still herd them properly."

As Ms. Wilcox explained the various documents - power of attorney, advance directives, will updates - Evie listened attentively, asking pointed questions that surprised even Maria.

"Now, about this power of attorney," Evie said, "I want to make sure Maria has the authority to make decisions, but I'd like to include my sister as a backup. Is that possible?"

Ms. Wilcox nodded, "Absolutely. We can set that up for you."

As they worked through each document, Maria marveled at her mother's clarity and foresight. There were moments of confusion, but Evie approached them with humor and determination.

By the end of the appointment, they had a clear plan in place. As they stood to leave, Evie turned to Maria. "See, honey? Nothing to worry about. We've got it all sorted."

Maria hugged her mother tightly. "Thanks, Mom. For doing this, for being so... you about it all."

As they left the office, Evie's eyes twinkled. "Now, I believe planning for the future calls for a celebration. Ice cream?"

Maria laughed, feeling a weight lift off her shoulders. "You read my mind, Mom."

Walking arm in arm, Maria felt grateful for her mother's strength and foresight. They had faced this challenge head-on, together, and she knew that whatever the future held, they were as prepared as they could be.

When faced with a dementia diagnosis, addressing legal and financial matters might seem like a secondary concern amidst the emotional turmoil and immediate health considerations. However, early planning is not just important —it's crucial in ensuring quality care and peace of mind for both the individual with dementia and their family. Time is of the essence in this process, as the ability to make sound decisions diminishes as the condition progresses.

The Importance of Early Action

Starting the planning process soon after diagnosis allows the individual to be actively involved in important decisions about their future care, finances, and legal matters. This early involvement not only ensures that their wishes are respected but also significantly reduces stress and potential conflicts down the line. As dementia advances, the capacity to make sound decisions diminishes, which can lead to legal complications if essential documents are not in place.

Early planning also provides more options in terms of financial strategies and care choices. It allows families to explore various care options, consider different financial scenarios, and make informed decisions without the pressure of an immediate crisis. This proactive approach can help preserve assets, ensure quality care, and reduce the emotional and financial strain on family members.

Power of Attorney and Guardianship

One of the first and most critical steps in legal planning is establishing a power of attorney (POA). This legal document allows an individual to appoint someone they trust to make decisions on their behalf. There are several types of POA to consider, each serving a specific purpose in the comprehensive care plan for someone with dementia.

A *durable power of attorney* remains in effect if the principal becomes incapacitated, making it particularly important in dementia care. Unlike a standard POA, which becomes invalid if the principal loses mental capacity, a durable POA continues to be effective, allowing the appointed agent to make decisions even as dementia progresses.

A *healthcare power of attorney* specifically covers medical decisions. This document allows the appointed agent to make healthcare decisions on behalf of the individual with dementia when they are no longer able to do so. This can include decisions about treatments, medications, and end-of-life care. It's crucial that the appointed agent is familiar with the individual's healthcare wishes and values to ensure decisions align with what the person would have wanted.

A *financial power of attorney* covers financial and legal matters. This allows the appointed agent to manage finances, pay bills, manage investments, and make other financial decisions. Given the potential for financial exploitation in dementia cases, it's vital to choose a trustworthy individual for this role and to consider setting up oversight mechanisms.

When setting up a POA, it's essential to choose a trustworthy agent who understands the individual's wishes and values. Many families choose to name different agents for healthcare and financial decisions, recognizing that different skills and knowledge may be required for each role. It's also wise to name backup agents in case the primary agent is unable to serve.

The powers granted by a POA can be as broad or as limited as the individual wishes. For example, a financial POA might grant the agent the power to manage all financial affairs, or it might be limited to specific tasks like paying bills or managing investments. Similarly, a healthcare POA can specify exactly what kinds of medical decisions the agent is empowered to make. It's important to discuss these details with a legal professional to ensure the POA aligns with the individual's wishes and needs.

In cases where a POA is not in place and the individual loses capacity, guardianship may become necessary. This is a more complex and potentially restrictive option, requiring a court process to establish. Guardianship should be considered a last resort, as it's generally more restrictive than a POA and can be more costly and time-consuming to establish.

The guardianship process involves a court hearing where evidence of the individual's incapacity is presented. If guardianship is granted, the court appoints a guardian to make decisions on behalf of the individual. This can be a family member or a professional guardian. The guardian is required to report to the court regularly on the individual's condition and care. While guardianship can provide necessary protection for individuals who can no longer make decisions for themselves, it also removes many of their legal rights, which is why it's generally considered only when other options have been exhausted.

Navigating the Financial Maze

Planning for the financial aspects of long-term dementia care can be daunting. The costs can be substantial, and navigating the various funding options can feel like solving a complex puzzle. The first step is to assess the current financial situation, getting a clear picture of all assets, income sources, and debts. This includes bank accounts, investments, real estate, pensions, social security benefits, and any other sources of income or assets.

Next, it's important to estimate future care costs based on current health and family history. This can be challenging, as the progression of dementia can vary widely between individuals. However, having a rough estimate can help in planning for future needs. Consider factors such as potential in-home care costs, adult day care, assisted living facilities, and nursing home care. Don't forget to factor in potential medical expenses, medications, and safety equipment that may be needed over time.

There are several potential ways to fund long-term care, each with its advantages and considerations:

Long-term care insurance, if purchased before diagnosis, can be a valuable resource. These policies can cover a range of care options, from in-home care to nursing home care. However, it's essential to understand the specifics of the policy, including what it covers, when benefits kick in, and how long they last. Some policies have elimination periods (similar to a deductible) before coverage begins, and many have limits on daily benefits or total lifetime benefits.

Some life insurance policies can be converted to pay for long-term care through what's known as a life settlement or viatical settlement. This involves selling the policy to a third party for a lump sum that can be used to fund care. While this can provide needed funds, it's important to consider the tax implications and the impact on any beneficiaries of the policy. These settlements often offer less than the full death benefit of the policy, so they should be considered carefully as part of a comprehensive financial plan.

For homeowners aged 62 and older, a reverse mortgage can provide income from home equity. This option allows homeowners to borrow against the equity in their home without having to make monthly mortgage payments. The loan is repaid when the homeowner sells the house, moves out, or passes away. While this can be a source of needed funds, it should be carefully considered as it can impact inheritance plans and may not be suitable if the individual is likely to need to move to a care facility in the near future.

Government programs can also play a role in funding care. Medicare, the federal health insurance program for people 65 and older, covers some health care costs but has significant limitations when it comes to long-term care. It covers skilled nursing facility care for a limited time following a qualifying hospital stay, and some home health care. Still, it does not cover the long-term custodial care often needed in later stages of dementia.

Medicaid, on the other hand, may cover long-term care for those who meet income and asset requirements. Medicaid is a joint federal and state program that provides health coverage to eligible low-income individuals. It is the primary payer for long-term care services in the United States. However, qualifying for Medicaid often requires spending down assets, which can be a complex process.

Medicaid planning can be intricate and often involves strategies to spend down or transfer assets in order to meet eligibility requirements. However, it's important to note that Medicaid has a five-year lookback period for asset transfers. This means that any transfers of assets made in the five years prior to applying for Medicaid will be scrutinized and may result in a period of ineligibility. Because of this, Medicaid planning needs to be done well in advance of needing care.

Given the complexity of these financial options, many families find it beneficial to consult with a financial advisor who specializes in elder care or long-term care planning. These professionals can help navigate the various options and develop a comprehensive plan that takes into account the individual's unique circumstances and needs.

Protecting Against Financial Exploitation

As dementia progresses, individuals become more vulnerable to financial exploitation and fraud. Implementing protective measures early on is crucial. This can include setting up online access to monitor bank and credit card accounts, reducing credit limits on cards, and closing unused accounts.

Other protective measures can include:

- Setting up automatic bill payments to ensure important bills are paid on time
- Using protective banking services designed for vulnerable adults, such as view-only access for family members or alerts for unusual transactions
- Educating family members about common scams targeting seniors, such as telemarketing fraud, Medicare scams, fake charity solicitations, and "grandparent" scams where the scammer pretends to be a grandchild in trouble
- Registering for the National Do Not Call Registry to reduce unwanted sales calls
- Regularly reviewing credit reports to check for any suspicious activity

It's also important to be cautious about who has access to financial information. While it's necessary for trusted individuals to have some access to manage care and finances, this access should be carefully controlled and monitored.

Advance Directives

Advance directives are another crucial component of legal planning for dementia care. These documents outline an individual's preferences for future medical care, ensuring their wishes are respected even if they become unable to communicate those wishes themselves. Advance directives typically include a living will and a healthcare power of attorney.

A living will specifies wishes for end-of-life care. It can address a range of medical interventions, including:

- Use of life support systems, such as ventilators or feeding tubes
- Preferences for pain management and comfort care
- Wishes regarding resuscitation attempts
- Desires for organ or tissue donation

Some individuals also choose to create a Do Not Resuscitate (DNR) order, which instructs healthcare providers not to perform CPR if the person's heart stops beating or they stop breathing. A more comprehensive document is the Physician Orders for Life-Sustaining Treatment (POLST), which provides specific medical orders for care preferences.

It's important to review and update advance directives regularly, especially after significant health changes. As dementia progresses, the individual's care needs and preferences may change. Regular reviews ensure that the directives continue to reflect current wishes.

Ensure copies of advance directives are provided to healthcare providers and family members. Many people choose to carry a card in their wallet, indicating that they have an advance directive and where it can be found. Some states have registries where you can file your advance directive, making it easily accessible to healthcare providers.

Estate Planning Considerations

Updating estate plans is crucial after a dementia diagnosis. This involves reviewing and updating wills to ensure they reflect current wishes and considering the impact of potential long-term care costs on the estate.

Trusts can be a valuable tool in estate planning for individuals with dementia. A revocable living trust can help manage assets and avoid probate, providing a smoother transition of assets after death. It can also provide for the management of assets during incapacity. A special needs trust might be appropriate for beneficiaries with disabilities, allowing them to receive an inheritance without jeopardizing their eligibility for government benefits.

It's also important to review beneficiary designations on life insurance policies, retirement accounts, and other assets. These designations typically supersede instructions in a will, so ensuring they're up to date is crucial.

Consider the potential tax implications of various estate planning strategies. For example, gifting assets during one's lifetime can be a way to reduce estate taxes. Still, it's essential to be aware of gift tax rules and how they might interact with Medicaid eligibility.

The Importance of Ongoing Review

Legal and financial planning for dementia care is not a one-time event. Regular review and adaptation are necessary as circumstances change and the condition progresses. These reviews should include:

1. Reassessing the individual's capacity and care needs
2. Reviewing and updating legal documents as necessary
3. Evaluating the effectiveness of financial strategies

4. Adjusting plans based on any changes in laws or regulations
5. Reviewing insurance coverage and benefits
6. Assessing the need for additional services or support

Consider scheduling annual reviews with legal and financial advisors to ensure plans remain current and effective.

Communicating Plans with Family

Clear communication about legal and financial plans can prevent misunderstandings and conflicts down the line. Holding family meetings to discuss plans and their rationale can help ensure everyone is on the same page. These discussions can be challenging, as they often involve confronting uncomfortable realities about the future. However, open and honest communication can prevent conflicts later on and ensure that everyone understands and respects the individual's wishes.

While transparency is important, it's also crucial to respect the individual's privacy. Balance openness with family members with the individual's right to keep certain matters private. The extent of information shared should be guided by the individual's wishes and what's necessary for effective care planning.

In conclusion, while legal and financial planning can seem overwhelming, it's a crucial step in ensuring quality care and peace of mind for both the individual with dementia and their family. By taking these steps early, reviewing them regularly, and communicating clearly with family members, you're providing a foundation of security and respect for your loved one's wishes. This comprehensive planning allows you to focus on what matters most - providing care and support throughout the dementia journey.

Remember, every situation is unique, and it's often beneficial to consult with legal and financial professionals who specialize in elder care and dementia issues. They can provide personalized advice tailored to your specific circumstances and help navigate the complex landscape of dementia care planning.

Caregiver's Corner

Planning ahead isn't just about paperwork—it's an act of love that provides security and peace of mind for both you and your loved one.

Key Takeaways:

- Early legal and financial planning is crucial for preserving autonomy and ensuring quality care
- Establishing power of attorney for healthcare and finances protects decision-making rights
- Learn what funding options may be available to help alleviate some of the financial burden

Quick Tip: Create a "financial emergency kit" with copies of important documents, account information, and contact details for financial advisors. Keep it secure in your patient care binder.

Reflection Question: How can you initiate a conversation about legal and financial planning with your loved one in a way that's sensitive to their feelings and concerns?

Resource Spotlight: Explore the National Academy of Elder Law Attorneys (NAELA) website to find specialized attorneys who can guide you through the complexities of elder law and dementia care planning.

Chapter 6
Building Your Care Team

A thick folder of medical records lay on Maria's lap. Evie fidgeted in the chair beside her, eyeing the various diplomas on the wall.

"So," Dr. Anderson began, "I understand you're here to discuss building a care team for your mother?"

Maria nodded, feeling overwhelmed. "Yes, I... I'm realizing I can't do this all on my own. But I'm not sure where to start."

Dr. Anderson smiled reassuringly. "That's a very natural feeling, and you're taking an important step. Let's talk about the different specialists who could help."

As the doctor began listing various healthcare professionals and how each one could offer unique assistance, Evie leaned over to Maria. "My goodness, are we assembling the Avengers?"

Maria couldn't help but chuckle. "Mom, please. This is important."

"I know, dear," Evie whispered back. "But if we're putting together a superhero team, the position of Wonderwoman has already been taken—by me."

Dr. Anderson, overhearing, laughed. "Well, Mrs. Thompson, I'd say you're certainly the star of this team. We're just here to support you."

As the appointment continued, Maria found herself taking copious notes. Neurologist, geriatrician, occupational therapist, social worker--the list seemed endless.

"It sounds like a lot," Dr. Anderson admitted, noticing Maria's overwhelmed expression. "But remember, you don't need everyone at once. We'll prioritize based on your mother's current needs."

Evie suddenly spoke up. "Doctor, in all this talk of teams and specialists, where does my daughter fit in? As far as I'm concerned, she's the real hero here."

Maria felt tears prick her eyes as Dr. Anderson nodded solemnly. "You're absolutely right, Mrs. Thompson. Caregivers like your daughter are the backbone of any care team. Which is why," he turned to Maria, "it's crucial that we also discuss support for you. Caregiver support groups, respite care options..."

As they left the office an hour later, Maria's head was spinning with information, but she felt a new sense of direction.

"Well," Evie said as they walked to the car, "if I'm going to have a whole team of people poking and prodding at me, at least I'll be well-entertained. Did you see the bowtie on that neurologist in the photo? Dapper fellow!"

Maria laughed, feeling some of the tension leave her shoulders. "Only you would be checking out the doctors' fashion choices, Mom."

Evie winked. "Got to keep things interesting, dear. Now, all this team-building talk has made me hungry. What do you say we stop for—"

"Ice cream?" Maria interrupted with a grin.

As they drove to the ice cream parlor, Maria reflected on the appointment. Building a care team would be a process, but she no longer felt alone in this journey.

"You know, Mom," Maria said as they pulled into the parking lot, "I think you're right. You are the Wonder Woman of this team."

Imagine the healthcare system for dementia as an orchestra, with each provider playing a unique and vital role. This chapter will introduce you to the various sections of this healthcare ensemble - from the primary care physician who often leads the group, to the specialists who provide crucial expertise. We'll explore how to assemble your team, coordinate their efforts, and ensure they work together effectively.

Primary Care Physician

The primary care physician often serves as the conductor of this healthcare symphony. They coordinate overall care, manage general health issues, and help determine when specialist care is necessary.

Regular check-ins with the primary care physician are invaluable. These visits allow for early detection and management of other health issues that could exacerbate dementia symptoms. Your loved one's primary care doctor can also help you understand how different health conditions interact with dementia and guide you in prioritizing treatments and interventions.

Neurologist

Specialists form the backbone of your care team, with neurologists playing a particularly crucial role. These brain experts are essential in determining the specific type of dementia and developing a targeted treatment plan. When visiting a neurologist, come prepared with a detailed account of the cognitive changes you've observed. This information, combined with medical tests and brain scans, helps the neurologist make an accurate diagnosis and recommend appropriate treatments.

Geriatrician

For older adults with dementia, a geriatrician can be a game-changer. These doctors specialize in healthcare for seniors and are adept at managing the complex interplay of multiple health conditions often seen in older adults. A geriatrician looks at the big picture, considering how dementia interacts with other age-related health issues. They can help balance treatments, adjust medications to minimize side effects, and provide guidance on maintaining overall health and quality of life as dementia progresses.

Phychiatrist

Mental health is a critical component of dementia care, making a psychiatrist, particularly one specializing in geriatric care, an essential team member. Behavioral symptoms like agitation, anxiety, or depression are common in dementia and can significantly impact quality of life. A psychiatrist can help manage these symptoms through a combination of non-pharmacological approaches and, when necessary, carefully prescribed medications. They can guide you in understanding the emotional and behavioral changes your loved one is experiencing and provide strategies for addressing challenging behaviors.

Occupational Therapist

Allied health professionals play vital roles in maintaining quality of life and functional abilities. Occupational therapists, for instance, are invaluable in helping your loved one maintain independence in daily activities. They can assess your home environment and suggest modifications to enhance safety and ease of navigation. An occupational therapist might recommend simple changes like removing clutter and improving lighting, or more significant adaptations like installing grab bars in the bathroom. They can also teach techniques for simplifying daily tasks, allowing your loved one to maintain a sense of independence and purpose for as long as possible.

Physical Therapist

Physical therapists focus on maintaining mobility and preventing falls, which become increasingly important as dementia progresses. They can design exercise programs tailored to your loved one's abilities and teach safe transfer techniques to reduce the risk of falls. A physical therapist can also assess the need for mobility aids like walkers or wheelchairs and provide training on how to use them effectively.

Speech Therapist

As dementia advances, communication difficulties often arise. This is where a speech and language therapist becomes crucial. They can provide strategies for maintaining meaningful communication even as verbal skills decline. This might involve teaching alternative communication methods, such as using gestures or picture cards. Speech therapists also play a vital role in managing swallowing difficulties, which are common in advanced dementia. They can recommend texture modifications for food and teach safe swallowing techniques to prevent aspiration.

Social Worker

Social workers are often the unsung heroes of the dementia care team. They provide emotional support, help navigate the complex world of community resources, and assist with long-term care planning. A social worker can be your guide to local support services, help you understand your options for respite care, and provide counseling to help you cope with the emotional challenges of caregiving.

Pharmacist

Don't underestimate the importance of a good pharmacist on your team. As the number of medications often increases with age and the progression of dementia, a pharmacist's expertise becomes invaluable. They can review all medications, including over-the-counter drugs and supplements, to check for potential interactions or side effects. A pharmacist can also suggest strategies for simplifying medication management, such as using pill organizers or exploring options for pre-packaged medications.

Building Your Healthcare Team

The process of assembling your healthcare team typically begins with your loved one's primary care physician (PCP). This doctor, who may have been caring for your loved one for years, often serves as the foundation of the team. If you don't have a PCP you trust, start by asking for recommendations from friends, family, or local senior care organizations. Look for a doctor with experience in geriatric care and a willingness to coordinate with other specialists.

From there, your PCP can provide referrals to necessary specialists. However, don't hesitate to do your research as well.

Resources for finding specialists include:

- Online directories from professional organizations (e.g., American Academy of Neurology)
- Local Alzheimer's Association chapters
- Geriatric care managers
- Hospital referral services

Once you've identified potential team members, coordinate an initial consultation. Use this opportunity to assess not just their medical expertise, but also their rapport with your loved one and their collaborative approach.

When choosing healthcare providers, consider the following criteria:

1. Experience with dementia patients
2. Communication style and willingness to explain complex concepts
3. Openness to working as part of a team
4. Accessibility and responsiveness
5. Acceptance of your loved one's insurance

Remember, building your team is an ongoing process. As your loved one's needs change, you may need to bring in new specialists or change existing team members.

Effective Communication: The Key to Quality Care

Navigating the healthcare system effectively requires clear communication with your team. Medical terminology can feel like a foreign language, especially when dealing with a complex condition like dementia. Never hesitate to ask healthcare providers to explain terms or concepts you don't understand. A good provider will be happy to break down complex information into more digestible terms.

Preparing for medical appointments can significantly enhance their effectiveness. Before each visit, take some time to reflect on any changes or concerns you've noticed since the last appointment. Write these down, along with any questions you have. Prioritize your list, focusing on the most pressing issues first, in case time runs short.

During appointments, don't be afraid to take notes or ask if you can record the conversation for later review. If you're uncomfortable doing this alone, consider bringing a trusted friend or family member to appointments. They can act as a second set of ears, often picking up on details you might miss or thinking of questions you hadn't considered.

After each appointment, take a few moments to review and summarize what was discussed. If you're using a patient portal, log in to review visit summaries and test results. If anything is unclear, don't hesitate to reach out to the healthcare provider for clarification. Remember, you are an essential part of the care team, and your understanding of the treatment plan is crucial for its success.

Insurance Options

Understanding insurance coverage is crucial for managing care costs, but it can feel like navigating a labyrinth. Medicare, with its various parts and coverage options, is particularly complex. Medicare Part A covers inpatient hospital stays, skilled nursing facility care, and some home health care. However, it's important to understand that this coverage is limited. For example, Medicare will cover up to 100 days in a skilled nursing facility following a qualifying hospital stay, but only if the patient requires skilled care. It doesn't cover long-term custodial care, which is often needed in advanced dementia.

Medicare Part B covers outpatient care, preventive services, and medical supplies. This can include doctor visits, diagnostic tests, and durable medical equipment. For individuals with dementia, Part B can cover cognitive assessments and care planning sessions with healthcare providers. These sessions can be invaluable for developing comprehensive care strategies and are separate from routine visits.

Part D, which covers prescription drugs, is crucial for managing the various medications often prescribed in dementia care. However, coverage can vary significantly between plans. Hence, it's important to review your loved one's medications annually during the open enrollment period to ensure they're on the most cost-effective plan.

For those who qualify based on income and assets, Medicaid can provide coverage for long-term care services not covered by Medicare. This can include nursing home care and, in many states, home and community-based services that allow individuals to receive care in their own homes. Understanding the interplay between Medicare and Medicaid can be crucial for long-term financial planning.

It's also worth exploring whether your loved one has any private long-term care insurance. These policies, if purchased before the onset of dementia, can provide significant support for long-term care costs. However, they often come with specific requirements for activating benefits, so it's important to understand the policy details.

Navigating these insurance options can be overwhelming. Don't hesitate to seek help from a social worker, elder law attorney, or financial advisor specializing in elder care. These professionals can provide invaluable guidance in understanding coverage options and planning for future care needs.

Being Your Loved One's Voice

Perhaps the most important role you'll play in navigating the healthcare system is that of an advocate. As dementia progresses, your loved one may lose the ability to communicate their needs and preferences effectively. Your role is to ensure their voice is heard and their rights are protected.

Keep detailed records of all medical interactions, including symptoms, medications, and treatment plans. These records can be invaluable when coordinating care between different providers or seeking second opinions. Don't hesitate to speak up if you notice inconsistencies or have concerns about the care being provided.

Remember, you know your loved one best. If you feel something isn't right, persist in expressing your concerns and requesting further evaluation. Trust your instincts – your day-to-day observations can often catch issues that might not be immediately apparent in a brief medical visit.

Navigating the healthcare system for dementia care is undoubtedly challenging, but it's a crucial part of providing comprehensive care for your loved one. By understanding the roles of various healthcare providers, effectively communicating with your care team, navigating insurance options, leveraging community resources, and being a strong advocate, you can ensure the best possible care and quality of life for your loved one with dementia.

Caregiver's Corner

You're not just coordinating care; you're orchestrating a symphony of support.

Your dedication and attention to detail can make a world of difference in your loved one's quality of life.

Key Takeaways:

- Assemble a diverse healthcare team, starting with a trusted primary care physician
- Each specialist plays a unique role in comprehensive dementia care
- Effective communication with healthcare providers is crucial for quality care
- Understanding insurance options is vital for managing long-term care costs
- Advocacy is an essential part of navigating the healthcare system for your loved one

Quick Tip:

Create a "healthcare team contact sheet" with the names, specialties, and contact information of all providers. Keep it in your patient care binder. Ensure that it's updated regularly and easily accessible.

Reflection Question:

Looking at your loved one's current care team, what gaps do you see? Which specialist or service might you need to add or modify next to address upcoming challenges in their dementia journey?

Resource Spotlight:

Explore the Family Caregiver Alliance's "Health Care Team" section on their website for additional tips on working effectively with healthcare professionals in dementia care.

Chapter 7
Medications, Therapies, & Healthy Habits

Maria sat in the neurologist's office, scribbling notes furiously as the doctor discussed treatment options. Evie, meanwhile, was more interested in a plastic model brain on the desk.

"So, as I was saying," the doctor continued, "we can start with cholinesterase inhibitors. They may help improve memory and cognitive function."

"Choli-what-now?" Evie interjected, picking up the brain model. "Sounds like broccoli. Is that the secret? Eat your veggies, and suddenly, you remember where you left your keys?"

Maria shot her mother a look. "Mom, please."

The doctor smiled patiently. "It's okay. Mrs. Thompson, these medications work by increasing certain chemicals in the brain that are important for memory and thinking."

Evie nodded, turning the brain model in her hands. "I see. So you're saying my rusty, old brain needs a tune-up. Maybe we could just spray some WD-40 in my ear and call it a day?"

"Mom!" Maria exclaimed, mortified.

The doctor chuckled. "Well, it's not quite that simple, but your mother's sense of humor is a great asset. Maintaining a positive attitude can be very beneficial."

As the doctor continued explaining various management strategies, Maria noticed her mother growing quieter, her jokes less frequent. Finally, Evie spoke up, her voice uncharacteristically soft.

"Doctor, will these treatments... will they make me 'me' again?"

The room fell silent. Maria reached for her mother's hand, her heart breaking at the vulnerability in Evie's voice.

The doctor leaned forward, his expression kind but serious. "Mrs. Thompson, these treatments can help manage symptoms, but they're not a cure. The most important thing is to focus on quality of life. And from what I've seen today, you have a wonderful support system in your daughter."

Evie squeezed Maria's hand, a small smile returning to her face. "Well, she does put up with my jokes. I suppose that counts for something."

As they left the office, treatment plan in hand, Evie turned to her daughter. "Well, that was quite the earful. Good thing I had my trusty translator with me."

Maria smiled, realizing how much she'd absorbed and processed during the appointment. She'd asked insightful questions, made detailed notes, and already started formulating a plan to implement the doctor's recommendations.

"You know, Mom," Maria said, "I think we make a pretty good team. Your jokes keep us laughing, and I'll keep us organized and on track with this treatment plan."

Evie patted her daughter's arm affectionately. "That we do, sweetheart. I may be forgetful, but I'll never forget how lucky I am to have you in my corner."

While there's no cure for most types of dementia, various approaches can help manage symptoms and improve quality of life. This chapter explores current treatment options, management strategies, and emerging research that offers hope for the future.

As we delve into these topics, remember that the goal of dementia treatment isn't just about addressing cognitive symptoms. It's about enhancing overall well-being, maintaining independence as much as possible, and supporting both the person with dementia and you, their caregiver. What works best can vary from person to person, so you'll likely need to work closely with healthcare providers to find the right combination of treatments for your loved one.

Current Medication Approaches

Medications play a significant role in managing dementia symptoms, though their effects can be modest and vary between individuals. The main types of drugs used in dementia care include cholinesterase inhibitors and memantine.

Cholinesterase inhibitors work by boosting levels of acetylcholine, a chemical messenger involved in memory and judgment. These medications may help improve memory, awareness, and ability to perform daily activities. They're generally well-tolerated, but side effects can include nausea, vomiting, loss of appetite, and increased frequency of bowel movements.

Memantine works by regulating the activity of glutamate, another brain chemical involved in information processing. It's typically used for moderate to severe Alzheimer's and may be prescribed alone or in combination with a cholinesterase inhibitor. Side effects are generally mild and can include dizziness, confusion, constipation, and headache.

It's important to note that these medications don't work for everyone, and their effectiveness can decrease over time as the disease progresses. Regular follow-ups with the prescribing doctor are crucial to monitor effectiveness and manage any side effects. Don't be discouraged if the first medication tried doesn't yield the desired results - it often takes some trial and error to find the proper medication or combination of medications that produces the desired effect.

As a caregiver, you play a vital role in medication management. Keep a detailed record of all medications, dosages, and any observed effects or side effects. This information can be invaluable during doctor visits and in assessing the treatment's effectiveness.

Disease-Modifying Drugs: A New Frontier

In recent years, a new class of drugs has emerged that targets the underlying disease process in Alzheimer's. These drugs, known as monoclonal antibodies, are designed to reduce the buildup of amyloid plaques in the brain, which are believed to contribute to Alzheimer's disease.

The first of these drugs, Aducanumab (brand name Aduhelm), was approved by the FDA in 2021. Since then, Lecanemab (brand name Leqembi) has also received approval in early 2023. Another drug in this class, Donanemab, is still undergoing clinical trials but has shown promising results.

These medications work by targeting and removing amyloid plaques from the brain, representing a shift from managing symptoms to potentially modifying the disease process itself. While this is an exciting new direction in Alzheimer's treatment, it's important to discuss the potential benefits and risks with healthcare providers.

These drugs can have significant side effects and may not be suitable for everyone. The most notable risks are amyloid-related imaging abnormalities (ARIA), which can involve brain swelling or small bleeds in the brain. Regular brain scans are typically required during treatment to monitor for these potential complications.

As a caregiver, it's crucial to stay informed about these new treatments. Ask your loved one's doctor about the latest developments and whether they might be appropriate options.

Consider asking about:

- The potential benefits and risks specific to your loved one's condition
- The frequency and nature of required medical monitoring
- How the treatment might impact daily life and care routines
- The cost and insurance coverage for these new treatments

Remember, while these new drugs offer hope, they're not miracle cures. They may slow the progression of Alzheimer's in some patients, but they don't reverse existing damage or stop the disease entirely. Managing expectations – both your own and your loved ones – is an essential part of the caregiving journey.

As research continues, we may see more drugs in this class become available, potentially offering more options for treatment. Staying in regular communication with healthcare providers will help ensure you're aware of the latest developments and can make informed decisions about your loved one's care.

Medications for Symptom Management

Dementia often brings with it a host of other symptoms that can significantly impact quality of life. Various medications may be prescribed to manage these specific symptoms. Antidepressants might be used to address depression, which is common in individuals with dementia and can exacerbate cognitive symptoms.

Antipsychotics may be prescribed for hallucinations, delusions, or aggression, though they're used cautiously due to increased risks in older adults with dementia. They should be used at the lowest effective dose for the shortest possible time.

Sleep disturbances and anxiety are also common in dementia. While non-pharmacological approaches are preferred, sometimes medications may be prescribed for these issues. It's crucial to remember that older adults with dementia can be more sensitive to medication side effects.

As a caregiver, your observations are invaluable. Keep notes of any changes in symptoms or new side effects, and don't hesitate to discuss concerns with your healthcare provider. Your role in monitoring and reporting on these medications is crucial for your loved one's well-being.

Non-Pharmacological Therapies

While medications play an important role, non-drug approaches are equally crucial in dementia care. These therapies can be remarkably effective in managing symptoms and improving quality of life, either alongside medication or on their own.

Cognitive Stimulation Therapy (CST) involves engaging in activities designed to stimulate thinking, concentration, and memory. This might include discussions of current events, word games and puzzles, or practical activities like baking or gardening. Many find that these sessions not only help maintain cognitive function but also provide enjoyable social interaction.

Reminiscence therapy is another powerful tool. By discussing past experiences, often with the aid of photographs, familiar objects, or music, this therapy can help maintain a sense of identity, improve mood, and enhance communication. As a caregiver, you can incorporate elements of reminiscence therapy into your daily interactions, creating moments of connection and joy.

Art and music therapy can provide avenues for emotional expression and cognitive engagement. Whether it's painting, sculpting, singing, or simply listening to favorite songs, these creative therapies can reduce anxiety and depression while stimulating cognitive function. They can be particularly beneficial for individuals who have difficulty communicating verbally.

Physical and occupational therapy also play vital roles. Physical therapy can help maintain mobility and reduce fall risk, while occupational therapy focuses on making daily tasks more manageable and homes safer. These interventions can significantly enhance independence and quality of life.

As a caregiver, you can support these therapies by encouraging participation and incorporating elements into daily life. Simple activities like looking at old photos together, singing familiar songs, or adapting household tasks to your loved one's abilities can make a big difference.

The Power of Healthy Habits

While pharmaceutical treatments are important, never underestimate the power of lifestyle factors in managing dementia. Regular physical activity, for instance, can help maintain cognitive function, improve mood, and reduce behavioral symptoms. This doesn't have to mean strenuous workouts – even simple activities like daily walks can be beneficial.

Diet plays a crucial role. A healthy, balanced diet rich in fruits, vegetables, whole grains, and lean proteins may help slow cognitive decline. Some studies suggest that Mediterranean-style diets may be particularly beneficial for brain health.

Social engagement is another crucial factor. Maintaining social connections can help preserve cognitive function and improve quality of life. Encourage participation in family gatherings, community activities, or support groups for people with dementia. Even simple social interactions, like regular phone calls or video chats with friends and family, can make a significant difference.

Engaging in mentally stimulating activities is equally important. Reading, doing puzzles, learning a new skill, or playing games can all help keep the mind active. The key is to choose activities that are enjoyable and not frustrating.

Maintaining good sleep hygiene and managing stress are also vital components of dementia care. As a caregiver, you can help by establishing regular routines, creating a calm environment, and introducing relaxation techniques like deep breathing or gentle yoga.

Remember, as you support your loved one in maintaining these healthy habits, it's equally important to take care of your health and well-being.

Emerging Research and Clinical Trials

The field of dementia research is dynamic and full of promise. New potential treatments are continually being explored, from immunotherapies targeting abnormal brain proteins to stem cell therapies aiming to replace damaged brain cells. Gene therapy and the repurposing of existing drugs for other conditions are also active areas of research.

For those interested in being at the forefront of dementia treatment, participating in clinical trials can provide access to cutting-edge treatments and expert medical care. It's an opportunity to contribute to the advancement of dementia research while potentially benefiting from new therapies. However, it's a decision that should be made carefully, considering all aspects of your loved one's health and care.

If you're considering a clinical trial, start by discussing the possibility with your healthcare provider. They may be aware of local studies that might be suitable. You can also explore options on reputable websites that provide searchable databases of clinical studies.

When considering a clinical trial, it's essential to ask questions about the study's goal, the tests and treatments involved, potential side effects, and how it might affect current care. As a caregiver, your role in this decision-making process is crucial, balancing the potential benefits with the realities of your loved one's condition and care needs.

Reason For Hope

As we continue to learn more about dementia and develop new treatments, there is reason for hope. While a cure remains elusive, current treatments and management strategies can significantly improve the quality of life for individuals with dementia and their caregivers.

Remember, every individual's journey with dementia is unique. What works best will depend on the specific type of dementia, the stage of the disease, and individual factors. Working closely with healthcare providers, staying informed about new developments, and remaining flexible in your approach will be key to providing the best possible care for your loved one.

In this chapter, we've explored a range of treatment options and management strategies for dementia. From current medications to lifestyle interventions and emerging research, there are many ways to support your loved one's well-being. As a caregiver, your role in implementing these strategies and advocating for your loved one is invaluable.

Stay informed, seek support when you need it, and remember to take care of yourself as well. With each passing day, we're learning more about dementia and developing better ways to manage it, bringing hope for more effective treatments in the future.

Caregiver's Corner

Your attentive care and love are potent medicines in and of themselves. Your efforts to implement these strategies make a profound difference in your loved one's quality of life.

Key Takeaways:

- Current medications can help manage dementia symptoms, but effectiveness varies
- New disease-modifying drugs offer the potential to slow Alzheimer's progression
- Non-pharmacological therapies play a crucial role in dementia care
- Lifestyle factors like diet, exercise, and social engagement are important
- Emerging research and clinical trials provide hope for future treatments

Quick Tip:

Create a "treatment diary" to track medications, therapies, and lifestyle interventions. Note any changes in symptoms or behavior. This record can be invaluable during healthcare appointments.

Reflection Question:

Considering the various treatment approaches discussed, which areas do you think could make the most significant positive impact on your loved one's daily life if implemented?

Resource Spotlight:

Explore the Alzheimer's Association's "TrialMatch" service to learn about clinical trials in your area that might be suitable for your loved one.

Chapter 8
Home Safety & Daily Care

Maria stood in the doorway of her mother's bathroom, surveying her handiwork. She'd spent the entire day installing grab bars, a shower seat, and non-slip mats. Now, she watched as Evie examined the changes with a critical eye.

"Well," Evie said, tapping one of the grab bars, "I see you've turned my bathroom into a jungle gym."

Maria sighed, "Mom, these are for your safety. The doctor said we need to make some changes around the house."

Evie raised an eyebrow. "I've been using this bathroom for 40 years without incident. I don't see why I need all this... equipment."

"Because things are different now, Mom," Maria said gently. "We need to prevent falls and make things easier for you."

Evie's face softened. "I know, sweetheart. It's just... all these changes. They make it so real, you know?"

Maria nodded, stepping closer to her mother. "I know, Mom. But think of it this way – we're not just making things safer. We're making your house work for you. It's like having a whole team of invisible helpers."

Evie chuckled. "Invisible helpers, eh? Do they pull weeds?"

As they shared a laugh, Maria noticed her mother unconsciously steadying herself on one of the new grab bars. A wave of relief washed over her – the changes were already making a difference.

"You know, Mom," Maria said, "I've been thinking. Maybe we could make some other changes too. Like setting up a medication system to help you remember your pills, or putting labels on some of the kitchen cabinets."

Evie considered this for a moment. "Well, I suppose a few labels wouldn't hurt. But I draw the line at child-proof locks. I may be forgetful, but I can still operate a darn cabinet!"

Maria smiled, realizing that each small victory—each safety measure accepted, each adaptation embraced—was a step towards ensuring her mother's wellbeing. As challenging as it was, she knew that her efforts were making a real difference in Evie's daily life and safety.

"Deal," Maria said, giving her mother a gentle hug. "No child-proof locks. But how about we work on a routine for your medications together?"

Evie nodded, returning the hug. "Alright, dear. Lead the way. After all, you seem to be getting pretty good at this caregiver business."

As dementia progresses, the world can become an increasingly confusing and potentially dangerous place for your loved one. Your role as a caregiver evolves into that of a guardian, tasked with creating a sanctuary of safety while preserving dignity and quality of life. It's a delicate balancing act. One that requires patience, creativity, and an unwavering commitment to your loved one's well-being.

Creating a Safe Home Environment

Transforming a home into a haven for someone with dementia requires both practical adjustments and a touch of creativity. Think of it as curating a space that not only protects but also comforts and orients. Your goal is to create an environment that reduces confusion, prevents accidents, and supports your loved one's changing abilities.

Lighting becomes your ally in this endeavor. Bright, even illumination can reduce shadows that might cause confusion or fear. Night lights can transform treacherous midnight paths to the bathroom into safe, reassuring routes. As you adjust the lighting, imagine how each space will appear through your loved one's eyes at different times of day. Consider using motion-sensor lights in key areas to ensure that pathways are always well-lit when needed.

The floors beneath their feet deserve special attention. Loose rugs that once added character to a room can become hazardous obstacles. Secure them firmly or consider removing them altogether. Transition areas between rooms, once unremarkable, may now require visual cues to prevent trips and falls. You might use contrasting colors or textured strips to clearly mark these changes. As you make these changes, you're not just removing risks – you're creating a space where your loved one can move with confidence.

In the living areas, consider creating a special "safe space" – a cozy corner filled with familiar objects and comfortable seating. This can become a retreat when the world feels overwhelming, a place of comfort amidst confusion. Include items that stimulate pleasant memories and provide sensory comfort, like a soft blanket or a photo album. This space can serve as an anchor, providing a sense of security and belonging.

The bathroom, once a private sanctuary, now requires thoughtful modification. Grab bars, non-slip mats, and a raised toilet seat aren't just safety features – they're tools of independence, allowing your loved one to maintain dignity in personal care for as long as possible. Walk-in showers are typically most user-friendly for those living with dementia, but a "transfer bench" can be used on a traditional tub arrangement to aid in getting in and out of the bath safely. Use color contrast to make important features stand out – for example, a dark-colored toilet seat on a white toilet can be easier to see and use.

In the kitchen, safety becomes paramount. As you childproof for grandchildren, you may find yourself "dementia-proofing" for your loved one. Simple changes like safety knobs on the stove or automatic shut-off devices can prevent potential disasters while still allowing for supervised participation in cooking activities that bring joy and purpose. Label cabinets and drawers with pictures as well as words to help your loved one find items independently. Consider removing rarely used appliances to reduce clutter and confusion.

Don't overlook the importance of outdoor spaces. A secure garden or patio can provide a valuable connection to nature and a safe space for exercise and relaxation. Ensure that outdoor areas are well-lit and free from tripping hazards. If wandering is a concern, consider installing secure fencing and gates with alarms.

As you make these changes, remember that the goal is not just to create a safer space, but also to maintain a sense of home. Try to incorporate safety features in a way that doesn't make the environment feel institutional. Personalize spaces with familiar items, photos, and cherished mementos to help your loved one feel secure and oriented.

Managing Daily Care

Personal care routines that were once second nature may now require gentle guidance and support. As you assist with hygiene and dressing, remember that you're not just cleaning and clothing a body – you're helping maintain your loved one's sense of self and dignity. These intimate tasks require patience, respect, and often, a good dose of creativity.

Approach these tasks with patience and respect. Lay out clothing and supplies in a logical order, turning the process into a series of manageable steps. Offer choices where possible – it may take a little longer, but the sense of control it provides is invaluable. For example, you might ask, "Would you like to wear the blue shirt or the green one today?" This simple choice can help preserve a sense of autonomy.

Bathing can be particularly challenging. Some individuals with dementia may fear water or become confused by the process. Create a soothing environment with warm temperatures, soft lighting, and perhaps gentle music. Use a hand-held showerhead to give your loved one more control over the water flow. Always explain what you're doing before you do it, to avoid startling or confusing them.

Mealtimes can become a source of both nourishment and connection. As you adapt to changing abilities and preferences, try to maintain the social aspect of eating together. A calm environment, contrasting colors to help distinguish food items, and adaptive utensils can all contribute to a more enjoyable and successful dining experience.

Be mindful of changing food preferences and abilities. As dementia progresses, your loved one may prefer finger foods or softer textures. They may also develop a preference for sweeter foods. While maintaining good nutrition is important, don't underestimate the comfort that favorite foods can bring. Sometimes, the joy of a familiar treat outweighs strict nutritional considerations.

The challenges of sleep disturbances can test even the most patient caregiver. Creating a soothing bedtime routine can help signal to the body and mind that it's time to rest. Soft music, gentle lighting, and perhaps a warm, non-caffeinated beverage can become comforting rituals. If nighttime wandering becomes an issue, safety measures like Bluetooth door alarms can provide peace of mind without feeling restrictive.

Consider the impact of daytime activities on sleep patterns. Exposure to natural daylight and engaging in appropriate physical activities during the day can promote better sleep at night. Limit daytime napping, especially late in the afternoon, as this can disrupt nighttime sleep.

Communication becomes an art form as dementia progresses. Your words, tone, and body language all play crucial roles in conveying messages and providing comfort. Speak clearly and patiently, using simple phrases and visual cues when needed. Remember that even when words fail, the warmth in your voice and a gentle touch can convey love and reassurance.

Be attentive to non-verbal cues from your loved one. As verbal skills decline, they may communicate discomfort, pain, or needs through facial expressions, gestures, or changes in behavior. Learning to read these cues can help you respond more effectively to their needs.

Addressing Specific Safety Concerns

The fear of falls can be paralyzing, but with thoughtful preparation, you can create an environment that encourages safe movement. Beyond physical safeguards, consider activities that improve balance and strength – even simple seated exercises can make a difference. Tai Chi or gentle yoga, adapted for those with limited mobility, can be beneficial for both physical health and relaxation.

Wandering, one of the most anxiety-inducing behaviors for caregivers, requires a blend of prevention and preparedness. Try to understand the underlying needs that might prompt wandering – is it boredom, a need for purpose, or an attempt to fulfill old routines? By addressing these needs proactively, you may reduce the urge to wander.

Engage your loved one in meaningful activities that provide a sense of purpose. This might involve simple household tasks, sorting objects, or engaging with memory books. Sometimes, the need to wander comes from a desire to "go home" or "go to work" – even if they are already home. In these cases, validation and redirection can be more effective than correction.

At the same time, have a plan in place for when wandering does occur. Identification jewelry, alert systems, and informed neighbors can all be part of your safety net. Consider enrolling in a safe return program, which can help locate individuals who have wandered and become lost.

The issue of driving is often laden with emotion, representing independence and normalcy. Approaching this subject requires sensitivity and often, a united front with healthcare providers. Focus on alternative ways to maintain independence and social connections, whether through family support, community services, or adapted activities closer to home.

When it's time to stop driving, frame the conversation around safety and responsibility rather than loss of ability. Explore alternative transportation options together, such as family members providing rides, community senior transport services, or rideshare apps designed for seniors. Sometimes, maintaining a parked car in the driveway can provide a sense of comfort and normalcy, even if it's no longer driven.

Assessing the Ability to Live Alone

One of the most heart-wrenching decisions you'll face is determining when it's no longer safe for your loved one to live independently. This isn't a single moment of judgment, but rather an ongoing process of observation and honest evaluation. It's a decision that often comes with a mix of emotions – concern for safety, sadness at the loss of independence, and perhaps even relief at addressing a situation that has become increasingly problematic.

You'll find yourself becoming acutely aware of changes in your loved one's behavior and capabilities. Are they forgetting to take medications or struggling with once-familiar tasks? Do you notice unpaid bills piling up or spoiled food in the refrigerator? These seemingly small details can paint a larger picture of their ability to manage daily life.

Your observations are invaluable, so remember to use your journal to keep tabs on any changes you see occurring. In moments of doubt, it can provide clarity and validation of your instincts.

At times when you have doubts or are unsure if changes you suspect are of significance, don't hesitate to seek professional opinions. An occupational therapist can offer practical insights into your loved one's daily functioning, while a geriatric care manager can provide a holistic view of their living situation. These expert perspectives can complement your observations, helping you make informed decisions about care and living arrangements.

As you evaluate your loved one's ability to live alone, consider their cognitive function, physical safety, personal hygiene habits, nutritional intake, and emotional well-being. Are they able to respond appropriately in emergencies? Can they manage their finances and avoid potential scams? Is there a risk of them wandering and becoming lost? Each of these factors plays a crucial role in determining the level of care and support needed.

If the time comes when independent living is no longer safe, remember that there are options that can still honor your loved one's desire for autonomy. From in-home care to assisted living facilities, the goal is to find a solution that provides necessary support while maintaining as much independence as possible. This transition, while challenging, will often lead to improved quality of life and peace of mind for both you and your loved one.

Conclusion

Creating a safe environment and managing daily care for a loved one with dementia is a profound act of love. It's a journey that will challenge you, change you, and ultimately reveal strengths you never knew you had. As you implement these strategies and adapt to ever-changing needs, remember that perfection is not the goal – love and safety are.

Your efforts, no matter how small they may seem in the moment, are making a world of difference. In the soft smile of recognition, the moment of connection over a shared memory, or the peaceful sleep of your loved one, you'll find the rewards of your dedication. Stay informed, remain flexible, and above all, be gentle with yourself. You are doing sacred, meaningful work, and your love shines through in every thoughtful adaptation and careful consideration.

As you navigate this journey, remember that you're not alone. Reach out to support groups, connect with other caregivers, and don't hesitate to seek professional help when needed. Your dedication to creating a safe and loving environment is a testament to the power of human compassion and resilience. Take pride in your role as a caregiver – you are making a profound difference in your loved one's life, one day at a time.

Caregiver's Corner

Your efforts to create a safe-haven for your loved one are acts of profound love. Remember that in the midst of adapting routines and modifying spaces, your presence and care are the most potent safety measures of all.

Key Takeaways:

- Creating a safe home environment involves practical adjustments and creative solutions
- Daily care routines require patience, respect, and adaptability
- Addressing specific safety concerns like wandering and driving requires proactive planning
- Assessing the ability to live alone is an ongoing process requiring careful observation
- The caregiver's role in ensuring safety is crucial and evolves with the progression of dementia

Quick Tip:

Create a "safety checklist" for each room in the house. Review and update it monthly to ensure you're addressing new challenges as they arise and maintaining a secure environment.

Reflection Question:

Consider a daily care routine that has become challenging. How might you redesign this routine to enhance both the safety and dignity of your loved one? What creative approaches could you try to make the experience more positive for both of you?

Resource Spotlight:

Explore the National Institute on Aging's "Home Safety Checklist for Alzheimer's Disease" for a comprehensive guide to creating a dementia-friendly living space.

Chapter 9

Effective Communication and Behavior Management

Maria stood in the kitchen, watching her mother stare blankly at the coffee maker. Evie had been standing there for several minutes, her hand hovering over the buttons.

"Mom?" Maria said gently. "Do you need help with the coffee?"

Evie turned, frustration etched on her face. "I can make a damn cup of coffee!" she snapped, then immediately looked contrite. "I'm sorry, honey. I just... I can't remember how to work this thing."

Maria took a deep breath, reminding herself that the outburst wasn't personal. "It's okay, Mom. Why don't we do it together?"

As they went through the steps of making coffee, Maria noticed her mother's hands shaking slightly. When the coffee was ready, they sat down at the kitchen table.

"Mom," Maria started carefully, "I've been thinking. Maybe we could put some labels on the buttons of the coffee maker? Just simple ones, like 'brew' and 'off'."

Evie was quiet for a moment, staring into her mug. "I suppose that might help," she said softly. Then, with a hint of her old humor, she added, "But let's make sure the labels are big enough. My eyes aren't what they used to be, you know. Wouldn't want to brew a pot of 'OFF' accidentally."

Maria chuckled, relieved to see a glimmer of her mother's wit. "Deal. We'll make them big and clear."

As they sipped their coffee, Evie reached across the table and took Maria's hand. "I'm sorry I snapped at you earlier. I get so frustrated sometimes."

"I know, Mom," Maria said, squeezing her hand. "It's okay to feel frustrated. We're in this together, remember? When you forget things, I'll be here to remind you. And when I forget to be patient, you can remind me."

Evie smiled, her eyes misty. "You're a good daughter, Maria. I don't know what I'd do without you."

At that moment, Maria realized that effective communication wasn't just about words or memory aids. It was about patience, understanding, and the unspoken language of love that flowed between them. Even as the dementia progressed, this connection would be their most vital lifeline.

"Now," Evie said, a mischievous glint in her eye, "how about we label the ice cream in the freezer as 'Health Food'? Might help me remember to eat more of it."

As they laughed together, Maria felt a renewed sense of purpose. With each challenge they faced, she was learning to adapt, to communicate better, and to cherish the moments of connection, no matter how small.

As your loved one's journey with dementia progresses, you'll likely find yourself facing new challenges in communication and behavior. These changes can feel like navigating a landscape where the terrain shifts beneath your feet. But take heart - with understanding, patience, and the right strategies, you can find new ways to connect and manage this evolving journey.

The Changing Landscape of Communication

Communication is the bridge that connects us to our loved ones, allowing us to share thoughts, feelings, and experiences. Dementia gradually erodes this bridge, making it increasingly difficult for individuals to express themselves and understand others. As a caregiver, adapting your communication approach becomes crucial in maintaining your connection and providing effective care.

In the early stages, you might notice your loved one struggling to find the right words or losing their train of thought mid-conversation. They may repeat questions or stories, not remembering they've already shared this information. While these changes can be frustrating, approaching them with patience and understanding is key.

As the disease progresses, communication challenges become more pronounced. Your loved one may have difficulty understanding complex sentences or abstract concepts. They might struggle to express their needs or emotions, leading to frustration and potentially challenging behaviors. In later stages, verbal communication may become limited or even non-existent.

However, it's crucial to remember that even when words fail, communication is still possible. Non-verbal cues like facial expressions, tone of voice, and touch become increasingly important. Your loved one may not understand everything you say, but they can often sense your emotional state and respond to your presence.

Understanding the Brain Behind the Words

To better navigate these communication challenges, it helps to understand how dementia affects the brain. Different types of dementia impact various brain regions, but many affect areas crucial for language and communication.

For instance, in Alzheimer's disease, the temporal lobe, involved in language comprehension and word finding, is often affected early. This is why your loved one might struggle to find the right words or understand complex sentences. The frontal lobe, important for organizing thoughts and controlling impulses, can also be impacted. This might lead to speaking out of turn, difficulty following conversations, or struggling to organize thoughts into coherent speech.

Understanding these brain changes can help you approach communication difficulties with more empathy and patience. Remember, it's not that your loved one isn't trying - their brain is literally changing in ways that make communication more challenging.

Strategies for Effective Communication

Adapting your communication style can significantly improve your interactions. As dementia progresses, simplifying your language becomes increasingly important. Instead of complex sentences with multiple clauses, opt for short, straightforward statements. For example, rather than asking, "Would you like to go for a walk in the park to enjoy the nice weather?" try saying, "Let's go for a walk. The weather is nice."

Avoid asking open-ended questions that might be overwhelming. Instead of "What would you like to do today?" try offering simple choices: "Would you like to read a book or listen to music?" This approach reduces confusion and helps your loved one feel more in control.

Non-verbal communication becomes even more critical as verbal skills decline. Maintain eye contact to show you're engaged in the interaction. Use a gentle touch, like holding hands or a reassuring pat on the arm, to convey care and support. Keep your voice calm and pleasant, even if you're feeling frustrated.

Creating a conducive environment can also enhance communication. Minimize distractions by turning off the TV or radio during important conversations. Choose a quiet, well-lit area where your loved one can focus on you without competing stimuli.

Visual aids can be incredibly helpful as language processing becomes more difficult. Use gestures to reinforce your words. For example, if you're asking if they want to eat, mimic the action of eating. Show objects related to your conversation – if you're discussing going for a walk, show them their shoes or coat.

Above all, practice patience and don't be afraid of repetition. Your loved one may take longer to process information and formulate responses. Resist the urge to finish their sentences or rush them. Give them time to express themselves, even if it takes longer than you're used to.

Navigating the Seas of Behavioral Changes

Behavioral changes are a common and often challenging aspect of dementia. These changes can be confusing and distressing for both your loved one and you as a caregiver. Understanding the reasons behind these behaviors is the first step in managing them effectively.

It's important to remember that behavioral changes in dementia are not random or intentional. They're often the result of your loved one trying to communicate a need or respond to something in their environment. Physical discomfort, environmental factors, cognitive changes, emotional responses, or unmet needs can all contribute to challenging behaviors.

When faced with a behavioral change, try to understand the underlying cause. Is your loved one in pain? Does their environment overstimulate them? Are they trying to express a need that they can't articulate?

For instance, if your loved one becomes aggressive, ensure everyone's safety first. Then, try to identify the trigger for the aggressive behavior. Is it a particular activity, time of day, or environmental factor? Respond calmly and reassuringly, using a soft, soothing voice and non-threatening body language.

Wandering, another common behavior, often stems from confusion, restlessness, or an attempt to fulfill a former obligation. To manage wandering, ensure your home environment is secure. Use door alarms or locks that are out of your loved one's line of sight. Try to address the underlying need – if they're restless, provide opportunities for safe, supervised movement.

Sundowning, or increased confusion and agitation in the late afternoon or evening, can be managed by maintaining a consistent daily routine, encouraging physical activity during the day, and creating a calm environment as evening approaches.

Repetitive behaviors, while frustrating, often stem from anxiety or a need for reassurance. Respond patiently, even if you've answered the same question multiple times. Try using written notes or signs to provide constant reminders for frequently asked questions.

Preserving Dignity and Connection

As you navigate these communication and behavioral challenges, it's crucial to remember that your loved one is still the person you've always known and loved. Dementia may change how they express themselves, but their need for love, respect, and connection remains.

Continue to involve them in decisions about their care as much as possible. Even in later stages, offering simple choices can help maintain a sense of control and dignity. Celebrate small victories and find joy in moments of connection, no matter how brief.

Try to focus on the abilities your loved one retains rather than what they've lost. Encourage them to participate in activities they can still do, even if they need some assistance. This could be as simple as folding laundry together or listening to their favorite music.

Maintain physical affection if your loved one responds well to it. A gentle hand massage, a hug, or simply sitting close together can provide comfort and reinforce your connection when words fail.

Remember to take care of yourself as well. Caregiving can be emotionally and physically exhausting. Seek support from family, friends, or professional counselors. Join support groups where you can share experiences and advice with others who understand your journey.

The Power of Presence

In the midst of all these strategies and challenges, never underestimate the power of your presence. Sometimes, simply being there, offering a reassuring touch or a warm smile, can communicate more than words ever could. Your loved one may not always remember your name or recognize your face, but they can often sense the love and care you provide.

Create moments of joy wherever you can. Put on their favorite music and dance together. Look through old photo albums, even if they don't remember the specific events - the emotions tied to happy memories often remain. Engage in sensory activities like gardening or baking, which can stimulate the senses and evoke positive feelings.

Remember, communication in dementia care isn't just about exchanging information - it's about maintaining a connection, providing comfort, and showing love. Every small moment of understanding, every smile, every peaceful interaction is a victory. These moments, strung together, form the tapestry of your caregiving journey.

As you face each new day, armed with patience, understanding, and these strategies, know that you're doing more than just providing care. You're preserving a relationship, honoring a life story, and ensuring that your loved one feels valued and respected, regardless of the challenges dementia presents.

This journey of caregiving will test you, teach you, and transform you. There will be difficult days, but there will also be moments of profound connection and unexpected joy. Hold onto these moments. They are the light that will guide you through the challenges, reminding you of the deep bond you share with your loved one.

By approaching communication and behavior management with patience, creativity, and compassion, you can maintain a meaningful connection throughout this journey. Remember, in the world of dementia care, love speaks louder than words, and your unwavering presence is the most powerful communication of all.

Caregiver's Corner

In the ebb and flow of dementia care, your patience and love create a language of their own. Remember, even when words fail, your presence speaks volumes. Every tiny moment of connection is a triumph worth celebrating.

Key Takeaways:

- Communication challenges evolve as dementia progresses, requiring adaptable strategies
- Understanding the brain changes behind communication difficulties fosters patience
- Behavioral changes often stem from unmet needs or environmental factors
- Preserving dignity and focusing on retained abilities is crucial
- Your presence and non-verbal communication become increasingly important

Quick Tip:

Start a "Daily Itinerary" where you jot down important information for the day ahead - like scheduled activities, expected visitors, or the day's menu. Review this with your loved one each morning and leave it accessible for them to reference. This routine can help orient them to the day and reduce anxiety about unknown events.

Reflection Question:

Think about a recent positive interaction with your loved one. What non-verbal cues or environmental factors contributed to its success? How can you recreate these conditions to foster more such moments?

Resource Spotlight:

Explore the Alzheimer's Association's "Communication and Alzheimer's" page for additional tips and downloadable resources to enhance your communication strategies.

Chapter 10

Promoting Health & Well-Being

Maria spread out a yoga mat in the living room, eyeing her mother skeptically. Evie stood nearby, dressed in a mismatched tracksuit and a headband that had seen better days.

"Mom, are you sure about this? We could start with something simpler, like a short walk around the block."

Evie waved her hand dismissively. "Nonsense! The doctor said exercise is good for the brain, and I intend to give my grey matter a run for its money. Now, where's that yoga tape?"

Maria hesitated, then pressed play on the remote. As the instructor's soothing voice filled the room, Evie attempted to mimic the poses on screen. Her "Warrior Pose" looked more akin to a "Wobbly Flamingo", while her "Downward Dog" would have been better named "Woman Who Lost A Contact Lens".

"Mom, maybe we should—"

"I've got this, dear. Just because my mind's a bit foggy doesn't mean my body can't bend like a pretzel... or... maybe... more like a slightly stale breadstick."

Suddenly, as Evie attempted a particularly ambitious twist, she lost her balance and toppled over. For a moment, Maria held her breath, worried her mother might be hurt. But then Evie burst into laughter, her whole body shaking with mirth.

"Nailed it!" Evie giggled, struggling to sit up. "I hope you enjoyed the new pose I invented – the Tumbling Tortoise!"

For several minutes, mother and daughter laughed until tears streamed down their faces, all thoughts of proper yoga technique forgotten. As their laughter finally subsided into occasional chuckles, Maria helped her mother up, both of them wiping their eyes.

"Well," Evie said, still catching her breath, "I may not remember much, but I'll never forget this yoga session."

Maria hugged her mom, feeling lighter than she had in weeks. "Me neither, Mom. Me neither."

Later, as they sat at the kitchen table with cups of herbal tea, Maria pulled out a crossword puzzle. "How about we give our brains a workout now?"

Evie peered at the puzzle. "Ah, yes. Let's see if we can jog my memory into remembering things I never knew in the first place."

They worked on the puzzle together, with Maria patiently offering clues and gentle reminders when Evie struggled. To her surprise, her mother occasionally came up with answers that even Maria couldn't figure out.

"Ha!" Evie exclaimed triumphantly after solving a particularly tricky clue. "Looks like there's still some spark in this old noggin after all."

Maria beamed at her mother's joy. "You're full of surprises, Mom. How did you know that one?"

Evie winked. "Just because I can't remember what I had for breakfast doesn't mean I've forgotten everything. Some things just stick, you know?"

As they continued with the puzzle, Maria realized that promoting her mother's health wasn't just about physical exercise or mental challenges. It was about finding activities that brought engagement, joy, and a sense of accomplishment. Whether it was attempting yoga poses or solving crossword clues, these moments of active participation were keeping her mother's spirit alive and her mind engaged.

"You know, Mom," Maria said, "I think we make a pretty good team. Your yoga moves might need some work, but your crossword skills are top-notch."

Evie grinned. "Well, dear, between your patience and my unpredictable memory, we're unstoppable. Now, what do you say we celebrate our athletic and intellectual achievements with some ice cream?"

As they shared a laugh and headed to the kitchen, Maria felt a warm sense of accomplishment. They were finding their way, one wobbly yoga pose and crossword clue at a time.

Physical health forms the foundation of overall well-being, and exercise plays a crucial role in dementia care. Movement is medicine for people with dementia, and even gentle, regular activity can have profound benefits. For those in the early to middle stages of dementia, a mix of aerobic exercise, strength training, and balance activities can be beneficial.

Walking

Walking, often underestimated in its simplicity, can be a powerful tool. Start with short walks and gradually increase the duration as tolerated. You might begin with a stroll to the end of your street and back. Over time, you could find yourselves enjoying a 30-minute loop around the neighborhood each morning. This not only provides physical benefits but also creates a special time of connection between you and your loved one.

As you establish a walking routine, pay attention to the environment. Choose routes with even surfaces to reduce the risk of falls. Parks or quiet residential areas can offer a pleasant, low-stress setting. Morning walks can be particularly beneficial, as the natural light exposure can help regulate sleep patterns. During your walks, engage your loved one in conversation about the surroundings – point out interesting plants, birds, or architecture. This combines physical activity with cognitive stimulation.

Swimming

If your loved one enjoys water, swimming or water aerobics can be excellent options, especially for those with joint issues. These activities provide a low-impact full-body workout. The buoyancy of water can make movement easier and more enjoyable for those who might struggle with land-based exercises. The sensory experience of being in water can also be calming and refreshing. Many community centers offer specialized water exercise classes for seniors or individuals with mobility issues.

Yoga

Gentle yoga or tai chi can improve balance, flexibility, and relaxation, while also providing a calming effect that can be particularly beneficial for individuals with dementia. These practices often incorporate breathing exercises, which can help reduce stress and anxiety. The slow, deliberate movements can improve body awareness and coordination. Look for classes specifically designed for seniors or those with cognitive impairments. Alternatively, there are many gentle yoga routines available on DVD or online that you can follow together at home.

Seated Exercises

For those with mobility issues, seated exercises can be incredibly valuable. Even from a chair, your loved one can perform movements that improve circulation, maintain flexibility, and provide some resistance training. Simple exercises like leg lifts, arm circles, or seated marches can be effective. You can even incorporate light weights or resistance bands for added benefit. Create a routine of 10-15 minutes of seated exercise twice a day. This could be done while watching a favorite TV show or listening to music to make it more enjoyable.

Keep Them Moving

The key is to keep your loved one moving in whatever way is safe and enjoyable for them. Even simple activities like gardening, light household chores, or dancing to favorite music can provide valuable physical activity. The goal is to make movement a regular, enjoyable part of daily life rather than a chore. Try to incorporate movement into everyday activities – for example, doing simple stretches while waiting for the kettle to boil, or marching in place during TV commercials.

Remember to always consult with a healthcare provider before starting any new exercise regimen, especially if your loved one has other health conditions or mobility issues. They can provide guidance on safe and appropriate activities.

Nourishing from Within

Proper nutrition is vital for overall health and can significantly impact cognitive function. However, individuals with dementia may face challenges with eating, such as forgetting to eat, losing the ability to use utensils, or having difficulty swallowing. As a caregiver, you can turn meals into opportunities for engagement, not just nutrition.

Consider involving your loved one in meal planning or preparation if possible. This can provide a sense of purpose and control. Even simple tasks like washing vegetables, stirring a pot, or setting the table can be meaningful. These activities can stimulate the senses and evoke memories associated with cooking and meal times. Use colorful plates that contrast with the food to make meals more visually appealing and easier to see. This can help with visual perception issues that often accompany dementia.

If using utensils becomes challenging, don't hesitate to provide finger foods. This allows your loved one to maintain some independence in eating. Foods like sandwiches cut into small pieces, cheese cubes, fruit slices, or vegetable sticks can be nutritious and easy to manage. You might also consider adaptive utensils with larger, easier-to-grip handles or plates with high sides to make scooping food easier.

When preparing meals, focus on nutrient-dense foods. Include a variety of fruits and vegetables for vitamins and antioxidants. Brightly colored fruits and vegetables are often high in antioxidants, which may help protect brain health. Berries, leafy greens, and sweet potatoes are excellent choices. Incorporate lean proteins like fish, chicken, or legumes to support muscle health. Fatty fish like salmon, mackerel, or sardines are particularly beneficial due to their high omega-3 content, which is associated with brain health.

Whole grains provide fiber and sustained energy. Options like oatmeal, quinoa, or brown rice can be easier to chew and swallow than some other grains. Omega-3 fatty acids, found in fish, walnuts, and flaxseeds, may have cognitive benefits. Consider adding ground flaxseed to smoothies or oatmeal for an easy omega-3 boost.

As dementia progresses, you might need to modify food textures to make eating easier and safer. This could mean chopping foods into smaller pieces, mashing certain foods, or using a food processor to create smoother textures. Always be aware of choking risks and adjust food consistency as needed.

The Critical Role of Hydration

Proper hydration is crucial for everyone, but it's particularly vital for individuals with dementia. As cognitive function declines, people may forget to drink water or lose the ability to recognize thirst, making dehydration a significant risk. This can lead to severe health complications and exacerbate the symptoms of dementia.

Adequate hydration is essential for numerous bodily functions. It regulates body temperature, aids digestion, maintains blood pressure, supports kidney function, and facilitates nutrient transportation to cells. For individuals with dementia, even mild dehydration can have pronounced effects, leading to increased confusion, dizziness, and fatigue.

Dehydration can also cause or worsen other health issues common in older adults. Urinary tract infections, for instance, are more likely to occur in dehydrated individuals and can cause sudden changes in behavior that might be mistaken for a progression of dementia. Constipation, another common issue, can be alleviated with proper hydration, potentially reducing discomfort and challenging behaviors.

It's essential to be vigilant for signs of dehydration. These can include dry mouth and lips, decreased urination or dark-colored urine, sunken eyes, increased confusion or irritability, and dizziness or headaches. In severe cases, dehydration can lead to hospitalization and serious complications, including kidney problems and an increased risk of falls due to dizziness and weakness.

To promote hydration, try offering drinks regularly throughout the day, not just at mealtimes. Using visual cues can be helpful; for example, a clear water bottle marked with times can serve as a reminder to drink. Variety is key - while water is excellent, herbal teas, low-fat milk, and foods with high water content like soups, fruits, and vegetables all contribute to hydration.

For those who have difficulty swallowing liquids, consider using thickeners as recommended by a speech therapist. These can make drinks easier to manage, reducing the risk of aspiration while ensuring adequate fluid intake.

Remember, the goal is to make hydration a consistent part of daily care. By prioritizing this often-overlooked aspect of health, you can help maintain your loved one's overall well-being and potentially reduce the risk of complications associated with dementia. Your attentiveness to hydration is a simple yet powerful way to enhance their quality of life and support their health in the face of cognitive challenges.

The Restorative Power of Rest

Sleep disturbances are common in dementia and can significantly impact both physical and cognitive health. Establishing good sleep hygiene can help manage these issues. Strive to maintain a consistent sleep schedule, even on weekends. The body's internal clock responds well to routine, so try to have your loved one go to bed and wake up at the same time each day.

Create a relaxing bedtime routine. This might include listening to calm music, reading a familiar story, or engaging in gentle stretching. These activities can signal to the body that it's time to wind down. Consider using aromatherapy, such as lavender-scented lotion or a diffuser with calming essential oils. The sense of smell is closely linked to memory and emotion, and familiar, soothing scents can help create a sense of comfort and relaxation.

Ensure the sleeping environment is conducive to rest. The bedroom should be dark, quiet, and at a comfortable temperature. If your loved one finds complete darkness disorienting, use a small night light. Consider using blackout curtains to block out early morning light if that's disrupting sleep. White noise machines or soft background sounds like gentle rain or ocean waves can help mask disruptive noises and create a soothing atmosphere.

Be mindful of daytime habits that can affect sleep. Limit caffeine intake, especially in the afternoon and evening. While a short nap can be refreshing, try to avoid prolonged or late-afternoon naps that might interfere with nighttime sleep. Aim to keep naps to 30 minutes or less and before 3 PM. Encourage physical activity during the day, but not too close to bedtime. Exposure to natural daylight, especially in the morning, can help regulate sleep-wake cycles.

If sleep problems persist, consult with a healthcare provider. Sometimes, underlying issues like sleep apnea or restless leg syndrome may be contributing to sleep disturbances. Medications can also affect sleep patterns, so a review of current prescriptions might be helpful. In some cases, a low dose of melatonin, under a doctor's guidance, might be beneficial.

Be prepared for nighttime wandering, which is common in dementia. Ensure the home is safe for nighttime movement – clear pathways, nightlights in hallways and bathrooms, and consider a bed alarm to alert you if your loved one gets up. If they do wake and wander, gently guide them back to bed with reassuring words and actions.

Remember that your rest is crucial, too. If nighttime caregiving is disrupting your sleep, consider options for respite care or taking turns with other family members. Your ability to provide care during the day is closely tied to the quality of your rest.

Stimulating the Mind

While dementia does cause progressive cognitive decline, engaging in mentally stimulating activities can help maintain cognitive function for longer and improve quality of life. The principles of Cognitive Stimulation Therapy (CST) offer valuable insights that you can incorporate into daily life.

Engage your loved one in activities that challenge thinking skills. This could include puzzles, word games, or simple problem-solving tasks. The key is to choose activities that are challenging enough to be stimulating but not so complex that they become frustrating. Crossword puzzles, jigsaw puzzles, or even simple math games can be effective. Start with easier versions and gradually increase the difficulty as able. Picture puzzles or matching games can be good options as verbal skills decline.

Importantly, encourage the expression of opinions rather than just factual recall. This approach values your loved one's thoughts and feelings, promoting a sense of self-worth. Ask open-ended questions about current events, family matters, or past experiences. Even if the responses aren't always accurate, the act of forming and expressing opinions is beneficial. This could be as simple as asking their opinion on a TV show you've watched together or what they think about a piece of music.

Use reminiscence activities, recalling past experiences positively. This not only provides cognitive stimulation but also helps maintain a sense of identity. Look through old photographs together, listen to music from their youth, or discuss favorite memories. These activities can evoke powerful emotions and memories, even in the later stages of dementia. Create a "memory box" filled with items from their past – photos, trinkets, or other meaningful objects. Exploring this box together can spark conversations and provide comfort.

Creative pursuits can be both cognitively stimulating and emotionally satisfying. Art activities like painting, coloring, or sculpting with clay allow for self-expression and can be adapted to various skill levels. The act of creating something can provide a sense of accomplishment and purpose. Don't focus on the end result – the process of creating is what's important. Simple crafts like stringing large beads or sorting colorful objects can be engaging and satisfying.

Music deserves special attention in cognitive stimulation. Whether listening to favorite songs, singing, or playing simple instruments, music can evoke memories and emotions, providing both cognitive and emotional benefits. Consider having daily 'concerts' where you listen to your loved one's favorite songs from their youth. You may see them light up, start tapping their foot, and sometimes even sing along. Music has a unique ability to reach people, even in the advanced stages of dementia. Try incorporating music into daily routines – perhaps a particular song for wake-up time, or calming classical music during meals.

The Healing Touch of Nature

Engaging with nature and sensory experiences can be both calming and stimulating. Gardening or plant care, even if it's just tending to a few potted plants, can provide a sense of purpose and connection to the natural world. The tactile experience of touching soil, the visual stimulation of colorful flowers, and the scent of herbs can all provide rich sensory input.

Consider setting up a small container garden, even if it's just on a patio or windowsill. Choose plants that are easy to care for and safe if ingested. Herbs like basil, mint, or lavender can be good choices, offering both visual appeal and pleasant aromas. The act of watering plants, removing dead leaves, or simply observing growth can be a peaceful and engaging activity. If outdoor gardening is possible, raised beds or vertical gardens can make the activity more accessible.

Bird watching, either outdoors or from a window, can be another way to connect with nature. Set up a bird feeder where it's easily visible. The activity of identifying different birds, observing their behaviors, and enjoying their colors and songs can be both cognitively stimulating and emotionally uplifting. Keep a simple bird identification guide nearby to look up different species together.

If possible, spend time outdoors regularly. A walk in a park, sitting in a garden, or even just feeling the sun and breeze can have profound effects on mood and well-being. The changing seasons provide ongoing opportunities for observation and discussion. Even if mobility is limited, sitting near an open window to feel the breeze and hear outdoor sounds can be beneficial.

Consider creating a sensory garden with plants of various textures, colors, and scents. Lamb's ear for its soft texture, bright marigolds for visual appeal, and fragrant rosemary can all provide different sensory experiences. This type of garden can be particularly engaging for individuals with dementia, stimulating multiple senses and evoking memories.

Nature-based activities can also be brought indoors. Arrange flowers together, plant herb seeds in small pots, or create nature collages using leaves and flowers. The texture of bark, the scent of pine needles, or the color of autumn leaves can all provide rich sensory experiences and topics for discussion.

Caregiver's Corner

Nurturing your loved one's physical and mental well-being is a powerful act of care. Remember, every small effort - from a short walk to a shared meal - contributes to their overall health and your connection with them.

Key Takeaways:

- Regular physical activity, even gentle exercises, can significantly benefit individuals with dementia
- Proper nutrition and hydration are crucial, with meals becoming opportunities for engagement
- Establishing good sleep hygiene can help manage common sleep disturbances in dementia
- Cognitive stimulation through various activities can help maintain mental function and improve quality of life
- Connecting with nature provides valuable sensory experiences and can be calming and stimulating

Quick Tip:

Create a "sensory box" filled with items of different textures, scents, and colors from nature. This can be an excellent tool for stimulation on days when outdoor activities aren't possible.

Reflection Question:

Think about your loved one's daily routine. Where can you incorporate more movement, sensory experiences, or cognitive stimulation? How might these additions enhance their overall well-being and your caregiving experience?

Resource Spotlight:

Check out the National Institute on Aging's "Go4Life" program, which offers free resources on exercise and physical activity specifically designed for older adults, including those with cognitive impairments.

Chapter 11

Navigating Common Challenges

Maria stood in the doorway of her mother's bedroom, watching as Evie rummaged through her dresser drawers, tossing clothes onto the floor.

"Mom? What are you doing?" Maria asked, stepping into the room.

Evie turned, clutching a handful of socks. "I can't find my blue sweater. Someone must have taken it."

Maria's heart sank. The sweater in question was draped over a chair in plain sight. "Mom, your sweater is right there," she said gently, pointing to the chair.

Evie blinked, confusion clouding her eyes. "But... I looked there. I don't understand."

As Maria helped her mother clean up the scattered clothes, she noticed Evie's hands trembling slightly. "Are you feeling okay, Mom?"

"I'm fine," Evie snapped, then immediately softened. "I'm sorry, dear. I just... I feel like I'm losing control. Things aren't where they should be. I forget... I forget so much."

Maria wrapped her arm around her mother's shoulders. "It's okay, Mom. We're in this together, remember?"

Evie nodded, leaning into her daughter's embrace. "I do remember that. At least, I think I do."

As they folded clothes together, Maria's mind raced with all the challenges they'd faced recently - the confusion, the mood swings, the repeated questions. Each day seemed to bring a new hurdle.

"You know what?" Maria said, trying to inject some cheerfulness into her voice. "Why don't we go for a walk outside? The fresh air might do us both some good."

Evie's face brightened. "Oh, yes. I'd like that. But... do you think we could have lunch first?"

Maria nodded despite knowing they'd already had lunch an hour ago. "Of course, Mom. A little snack before our walk sounds perfect."

As they headed to the kitchen, Evie suddenly chuckled. "You know, Maria, there's one good thing about this forgetfulness."

"What's that, Mom?" Maria asked, curious.

Evie grinned mischievously. "I get to hide my own Easter eggs!"

Maria couldn't help but laugh, grateful for her mother's enduring sense of humor. As she prepared a light snack, she made a mental note to call her mother's doctor. They needed some new strategies to cope with these growing challenges.

Caregiving for a loved one with dementia is a journey filled with unique challenges. While each experience is personal, there are common hurdles that many caregivers face. Understanding these challenges and having strategies to address them can make your caregiving journey more manageable and rewarding.

Resistance to Personal Care

One of the most common and emotionally taxing challenges is resistance to personal care. As dementia progresses, your loved one may forget the importance of hygiene or feel vulnerable during bathing and dressing.

The key to overcoming this challenge lies in creating a sense of comfort and control. Instead of announcing "It's bath time," try offering choices: "Would you prefer a bath or a shower today?" This simple shift gives your loved one a sense of autonomy.

Creating a pleasant environment can also make a significant difference. Play their favorite music softly in the background, use scented products they enjoy, or decorate the bathroom with familiar objects. These sensory cues can help create a more relaxing atmosphere.

Respecting modesty is crucial. Use a bath blanket or towel to cover areas not being washed, and explain each step before you do it. This approach can help reduce anxiety and resistance.

Establishing a consistent routine is also beneficial. Try to schedule personal care at the same time each day, preferably when your loved one is most cooperative. Over time, this routine can become a comforting ritual rather than a source of stress.

Aggressive Behavior

Aggression in dementia patients often stems from fear, confusion, or discomfort. When faced with aggressive behavior, your first instinct might be to react emotionally, but staying calm is crucial. Your tranquil demeanor can influence their mood and help de-escalate the situation.

Identifying triggers is a proactive approach to managing aggression. Keep a behavior log noting the time of day, surrounding circumstances, and any potential triggers when aggressive episodes occur. This information can help you anticipate and prevent future incidents.

Redirection is a powerful tool. When you sense tension building, try changing the subject or environment. Something as simple as suggesting a walk or offering a favorite snack can shift their focus and diffuse the situation.

Always check for underlying discomfort. Is your loved one in pain? Are they hungry or thirsty? Do they need to use the bathroom? Addressing these basic needs can often resolve aggressive behavior.

Validation therapy can be particularly effective. This approach involves acknowledging your loved one's feelings without arguing or trying to correct them. For instance, if they're upset about a long-deceased relative not visiting, instead of pointing out the reality, you might say, "You miss your mother very much, don't you? Tell me about her."

Sundowning

Sundowning, characterized by increased confusion and agitation in the late afternoon or evening, affects many dementia patients. Managing this challenge requires a multi-faceted approach.

Maintaining a predictable daily routine can help reduce the anxiety and confusion that often trigger sundowning. Try to schedule more demanding activities earlier in the day when your loved one is likely to be more alert.

Diet plays a crucial role. Limit caffeine and sugar intake, especially later in the day. Instead, offer a light, early dinner, and a small, protein-rich snack before bed to prevent hunger-related disturbances.

Creating a calm evening environment is essential. As the day winds down, reduce noise and activity levels in the house. Dim the lights gradually and close the curtains to minimize shadows, which can be confusing or frightening for someone with dementia.

Light therapy has shown promise in managing sundowning. Exposure to bright light during the day and softer lighting in the evening can help regulate the body's internal clock. Consider investing in a light therapy box or adjustable lighting system.

Engaging in calming bedtime activities can help signal that it's time to wind down. This could involve listening to soft music, gentle stretching, or looking at family photos together.

Wandering

Wandering is a common and potentially dangerous behavior in dementia patients. Creating a safe environment is paramount. Install door alarms or locks that are out of your loved one's line of sight. You might also consider camouflaging doors with curtains or removable mural stickers.

Creating safe walking areas can help satisfy the urge to wander. If possible, secure an outdoor space where your loved one can walk safely. Indoors, create a circular path free of obstacles for pacing.

Addressing underlying needs is crucial. Wandering often stems from boredom, restlessness, or a desire to "go home" (even when they are home). Regular, engaging activities and reassuring conversations can help mitigate these feelings.

Ensure your loved one always wears an ID bracelet or consider a GPS tracker for added security. Inform neighbors and local authorities about the wandering risk, and have a recent photo on hand in case of emergencies.

Regular physical activity can significantly reduce restlessness and the urge to wander. Try to incorporate exercises or activities your loved one enjoys into your daily routine.

Repetitive Behaviors

Repetitive behaviors, such as asking the same question repeatedly or performing the same action over and over, can be frustrating for caregivers. Understanding that these behaviors often stem from anxiety or uncertainty can help you respond with patience and compassion.

When faced with repetitive questions, respond calmly, even if you're repeating yourself for the hundredth time. Your loved one isn't trying to annoy you; they genuinely don't remember asking before.

Visual cues can be incredibly helpful. Create a large, visible daily schedule or use a whiteboard for important reminders. These visual aids can provide reassurance and reduce repetitive questions about plans or events.

Engaging in meaningful activities can serve as an effective distraction from repetitive behaviors. Find activities that your loved one enjoys and that provide a sense of purpose, such as sorting objects, folding laundry, or looking through photo albums.

Remember to take breaks when needed. Constant repetition can be mentally exhausting, and it's okay to step away for a few moments to recharge.

Eating Difficulties

As dementia progresses, eating can become challenging. Difficulty using utensils, forgetting to eat, or not recognizing food can all contribute to poor nutrition.

Offering finger foods can promote independence and make eating easier. Cut sandwiches into small, manageable pieces or provide bite-sized fruits and vegetables.

Visual contrast can make food more recognizable. Use plates that contrast with the color of the food, and avoid patterned tablecloths that might be visually confusing.

Minimize distractions during mealtimes. Turn off the TV, clear unnecessary items from the table, and create a calm eating environment.

Eating together can be beneficial. Your loved one can model your behavior, and mealtimes become opportunities for social interaction.

For those with coordination issues, adaptive utensils with larger handles or angled designs can make self-feeding easier. An occupational therapist can recommend appropriate tools.

Sleep Disturbances

Sleep problems are common in dementia and can be exhausting for both the patient and caregiver. Establishing consistent sleep schedules and bedtime routines is crucial. Try to maintain the same wake-up and bedtime every day, even on weekends.

Limit daytime napping, especially late in the day. If your loved one needs to rest, try to keep naps short and early in the afternoon.

Ensure regular daytime physical activity. Even simple exercises or short walks can improve sleep quality. However, avoid strenuous activity close to bedtime.

Create a sleep-friendly environment. Keep the bedroom cool, dark, and quiet. Use comfortable, breathable bedding and consider blackout curtains if outside light is an issue.

Nightlights in the bedroom, bathroom, and hallways can prevent disorientation if your loved one wakes up at night.

If sleep disturbances persist, consult a doctor. They can rule out sleep disorders or medication side effects that might be contributing to the problem.

Communication Difficulties

As dementia progresses, language skills often deteriorate, making it challenging for patients to express themselves and for caregivers to understand their needs. Patience and creative communication strategies are key.

Use simple, clear language and speak slowly. Break complex instructions into smaller steps. Non-verbal communication becomes increasingly important; pay attention to facial expressions and body language.

Visual aids can be helpful. Use gestures, demonstrate actions, or point to objects when words fail. Picture cards or a communication board with common needs and activities can be invaluable tools.

When your loved one struggles to find words, offer gentle prompts or suggestions, but be careful not to rush or pressure them. Allow plenty of time for responses and show that you're listening attentively.

Hallucinations and Delusions

Many dementia patients experience visual hallucinations or hold false beliefs, which can be distressing for both the individual and their caregiver. It's important to remember that these experiences feel very real to your loved one.

Avoid arguing or trying to convince them that what they're seeing isn't real. Instead, acknowledge their feelings and offer reassurance. You might say, "I know you're scared. You're safe here with me."

Check the environment for triggers. Sometimes, hallucinations can be sparked by poor lighting, reflections, or background noise. Address any potential causes you can identify.

If hallucinations or delusions are frequent and distressing, consult with your loved one's doctor. Sometimes, medication adjustments can help manage these symptoms.

Incontinence

Loss of bladder and bowel control is common in later stages of dementia and can be particularly challenging to manage. Establishing a regular toileting schedule can help prevent accidents. Encourage bathroom visits every few hours, even if your loved one doesn't express the need.

Make the bathroom easily accessible and recognizable. Use clear signage, keep the path well-lit, and remove any obstacles. Consider adaptive equipment like raised toilet seats or grab bars for safety and ease of use.

Choose clothing that's easy to remove, such as pants with elastic waistbands. Waterproof mattress covers and furniture protectors can ease your mind about potential accidents.

Remember, incontinence can be embarrassing for your loved one. Always approach the situation with dignity and respect, avoiding any language or reactions that might cause shame.

Hoarding and Hiding Objects

Some individuals with dementia may obsessively collect items or hide things, leading to clutter and frustration when important items go missing. Try to identify any patterns in the behavior. Are certain types of objects more likely to be hoarded or hidden?

Create a designated "rummaging" area where your loved one can sort through and arrange items safely. This can help satisfy the urge to collect while containing the behavior to one area.

For frequently misplaced important items like glasses or keys, buy multiples and keep spares in secure locations. Consider installing location devices on crucial objects.

When searching for hidden items, check common hiding spots like drawers, pockets of clothing, and under pillows or mattresses. Try to involve your loved one in the search, framing it as a team effort rather than an accusation.

Loss of Inhibition

Dementia can cause individuals to lose their social filters, potentially resulting in inappropriate behavior or speech. Remember that this behavior isn't intentional; it's a symptom of the disease.

When inappropriate behavior occurs, try to redirect your loved one's attention calmly and quickly. Have a few go-to distraction techniques ready, such as suggesting a favorite activity or changing the subject to a topic they enjoy.

In social situations, it can help to briefly explain to others that your loved one has dementia. Most people will be understanding if they're aware of the situation.

For consistent problems, like disrobing in public, consider adaptive clothing with fastenings in the back or clothing layered in a way that makes it more difficult to remove inappropriately.

Apathy and Loss of Initiative

Many dementia patients lose interest in activities they once enjoyed and may require significant encouragement to engage in daily activities. While it's important to encourage activity, be mindful not to overwhelm your loved one.

Start with simple, achievable tasks that provide a sense of accomplishment. This could be as basic as helping to fold a towel or arranging flowers in a vase.

Try to engage your loved one in activities that connect to their past interests or skills. If they were a gardener, they might enjoy helping to pot plants or arrange flowers. If they loved music, playing favorite songs might spark engagement.

Sometimes, simply sitting with your loved one and describing what's happening around you can provide stimulation without requiring active participation from them.

Paranoia and Suspicion

Individuals with dementia may become suspicious of those around them, including their caregivers, which can strain relationships and make care more difficult. It's crucial to remember that these feelings of paranoia are a symptom of the disease, not a reflection of your caregiving.

Avoid arguing or trying to use logic to dispel suspicions. Instead, acknowledge their feelings and offer reassurance. You might say, "I can see you're worried. I'm here to help keep you safe."

If your loved one frequently misplaces items and suspects theft, consider keeping a spare set of commonly lost objects. This way, you can "find" the item quickly and ease their concerns.

Try to identify any triggers for paranoid thoughts. Sometimes, confusion about time or place can lead to suspicion. Keeping a visible calendar and clock, and gently orienting your loved one to their surroundings can help.

Remember, every person with dementia is unique, and what works for one individual may not work for another. Be patient as you find strategies that work best for your situation. Don't hesitate to reach out to healthcare providers, support groups, or fellow caregivers for additional support and ideas. Your journey as a caregiver is challenging but immensely important. By addressing these common challenges with creativity, patience, and compassion, you can enhance the quality of life for both you and your loved one.

Caregiver's Corner

Remember, behind every challenging behavior is a person trying to communicate a need or emotion. Your patience, creativity, and compassion are powerful tools in navigating these difficulties.

Key Takeaways:

- Resistance to personal care can be managed by creating comfort and offering choices
- Aggressive behavior often stems from unmet needs or confusion and requires calm, patient responses
- Sundowning can be mitigated through routine, diet management, and creating a calm environment
- Wandering behaviors need safety measures and addressing underlying causes
- Communication difficulties require patience, simplicity, and use of non-verbal cues

Quick Tip: Create a "calming kit" with items that soothe your loved one. Perhaps a favorite photo, a soft blanket, or a scented item they enjoy. Having this readily available can help de-escalate challenging situations quickly.

Reflection Question: Think about a recent challenging behavior you've encountered. What might your loved one have been trying to communicate through this behavior? How could you approach a similar situation differently next time?

Resource Spotlight: Explore the Alzheimer's Association's "Caregiver Center" online for detailed strategies on managing specific behaviors and challenges in dementia care. They offer printable tip sheets and online training modules that can be invaluable resources.

Chapter 12
The Caregiver Self-Care Guide

Maria slumped onto the couch, her eyes heavy with exhaustion. She'd been up since dawn, juggling medication schedules, doctor's appointments, and household chores. As she closed her eyes for just a moment, she felt a gentle tap on her shoulder.

"Maria, dear?" Evie's voice was unusually clear. "When was the last time you left this house?"

Maria blinked, trying to remember. "I... I'm not sure, Mom. There's just so much to do here."

Evie shook her head, a determined look in her eye. "That settles it. You're going out today."

"But Mom, I can't just—"

"Nonsense," Evie interrupted in a voice of motherly authority. "I may not remember how to tie my shoes, but I do remember our neighbor Sarah saying she'd be happy to help anytime. So, you're going to call her, and then you're going to leave this house for at least two hours."

Maria started to protest, but the firmness in her mother's voice stopped her. With a mix of guilt and relief, she made the call to Sarah.

An hour later, Maria found herself on a park bench, the afternoon sun warm on her face. She took a deep breath, realizing how long it had been since she'd simply sat and enjoyed the outdoors. The guilt of leaving her mother started to fade as she watched children play and dogs chase frisbees.

As the sun began to dip lower in the sky, Maria felt a sense of renewal washing over her. The weight on her shoulders felt a little lighter, her mind a little clearer. She stood up, stretched, and began the walk home.

Approaching her front door, Maria paused. For the first time in weeks, she felt genuinely excited to see her mother. She walked in to find Evie and Sarah laughing over a photo album.

"There's my girl!" Evie exclaimed. "My goodness, you look like you've had a facelift. Amazing what a little fresh air can do, isn't it?"

Maria couldn't help but laugh. "You were right, Mom. I needed that break more than I realized."

As she sat down to join them, Maria felt a new surge of energy. She was ready to face whatever challenges lay ahead, armed with the knowledge that taking care of herself wasn't selfish – it was essential.

Evie patted her hand. "Remember, dear, you can't pour from an empty cup."

As a dementia caregiver, you're navigating a challenging journey that demands immense physical and emotional energy. This chapter explores the critical importance of self-care in maintaining your well-being and enhancing your caregiving capabilities. We'll delve into strategies to overcome common obstacles, techniques for mental health management, and ways to create a personalized self-care plan that works for your unique situation.

Caregiver's Self-Care Guide

Self-care isn't a luxury for caregivers; it's an absolute necessity. By taking care of yourself, you ensure that you have the physical energy, emotional resilience, and mental clarity to provide the best possible care for your loved one with dementia. The demanding nature of dementia caregiving often leads to neglect of personal well-being. As the disease progresses and your responsibilities increase, you might find yourself exhausted, irritable, and feeling like you're failing at everything.

In the early stages of caregiving, you might pride yourself on your ability to juggle multiple responsibilities. However, as time passes, you may find yourself constantly tired, easily frustrated, and making mistakes in various aspects of your life. This is a common experience for many caregivers who prioritize everyone else's needs above their own.

Understanding Caregiver Burnout

Burnout in caregivers is not just a temporary state of fatigue; it can lead to serious health issues, depression, and a breakdown in the caregiving relationship. When you're well-rested, well-nourished, and emotionally balanced, you're better equipped to handle the challenges of caregiving. You'll find yourself more patient, more attentive, and better able to make important decisions that affect both you and your loved one.

Moreover, practicing self-care models healthy behavior for your loved one and others around you. This is particularly important in a dementia care context, where your loved one may be struggling with their sense of self and daily routines. You're demonstrating that it's important to value and care for oneself, even under challenging circumstances.

Are You at Risk of Burnout?

It's crucial to recognize the signs of burnout early. Take a moment to reflect on your current state.

- Do you often feel overwhelmed by your caregiving responsibilities?
- Have you lost interest in activities you once enjoyed?
- Do you frequently feel tired, even after sleeping?
- Are you easily irritated or angered?
- Do you often feel anxious or depressed?
- Are you neglecting your own health needs?
- Do you have trouble sleeping?
- Have you become isolated from friends and family?

If you find yourself answering "yes" to several of these questions, you may be at risk of caregiver burnout. It's crucial to take steps to care for yourself.

Practical Self-Care Strategies

Even on the busiest of days, it's possible to find small pockets of time for self-care. These quick activities can make a significant difference in your overall well-being. Practice deep breathing exercises whenever you feel stress mounting. Inhale deeply for four counts, hold for four, and then exhale for four. This simple technique can help calm your nervous system and reduce stress hormones.

Physical movement, even for just a few minutes, can boost your energy and mood. Take a moment to do a quick stretch routine, focusing on areas that often hold tension like your neck, shoulders, and back. If possible, step outside for a breath of fresh air and sunlight. The change of scenery and natural light can help reset your mind and improve your mood.

Music can be a powerful tool for emotional regulation. When you're feeling overwhelmed, take a moment to listen to a favorite uplifting song. The familiar melody and positive associations can help shift your emotional state. Alternatively, practicing gratitude can help reframe your mindset. Take a few minutes to write down three things you're grateful for, no matter how small they might seem.

Physical Self-Care

Regular physical activity is crucial for maintaining your health and energy levels as a caregiver. However, finding time for exercise can be challenging. The key is to start small and be consistent. If you can't dedicate large blocks of time to exercise, try incorporating movement into your daily routine.

Chair exercises can be done while your loved one is resting or watching television. Simple movements like leg lifts, arm circles, and seated twists can help improve circulation and flexibility. Walking is another excellent form of exercise that doesn't require special equipment. Aim to start with a 10-minute walk daily, gradually increasing the duration as you build stamina.

Strength training doesn't necessarily require a gym membership. Use household items as weights for simple exercises like bicep curls or squats. Canned goods, water bottles, or even books can serve as makeshift weights. Yoga is another versatile form of exercise that can be adapted to your schedule and space constraints. Simple poses like *child's pose* or *cat-cow stretch* can help improve flexibility and provide stress relief.

Nutrition is equally important in physical self-care. As a caregiver, you might find yourself skipping meals or relying on unhealthy convenience foods. However, proper nutrition is essential for maintaining your energy and health. Plan for quick, nutritious meals that can be prepared in advance. Overnight oats with fruits and nuts can make for a hearty breakfast that's ready when you wake up. Greek yogurt parfaits with granola provide a good balance of protein and carbohydrates. For lunch or dinner, consider making veggie and hummus wraps or using an instant pot to prepare soups or stews in bulk that can be frozen for later use.

Mental and Emotional Self-Care

Caring for your mental and emotional well-being is just as important as physical self-care. Mindfulness and meditation can be powerful tools for managing stress and improving emotional regulation. If you're new to these practices, consider using apps like Headspace or Calm, which offer guided meditations and mindfulness exercises tailored for beginners.

Journaling is another effective tool for emotional self-care. Spend 5-10 minutes daily writing down your thoughts and feelings. This practice can help you process emotions, identify patterns in your mood and behavior, and gain clarity on challenging situations. Don't worry about perfect grammar or eloquent prose – the act of writing itself is what matters.

Cognitive Behavioral Techniques can help you manage negative thought patterns that often accompany caregiving stress. When you find yourself thinking, "I'm a terrible caregiver," try to counter that thought with evidence of times you've provided good care. Remember the times you've patiently repeated information, helped with daily tasks, or shared a moment of connection with your loved one.

Social connection is vital for emotional well-being, but caregivers often become isolated. Make an effort to stay connected with friends and family, even if it's just for short periods. Use video chat apps to have virtual coffee dates or join online communities for caregivers to share experiences and support.

Setting Boundaries

Setting healthy boundaries is crucial for preventing burnout, but it can be one of the most challenging aspects of self-care for caregivers. Many caregivers struggle with guilt when they try to set limits, feeling that they should be able to do it all. However, boundaries are not selfish—they're necessary for sustainable caregiving.

Start by learning to say no to additional responsibilities when you're already stretched thin. This might mean declining to host family gatherings, stepping back from volunteer commitments, or reducing your workload if possible. Remember, saying no to some things allows you to say yes to what's most important—your health and your ability to care for your loved one.

Delegation is another important aspect of boundary setting. Make a list of tasks that others can help with, and don't hesitate to ask for assistance. This might include grocery shopping, lawn care, or even sitting with your loved one for a few hours so you can have a break. Many people want to help but don't know how; giving them specific tasks can make it easier for them to support you.

Scheduling personal time is also a form of boundary setting. Block out time in your calendar for self-care activities and treat it as non-negotiable. This might be time for exercise, a hobby, or simply rest. Communicate clearly with family members about this time and ask for their support in protecting it.

Clear communication is key to successful boundary setting. Express your needs and limits to family members, friends, and healthcare providers. Be specific about what you can and cannot do, and what kind of support you need.

Technology-Based Solutions

In today's digital age, technology can be a valuable ally in caregiving and self-care. Caregiver organization apps like *Caring Village* or *Lotsa Helping Hands* can help you coordinate care tasks with family and friends. These apps allow you to create shared calendars, to-do lists, and communication channels, reducing the mental load of managing everything on your own.

Medication management can be one of the most stressful aspects of caregiving, especially when dealing with multiple prescriptions. Apps like *Medisafe* or *Mango Health* can help track medications and dosages, sending reminders when it's time for the next dose. This can provide peace of mind and reduce the risk of medication errors.

For quick stress relief throughout the day, consider using relaxation apps. *Insight Timer* offers a wide range of guided meditations and calming music, while *Breathe2Relax* provides guided breathing exercises. These tools can be particularly helpful during moments of acute stress or when you're having trouble falling asleep.

Online support groups can provide valuable emotional support and practical advice. Join virtual communities on Facebook or specific dementia care forums to connect with other caregivers who understand your experiences. These groups can be a source of validation, advice, and even humor—all important elements for maintaining emotional well-being.

Budget-Friendly Self-Care

Self-care doesn't have to be expensive. There are many low-cost or free options available if you know where to look. Local community centers often offer free or low-cost exercise classes. These can be a great way to stay active and meet other people in your community. Many libraries provide free access to e-books, audiobooks, and online courses. This can be a valuable resource for both entertainment and learning new skills.

The internet is a treasure trove of free resources. YouTube, for example, has a wealth of free workout videos, meditation guides, and educational content. You can find everything from gentle yoga routines to intensive cardio workouts, all tailored to different fitness levels and time constraints.

Nature can be one of the most effective (and free) stress relievers. Take advantage of local parks or hiking trails for walks or hikes. The combination of physical activity and exposure to nature can significantly boost mood and reduce stress. If mobility is an issue, even sitting in a garden or by a window with a view of nature can have calming effects.

Many museums and art galleries offer free admission days. These can provide a much-needed mental break and exposure to beauty and culture. Check local listings for these opportunities and schedule them into your calendar as part of your self-care routine.

Crisis Management Strategies

Despite our best efforts at self-care, there may be times when you feel overwhelmed and on the brink of a crisis. In these moments, having a plan can make all the difference.

It's crucial to have a list of emergency contacts readily available. This should include a trusted friend or family member who can provide immediate support, your doctor or therapist, and local crisis hotline numbers. Keep this list somewhere easily accessible, like on your phone or posted on the refrigerator.

Consider creating a "crisis kit" with items that help you calm down. This might include a stress ball or fidget toy to keep your hands busy, essential oils with calming scents, a favorite book of quotes or poems, or photos of happy memories or loved ones. The act of engaging with these items can help ground you and provide a sense of comfort during difficult moments.

Knowing your personal triggers and early warning signs of a crisis is also important. These might include physical symptoms like headaches or stomach upset, emotional signs like increased irritability or sadness, or behavioral changes like withdrawing from others or neglecting self-care. Create a plan for what to do when you notice these signs, such as calling a supportive friend, practicing deep breathing, or taking a brief break from caregiving duties if possible.

Creating Your Self-Care Action Plan

Developing a personalized self-care plan can help you prioritize your well-being and make self-care a consistent part of your routine. Start by assessing your needs. Reflect on areas of your life that need attention, considering all aspects of your well-being: physical, emotional, social, and spiritual.

Based on your assessment, set specific, achievable goals. Make sure your goals are SMART: Specific, Measurable, Achievable, Relevant, and Time-bound. For example, instead of a vague goal like "I want to exercise more," a SMART goal would be: "I will practice 10 minutes of meditation using the *Calm* app three times a week (Monday, Wednesday, Friday) at 7 AM for the next month."

This goal is specific (10 minutes of meditation), measurable (three times a week), achievable (only 10 minutes at a time), relevant (meditation can help reduce caregiver stress), and time-bound (for the next month). By setting SMART goals, you drastically increase your chances of success and can more easily track your progress.

Remember to start small and build up gradually. As you achieve these goals, you'll gain confidence and motivation to tackle larger self-care objectives. Be patient with yourself and celebrate every small step you take towards better self-care.

Seeking Professional Support

While self-care strategies can be incredibly helpful, sometimes professional support is necessary. There's no shame in seeking help; in fact, it's a sign of strength and commitment to your role as a caregiver. Consider professional help if you feel overwhelmed, anxious, or depressed for an extended period, have trouble sleeping or are experiencing physical symptoms of stress, struggle to manage your loved one's care or challenging behaviors, feel isolated or have difficulty maintaining relationships, or find yourself turning to unhealthy coping mechanisms.

Professional support can take many forms. Individual therapy provides a safe space to process your emotions and develop coping strategies. Cognitive Behavioral Therapy (CBT) can be particularly helpful for managing stress and negative thought patterns. For dementia caregivers, therapy can also help in processing grief related to the gradual loss of your loved one's cognitive abilities.

Support groups, led by professionals, allow you to connect with other caregivers, share experiences, and learn new coping strategies. Dementia-specific support groups can offer targeted advice and understanding of your unique challenges. Respite care services can provide temporary relief, allowing you time to rest and recharge. This can range from a few hours of in-home care to short-term residential care for your loved one.

Care coordinators can help manage the logistical aspects of caregiving, reducing your stress by assisting with healthcare navigation, appointment coordination, and future care planning. If you're experiencing significant anxiety or depression, a psychiatrist can evaluate whether medication might be helpful alongside other treatments. They can also help manage any sleep issues you might be experiencing.

Occupational therapists can provide advice on modifying your home environment and daily routines to make caregiving tasks easier and safer. Nutritionists can help you plan quick, nutritious meals and snacks to support your health when caregiving demands are high.

Caregiver's Corner

Taking care of yourself isn't selfish—it's a vital part of your caregiving role. Your well-being directly impacts the quality of care you can provide. By nurturing yourself, you're also nurturing your ability to care for your loved one.

Key Takeaways:

- Self-care is essential for maintaining your ability to provide quality care
- Recognizing signs of burnout early is crucial for preventing caregiver fatigue
- Physical, mental, and emotional self-care are all important aspects of overall well-being
- Setting boundaries and delegating tasks are vital skills for sustainable caregiving
- Seeking professional support when needed is a sign of strength, not weakness

Quick Tip:

Create a "Self-Care Emergency Kit" with items that quickly help you relax or boost your mood. Include things like a favorite tea bag, a small bottle of essential oil, a stress ball, or a photo that makes you smile. Keep this kit easily accessible for those moments when you need a quick self-care boost during your caregiving day.

Reflection Question:

Think about your typical week. Where are the small pockets of time that you could reclaim for self-care activities? How might you use these moments to recharge and care for yourself?

Resource Spotlight:

Explore the Caregiver Action Network's website (caregiveraction.org) for free resources on self-care, including webinars, tip sheets, and a supportive online community of fellow caregivers.

Chapter 13
The Power Of Connection

Maria slowly walked with Evie into the community center, the sounds of laughter and chatter growing louder as they approached the main hall.

"Remind me again where we're going?" Evie asked, a hint of nervousness in her voice.

"It's the weekly Senior Social, Mom," Maria explained patiently. "Remember? We thought it might be nice to meet some new people."

As they entered the bustling room, Maria's heart sank. Maybe this was a mistake. Evie had been increasingly withdrawn lately, and the crowd seemed overwhelming.

But before she could suggest leaving, a cheerful woman approached them. "Well, hello there! I'm Grace. Is this your first time joining us?"

Maria nodded, introducing herself and Evie. To her surprise, Evie piped up, "Lovely to meet you, Grace. I must say, that's a smashing brooch you're wearing."

Grace beamed, launching into a story about the brooch. As she spoke, an elderly gentleman wheeled over. "Grace, are you monopolizing the newcomers? I'm Frank," he said, extending his hand to Evie.

"Charmed, I'm sure," Evie replied with a twinkle in her eye. "Tell me, Frank, do you play cards? I have a sudden urge to fleece someone at gin rummy."

Frank laughed heartily. "Oh, you're on! But I warn you, I'm not easily fleeced."

Before Maria knew it, Evie was settled at a card table with Frank and two other seniors.

As Grace and Evie chatted, a kind-faced woman approached Maria. "First time here? I'm Susan. Is that your mother?"

Maria nodded, feeling a bit overwhelmed. "Yes, I'm her caregiver. I wasn't sure about coming, but..."

Susan's eyes lit up with understanding. "Oh, you're a caregiver too? Come on, there's a group of us over here. We meet while our loved ones socialize.

Surprised and slightly hesitant, Maria followed Susan to a small circle of people. As they introduced themselves, Maria felt a weight lifting off her shoulders. Here were people who understood her daily struggles, her fears, her exhaustion.

"I... I didn't realize there were so many of us," Maria admitted. "Sometimes I feel so alone in this."

A chorus of understanding murmurs rose from the group. "We've all been there," one man said gently. "But you're not alone. Not anymore."

As the afternoon progressed, Maria found herself opening up, sharing stories and receiving advice. She laughed, she cried a little, and for the first time in months, she felt truly understood. Additionally, Maria watched in amazement as her mother laughed, joked, and yes—thoroughly trounced Frank at gin rummy.

On the drive home, Maria felt a new sense of energy. Evie hummed contentedly beside her. "You know, dear," Evie said, "I may not remember my own birthday, but I'll remember this afternoon for a long time. Thank you for bringing me."

Social engagement is a fundamental human need that doesn't diminish with a dementia diagnosis. In fact, it becomes even more crucial as the disease progresses. For your loved one, social interaction can help maintain cognitive function, reduce feelings of isolation and depression, and contribute significantly to overall quality of life. Research supports this view, with studies showing that social engagement can slow cognitive decline in older adults, including those with dementia.

For you as a caregiver, maintaining social connections is equally important. The demands of caregiving can often lead to social isolation, but staying connected with friends, family, and community can provide essential emotional support, practical help, and a much-needed sense of normalcy amidst the challenges of caregiving.

Nurturing Relationships in the Face of Change

As dementia progresses, relationships inevitably change, but they remain important. Adapting your approach to social interactions can help maintain these vital connections. Open communication is key. Consider educating friends and family about the condition. Explain that your loved one might repeat stories or questions, and guide them on how to respond patiently. Suggest they answer as if it's the first time they've heard the question. This helps your loved one feel heard and respected, and once people understand, they're often much more patient, leading to more positive interactions.

It's important to prepare visitors for what to expect. Let them know about any changes in your loved one's appearance or behavior. Suggest topics for conversation or activities that your loved one enjoys. This preparation can help visitors feel more comfortable and make their visits more successful.

Adapting social activities to suit your loved one's current abilities is crucial. This might mean choosing quieter, less crowded venues for get-togethers or planning shorter visits to prevent fatigue. Engage in activities that match your loved one's current abilities and interests. If they always loved gardening but can no longer manage complex tasks, involve them in simple activities like watering plants or arranging flowers. It might not be the same as before, but it can still bring joy and a sense of purpose.

Consider creating a 'memory box' filled with objects that hold special meaning for your loved one. This can be a great conversation starter during visits, helping to trigger memories and encouraging interaction. Include items like old photographs, souvenirs from trips, or small objects related to their former hobbies or career.

Navigating Family Dynamics

Dementia often leads to significant shifts in family dynamics. You may find yourself taking on a parental role for your parent, or transitioning from a spouse to a caregiver. These changes can be emotionally challenging for everyone involved.

Open communication is key to navigating these changes. Have conversations with family members about care responsibilities. Consider creating a shared online calendar where family members can sign up for specific tasks, like accompanying your loved one to medical appointments or helping with household chores. This can help distribute responsibilities more evenly and ensure everyone feels involved.

Acknowledge that family members may react differently to the situation. Some may dive into hands-on care, while others might struggle to accept the diagnosis and distance themselves. Respect varying levels of involvement while encouraging support from all family members in whatever way they can provide it.

It's important to have regular family meetings to discuss care plans, share updates, and address any concerns. These meetings can be in person or via video call to include distant family members. Having a neutral facilitator, like a social worker or family counselor, can help keep these discussions productive and focused.

If conflicts arise, consider seeking mediation. Family counseling can be beneficial in navigating these complex dynamics. Sometimes, a neutral third party, like a social worker or therapist, can facilitate discussions and help find solutions that work for everyone.

Combating Social Isolation

Social isolation can be a significant risk for both your loved one and you as a caregiver. Fortunately, many communities offer resources to help combat this isolation. Look into programs at local senior centers specifically designed for individuals with dementia. These might include memory cafes, which provide a safe and supportive environment for socializing, or specialized exercise classes that combine physical activity with cognitive stimulation.

Adult daycare centers can provide valuable socialization opportunities for your loved one while also giving you a much-needed break. These centers typically offer structured activities, meals, and professional care in a safe environment. Many also provide transportation services, which can be a significant help if driving has become difficult.

Consider joining or starting a dementia-friendly social group in your community. This could be a regular coffee meetup, a gentle exercise class, or an art group. The key is to create a welcoming, understanding environment where people with dementia and their caregivers can socialize without fear of stigma or misunderstanding.

Celebrating Moments of Joy

Amidst the challenges of dementia care, it's crucial to recognize and celebrate positive moments. These moments of joy, no matter how small, can provide emotional nourishment for both you and your loved one.

Make a point of acknowledging daily accomplishments. If your loved one remembers a name or completes a task, celebrate it. These small victories can boost mood and self-esteem for both of you. Create opportunities for joy by engaging in favorite activities or hobbies, adapted as needed to suit current abilities. This might involve listening to loved music, watching beloved films, or spending time in nature. Even if your loved one can't participate as they once did, the familiar sights, sounds, and experiences can evoke positive emotions and memories.

Consider starting a joy journal where you record these positive moments. On difficult days, reading through this journal can provide comfort and perspective, reminding you of the good times amidst the challenges.

Capture these happy moments to revisit later. Take photos of good times and keep a journal of positive experiences or interactions. These can serve as reminders of good days during more difficult times and can be comforting to look back on. Creating a scrapbook or memory album together can be a wonderful bonding activity and a treasure for the whole family.

Maintaining Social Connections

Social interaction is a vital component of well-being for both you and your loved one with dementia. As the disease progresses, maintaining social connections can become more challenging, but it remains crucial for emotional health and cognitive stimulation. Isolation can exacerbate symptoms of dementia and increase caregiver stress. From creating visitor schedules to exploring technology-assisted communication, these approaches aim to enrich your loved one's social life while also providing you with much-needed support and respite.

Create a visiting schedule: Encourage friends and family to visit regularly by setting up a loose schedule. This ensures your loved one has consistent social interaction and gives you a break. Consider creating a visitor's log where guests can write notes about their visit. This can help you keep track of social interactions and provide conversation starters for future visits.

Plan dementia-friendly outings: Research local attractions that are suitable for individuals with dementia. Many museums and gardens offer special programs or quiet hours. Start with short trips to familiar places and gradually expand as you both become more comfortable.

Join a support group: This provides socialization for you and an opportunity to share experiences with others who understand your journey. Many support groups also offer educational components, bringing in speakers to discuss various aspects of dementia care.

Explore volunteer opportunities: If possible, find ways for your loved one to contribute to the community. This could be as simple as helping to sort items for a food bank from home. Feeling useful and needed can significantly boost self-esteem and provide a sense of purpose.

Utilize technology: Set up easy-to-use video calling systems to keep in touch with distant family and friends. Consider using digital assistants like Alexa or Google Home to set reminders, play music, or even make calls, which can help your loved one feel more independent.

Create a memory book: Work with your loved one to create a book of important people, places, and memories. This can be a great conversation starter during visits and a comforting resource for your loved one to look through independently.

Host small gatherings: Invite a few close friends or family members for short, low-key get-togethers. Consider themed gatherings based on your loved one's interests, like a tea party or a sports viewing event.

Engage in intergenerational activities: If there are young children in the family, plan simple activities they can do with your loved one, like looking at picture books or doing simple crafts. The energy of children can be invigorating, and these interactions often bring out the best in people with dementia.

Explore pet therapy: If having a full-time pet isn't feasible, look into visiting pet therapy programs. The unconditional love and non-verbal interaction with animals can be incredibly soothing and joyful for people with dementia.

Maintain traditions: Continue to celebrate holidays and family traditions, adapting as necessary. These familiar rituals can provide comfort and a sense of continuity.

Remember, while dementia changes relationships, it doesn't erase the need for human connection. With patience, creativity, and support, you can help your loved one maintain meaningful social engagement throughout their journey with dementia. These connections not only enrich your loved one's life but can also provide you with much-needed support and moments of joy in your caregiving journey. You're not alone in this - there's a whole community of support ready to walk alongside you. By fostering these social connections, you're not just improving quality of life; you're creating a network of understanding and support that can sustain both you and your loved one through the challenges ahead.

Caregiver's Corner

Every social interaction, no matter how small, can brighten your loved one's day and yours. Your efforts to maintain these connections are invaluable, even when the results aren't always immediately apparent.

Key Takeaways:

- Social engagement is crucial for both the person with dementia and their caregiver
- Adapting social activities to current abilities helps maintain connections
- Open communication with family and friends about dementia can improve interactions

- Combating social isolation through community programs and support groups is essential
- Celebrating small moments of joy can provide emotional nourishment

Quick Tip:

Create a "Social Calendar" in a prominent place in your home. Use colorful markers or stickers to highlight upcoming visits, outings, or activities. This visual reminder can help your loved one anticipate social engagements, reducing anxiety and providing a sense of structure. It also serves as a helpful tool for family members and visitors to see when they might drop by or plan future interactions.

Reflection Question:

Think about a recent positive social interaction involving your loved one. What made it successful? How can you recreate similar conditions for future engagements?

Resource Spotlight:

Explore the Memory Cafe Directory (memorycafedirectory.com) to find a memory cafe near you. These cafes offer a supportive environment for people with dementia and their caregivers to socialize and enjoy activities together.

Chapter 14

Modern Tools For Dementia Care

Maria sat at the kitchen table, surrounded by gadgets and instruction manuals. She'd spent the morning installing a new smart home system, hoping it would help keep her mother safe and give her some peace of mind.

Evie shuffled into the kitchen, eyeing the technological maze with suspicion. "What's all this, dear? Are we opening an electronics store?"

Maria chuckled, "No, Mom. These are some new tools to help us out around the house."

She held up a small, puck-shaped device. "This is Alexa. She can remind you to take your medication, play your favorite music, or even tell you jokes."

Evie raised an eyebrow. "A little box that tells jokes? Now I've heard everything."

"Alexa," Maria called out, "tell us a joke."

The device lit up. "Why don't scientists trust atoms?"

Evie and Maria waited for the punchline.

"Because they make up everything!"

Evie burst out laughing. "Well, I'll be. It's funnier than some of the fellas I dated —smarter too!"

Encouraged, Maria demonstrated the other devices. A digital pill dispenser, a GPS tracker disguised as a stylish bracelet, and sensors that would alert Maria if Evie left the house unexpectedly.

"And look at this, Mom," Maria said, pulling out her smartphone. "This app connects to all these devices. I can check on you even when I'm not here."

Evie's smile faded slightly. "That's an awful lot of... supervision, isn't it?"

Maria paused, realizing how overwhelming this might seem. "I know it's a lot, Mom. But it's to help keep you safe and independent. And to give me some peace of mind when I can't be here."

Evie nodded slowly, then a mischievous glint appeared in her eye. "Well, if this fancy bracelet can track me, maybe we can finally figure out where I hid that secret chocolate stash!"

Maria laughed, relieved at her mother's humor. "Maybe so, Mom. Want to test it out?"

As they spent the afternoon exploring the new technology, Maria marveled at how quickly Evie adapted. There were moments of frustration, but also moments of delight – like when Evie discovered she could ask Alexa to play her favorite Frank Sinatra songs anytime she wanted.

Later that evening, as they sat together in the living room, Evie called out, "Alexa, what's the weather like tomorrow?"

Alexa's cheerful voice responded, "Tomorrow will be sunny with a high of 75 degrees Fahrenheit."

Evie winked at her daughter. "See? I'm getting the hang of this modern stuff. Maybe tomorrow we can take a walk in that sunshine."

Maria smiled warmly. "That sounds wonderful, Mom. We could even pack a picnic."

"Alexa," Evie said with a mischievous grin, "remind us to stop for ice cream after the picnic."

As Alexa confirmed the reminder, Maria couldn't help but laugh. "Ice cream, huh? I see how you're going to use this technology."

Evie patted her daughter's hand. "Well, dear, if I'm going to have all these gadgets watching over me, I might as well put them to good use. Now, how about we ask Alexa for one more joke before bed?"

As they shared another laugh over Alexa once again proving to have a better sense of humor than Evie's old boyfriends, Maria felt a comfort spread through her. The technology wasn't a cure-all, but it offered a new layer of safety and connection. And more importantly, it had given Evie a sense of control and engagement with her surroundings.

Maria smiled to herself, grateful for these moments of joy and connection. In this journey of caregiving, every little bit of help and every shared laugh was a precious gift.

As a caregiver for someone with dementia, you face unique challenges daily. Your role is demanding, often exhausting, but deeply important. While technology can't replace your compassion and dedication, it can offer valuable support in your caregiving journey. This chapter explores how various technologies can assist you, grouped by specific needs.

The goal of incorporating technology into dementia care is to enhance safety, improve communication, and potentially ease some of the stress of caregiving. However, it's crucial to remember that every caregiving situation is unique. What works well for one family may not be the right fit for another, and that's perfectly okay. Consider these technologies as potential aids in your caregiving toolkit, to be adopted if and when they feel suitable for your situation.

Safety and Security

In caring for a loved one with dementia, ensuring their safety is paramount. As cognitive abilities decline, individuals may become more prone to accidents, wandering, or confusion about their surroundings. Fortunately, modern technology offers a range of solutions to enhance safety while maintaining dignity and independence.

- **GPS Tracking Devices:** Wearable pendants or watches can help locate a loved one prone to wandering. Some include SOS buttons for emergencies. When choosing a device, consider battery life (ideally lasting several days), water resistance for shower use, and tracking frequency. Some devices update their location every few minutes, while others may only do so when requested.
- **Geofencing Alerts:** These advanced systems alert caregivers if their loved one leaves a designated safe area. You can set up multiple geofences - for example, one around the house and another around the neighborhood - with different alert levels. This technology can provide peace of mind while allowing your loved one some independence.

- **Smart Home Security:** Smart door locks, doorbell cameras, and motion sensors can enhance home security. Many systems allow remote monitoring and control via smartphone apps. For instance, you could receive an alert if the front door opens at an unusual time, or lock/unlock doors remotely for authorized visitors.
- **Comprehensive Home Monitoring Systems:** These use sensor networks to track movement and behavior patterns throughout the home. They can alert caregivers to potential issues, such as if a person has been in the bathroom for an unusually long time or hasn't opened the refrigerator all day. Some systems can learn normal patterns of behavior over time and alert caregivers to significant deviations. When considering such a system, carefully balance the benefits of increased safety with privacy concerns.
- **Smart Appliance Monitoring:** Internet-connected appliances allow remote monitoring of stoves, refrigerators, and other potentially hazardous items. Some smart stoves can automatically shut off if left unattended for too long, while smart refrigerators can send alerts if the door is left open or if frequently used items are running low. These features can help prevent accidents and ensure your loved one is eating regularly.

Medication Management

Missed doses, incorrect dosages, or overmedication can have serious health consequences. Technology has stepped in to address this critical aspect of care, offering solutions ranging from simple reminder systems to advanced automated dispensers. These tools can help ensure medication compliance, reduce errors, and alleviate some of the stress associated with managing complex medication regimens. Here are some technological solutions to consider:

- **Basic Medication Reminders:** Simple apps or devices can help ensure medications are taken on time. Options range from alarm clocks with medication reminders to smart pill bottles that track when they're opened. Some apps allow you to input complex medication schedules and can send reminders to both the patient and caregiver.
- **Advanced Medication Management Systems:** These systems offer automatic dispensing, remote monitoring of medication adherence, and alerts to caregivers if doses are missed. Some can dispense pre-sorted medications at scheduled times, only allowing access to the current

dose. When choosing a system, consider factors like the number of medications it can manage, ease of refilling, and how it handles dosage changes.

- **Smart Watches with Medication Alerts:** Some smartwatches can be programmed with medication reminders, combining this function with other health monitoring features. The advantage here is that the reminder is always with the wearer, reducing the chance of missed doses due to being away from a stationary reminder system.

Communication and Social Connection

Maintaining social connections is vital for the emotional well-being of individuals with dementia, yet it often becomes more difficult as the disease advances. Isolation can exacerbate symptoms and diminish quality of life. Thankfully, various technologies can help bridge communication gaps, keep loved ones connected, and provide cognitive stimulation. From simplified communication devices to interactive digital frames, these tools can help maintain meaningful relationships and provide comfort. Let's look at some technological aids that can support communication and social connection:

- **Simplified Smartphones and Tablets:** Devices with simplified interfaces, large buttons, and straightforward menus can help your loved one stay connected. Look for models with long battery life, durable construction, and the ability to limit functions to prevent confusion. Some devices allow caregivers to remotely manage settings and contacts.
- **Video Chat Platforms:** While not dementia-specific, video calls can help maintain connections with family and friends. Use larger screens if possible, ensure good lighting, and keep calls relatively short to prevent fatigue. Some caregivers find it helpful to have props or topics prepared to stimulate conversation during these calls.
- **Digital Photo Frames:** These display rotating galleries of family photos, stimulating memories and providing comfort. Some advanced frames allow for short video clips or recorded messages alongside images. When setting up a digital photo frame, place it in a prominent location and pay attention to which types of images elicit the most positive responses.
- **Voice-Activated Assistants:** Smart speakers can provide companionship through conversation, music, and information access, potentially reducing feelings of isolation. They can also control smart

home devices, making it easier for individuals with dementia to manage their environment.

Cognitive Stimulation and Daily Structure

As dementia progresses, maintaining cognitive function and daily routines becomes increasingly important. Engaging the mind and providing structure can help slow cognitive decline, reduce anxiety, and improve overall quality of life. Technology offers a variety of tools to support cognitive stimulation and help maintain daily routines. From brain training apps to smart labeling systems, these solutions can provide engaging activities and help with daily organization and scheduling.

- **Cognitive Stimulation Apps:** Apps like Lumosity, BrainHQ, and MindMate offer games and exercises targeting different cognitive skills. Start with simpler activities and gradually increase complexity as appropriate. While these apps won't cure dementia, they can provide engaging activities that support cognitive function and offer a sense of accomplishment.
- **Digital Calendars with Shared Access:** Online calendars accessible by multiple caregivers can help coordinate appointments, medication schedules, and daily routines. Many offer color-coding and reminders to multiple devices. Some caregivers find it helpful to use a digital calendar in conjunction with a large, physical calendar in the home for their loved one to reference.
- **Label Makers and QR Code Labels:** Clear, large-print labels on drawers, cabinets, and doors can help maintain independence and reduce confusion. For more tech-savvy caregivers, QR code labels linked to instructional videos can guide complex tasks. When creating labels, use high-contrast colors and simple language for clarity.
- **AI-Powered Virtual Assistants:** Specialized AI assistants can provide sophisticated reminders, engage in simple conversations, and even alert caregivers to changes in behavior patterns. While promising, it's important to approach AI technology with a critical eye, understanding its limitations and potential privacy implications.

Home Automation and Daily Living Assistance

For individuals with dementia, managing daily tasks and navigating their home environment can become challenging over time. Home automation and assistive technologies can play a crucial role in maintaining independence, enhancing safety, and improving quality of life. These solutions range from simple voice-activated controls to complex smart home systems that can learn and adapt to an individual's needs. By automating certain aspects of daily living, these technologies can help reduce stress for both the individual with dementia and their caregivers.

- **Smart Home Devices:** Automated lighting, thermostats, and appliances can improve safety and comfort. For example, you could set up a nighttime routine that gradually dims the lights, locks the doors, and adjusts the thermostat to a comfortable sleeping temperature. Motion-activated lighting can help prevent falls during nighttime trips to the bathroom.
- **Voice-Activated Controls:** Smart speakers can control various home functions through voice commands, making it easier for individuals with dementia to manage their environment. This can help maintain a sense of independence and control.
- **Smart Watches for Health Monitoring:** Some smartwatches offer heart rate monitoring, fall detection, and activity tracking. Look for models with long battery life, easy-to-read displays, and interfaces that can be simplified for users with cognitive impairments. Some watches can automatically alert emergency services or designated contacts in case of a detected fall.
- **Complex Smart Home Automation:** Advanced systems can create sophisticated routines and learn patterns over time, automatically adjusting the home environment to suit the individual's needs. For example, if your loved one typically gets up at night to use the bathroom, the system could automatically light a path to guide them safely.

Implementing Technology with Care

Selecting the right technology for dementia care isn't just about features; it's about finding tools that seamlessly integrate into your caregiving journey. Think of it as curating a personalized toolkit, where each item serves a purpose and works in harmony with the others.

Start by envisioning your ideal caregiving scenario. What tasks consume most of your time? Where do you feel the most stressed? What are your most significant day-to-day concerns for your loved one? In what ways can technology potentially make their lives easier? These pain points are your compass, guiding you toward technologies that can truly make a difference.

When evaluating options, look beyond the shiny features. Seek out intuitive designs that speak to both you and your loved one. A sleek interface means little if it leaves you both frustrated. Instead, prioritize technologies that feel like natural extensions of your care routine – ones that whisper solutions rather than shout complications.

Consider the future, too. Dementia is a progressive condition, so choose adaptable technologies that can evolve alongside your needs. A scalable system might seem like overkill today, but it could become a lifeline tomorrow.

Start small, perhaps with a single device or solution that addresses your most pressing need. Allow time for both you and your loved one to adapt to the new changes before considering additional technology enhancements.

Cost Considerations and Financial Assistance

The cost of assistive technology can vary widely, from a few dollars for a simple app to thousands for comprehensive home monitoring systems. Here are some avenues to explore for financial assistance:

1. **Insurance:** Some assistive devices may be covered by Medicare, Medicaid, or private insurance. Check with your insurance provider for details on what's covered and any required documentation.
2. **Veterans Benefits:** If your loved one is a veteran, they may be eligible for certain assistive technologies through the VA.
3. **State Assistive Technology Programs:** Many states have programs that provide information, funding, or loans for assistive technology.
4. **Non-Profit Organizations:** Some organizations, like the Alzheimer's Association, offer grants or financial assistance for caregiving needs.
5. **Tax Deductions:** Some assistive technologies may qualify as medical expenses for tax purposes. Consult with a tax professional to understand what might be deductible in your situation.
6. **Manufacturer Programs:** Some technology companies offer discount programs or payment plans for their assistive devices.

Remember to thoroughly research any financial assistance options and understand all terms and conditions before committing to a purchase or program.

The Irreplaceable Human Element

While technology can provide valuable assistance, it's crucial to remember that its role is to enhance, not replace, human interaction and care. Use technology as a tool to facilitate more meaningful interactions and to free up time for personal connection or self-care.

As you integrate technology into your caregiving routine, continuously evaluate its impact. Is it genuinely making life easier and safer? Is it supporting your loved one's dignity and independence? Is it allowing for more quality time together? These are the key questions to keep in mind.

It's also important to be aware of the potential downsides of technology. Too much reliance on devices can lead to decreased human interaction or a sense of being constantly monitored. Strive for a balance that enhances care without compromising personal connection.

Caregiver's Corner

Technology is a tool to enhance your caregiving, not replace your compassion. The most powerful technology in dementia care remains the human touch - your patience, love, and understanding.

Key Takeaways:

- Technology can enhance safety, improve communication, and ease caregiving stress
- Solutions range from GPS tracking devices to medication management systems
- Communication tools can help maintain social connections for those with dementia
- Cognitive stimulation apps and home automation can support daily living
- When implementing technology, start small and prioritize intuitive designs

Quick Tip:

Consider starting something like a "Tech Tuesday" tradition where you spend one hour each week exploring a new caregiving technology. Involve your loved one in the process to see how they respond. This consistent, manageable approach helps you discover practical tools while keeping both of you engaged and involved.

Reflection Question:

Consider your daily caregiving routine. What is one task or concern that causes you the most stress? How might technology potentially address this challenge?

Resource Spotlight:

Explore the Alzheimer's Association's online resource center (alz.org/help-support/caregiving/care-options/technology) for up-to-date information on technology in dementia care, including reviews and implementation tips.

Chapter 15

Considering Long-Term Care Options

Maria sat at the kitchen table, surrounded by brochures from various assisted living facilities. She'd been putting off this decision for months, but after Evie's latest wandering incident, she knew she couldn't delay any longer.

Evie shuffled into the kitchen, her bathrobe askew. "Good morning, dear. What's all this paper for? Are we planning a trip?"

Maria's heart clenched. "No, Mom. Remember? We talked about possibly moving you somewhere safer."

"Moving?" Evie's brow furrowed. "But this is my home. Our home."

"I know, Mom," Maria said gently, guiding Evie to a chair. "But it's getting harder for me to keep you safe here. Remember last week when you went for a walk and couldn't find your way back?"

Evie's face clouded with confusion, then cleared. "Oh, yes. That nice policeman brought me home. Such a handsome young man."

Despite the seriousness of the situation, Maria couldn't help but smile. "Yes, he was. But Mom, we can't risk that happening again. I think... I think it might be time to consider one of these assisted living places."

As Maria explained the features of different facilities, Evie listened quietly, her usual humor subdued. Finally, she spoke up. "Will you still visit me if I move to one of these places?"

Maria felt tears welling up in her eyes. "Oh, Mom. Of course I will! Every day if you want."

Evie nodded slowly. "Well, I suppose if I have to live somewhere else, it might as well be somewhere with other people to appreciate my jokes. Lord knows you've heard them all by now."

Maria laughed softly, relieved to see a glimmer of her mother's spirit. "Trust me, Mom. You'll be the star of the place in no time."

As they looked through the brochures together, discussing the pros and cons of each facility, Maria felt a mix of sadness and relief. This wasn't an easy decision, but she knew it was the right one for both of them.

"You know, dear," Evie said as they finished reviewing the last brochure, "I may not always remember where I am, but I'll always know who you are. You're my Maria, my wonderful daughter who takes such good care of me."

Maria hugged her mother tightly, tears flowing freely now. "And you'll always be my mom, no matter where you live."

As they held each other, Maria knew that while their living situation might change, their bond never would.

As dementia progresses, there often comes a time when care needs exceed what can be safely provided at home. This realization can be one of the most challenging moments for families facing dementia. Recognizing when home care is no longer adequate is crucial for the safety and well-being of both the person with dementia and their caregiver. It's important to approach this decision with careful consideration, compassion, and a clear understanding of the available options.

Recognizing the Signs

The decision to transition to long-term care is rarely a sudden one. More often, it's a gradual realization that comes as the demands of care increase and the ability to meet those demands at home diminishes. Being aware of the signs that indicate a need for more comprehensive care can help you make this decision proactively, rather than in the midst of a crisis.

Safety concerns are often at the forefront when considering long-term care. Frequent falls become a serious risk as dementia affects balance and spatial awareness. Nighttime wandering, a common behavior in dementia, can lead to dangerous situations if the person leaves the home unattended. The inability to manage daily activities like bathing and dressing not only impacts quality of life but can also lead to hygiene issues and skin problems if not appropriately addressed.

Behavioral changes can also signal a need for specialized care. Increased aggression, though often not intentional, can pose risks to both the person with dementia and their caregivers. Severe sundowning syndrome, where confusion and agitation worsen in the late afternoon and evening, can be particularly challenging to manage at home, especially if it disrupts sleep patterns for the entire household.

It's crucial to remember that the need for long-term care isn't just about the person with dementia; caregiver stress is a serious issue that must be considered. If you find yourself constantly exhausted, irritable, or unable to enjoy any aspects of your life, it's a sign that the current care situation may not be sustainable. Caregiver burnout is real and can have severe consequences for both the caregiver and the person with dementia.

Key indicators that it might be time to consider long-term care include:

- **Safety concerns:** Beyond falls and wandering, this might include leaving appliances on, getting lost in familiar places, or being vulnerable to scams or exploitation.
- **Health management difficulties:** As medical conditions become more complex, managing medications and treatments at home can become overwhelming. Missed medications or appointments can have serious health consequences.
- **Personal care challenges:** When bathing, dressing, or managing incontinence becomes a daily struggle, it affects not just hygiene but also dignity and quality of life.
- **Behavioral changes:** Aggression, paranoia, or severe mood swings can create a tense and potentially unsafe home environment.
- **Caregiver burnout:** Persistent exhaustion, stress, or an inability to meet caregiving demands can lead to health problems for the caregiver and suboptimal care for the person with dementia.
- **Social isolation:** Lack of opportunities for the person with dementia to engage in social activities can accelerate cognitive decline and impact emotional well-being.
- **Home safety issues:** If your home can't be easily modified to meet changing needs (e.g., installing grab bars or removing trip hazards), it might be time to consider a purpose-built care environment.
- **Financial strain:** If the cost of in-home care is becoming unsustainable, a long-term care facility might actually be a more cost-effective option.

While these signs can serve as important indicators, it's crucial to remember that every situation is unique. The decision to transition to long-term care should be made thoughtfully, considering not only the physical and medical needs of the person with dementia but also the emotional and psychological well-being of both the individual and their caregivers.

As you consider this transition, take time to involve your loved one in the decision-making process as much as possible, respecting their wishes and preferences. Start exploring options early, before a crisis forces a rushed decision. By being proactive and informed, you can make a choice that best supports your loved one's needs while also addressing the well-being of the entire family.

Exploring Options

When it's time to explore long-term care options, the array of choices can seem overwhelming. It's important to understand that there's no one-size-fits-all solution. The right choice depends on your loved one's specific needs, preferences, and the progression of their condition.

Start by assessing current and future care needs. Consider the level of medical care required, the need for specialized dementia care, and the importance of social engagement opportunities. It's also crucial to think about potential future needs. Dementia is progressive, so you want to choose a facility that can accommodate increasing care requirements over time.

Here's a more detailed look at the main types of long-term care facilities:

Assisted Living Facilities

These facilities provide help with daily activities but not extensive medical care. They often offer apartment-style living with communal dining and activities. Some have specialized memory care units for those with dementia. Assisted living can be a good option for individuals in the early to middle stages of dementia who need some assistance but still maintain a level of independence.

Pros:

- More homelike environment
- Encourages independence where possible
- Social activities and communal spaces
- Less expensive than nursing homes

Cons:

- It may not be suitable for advanced dementia care
- Limited medical care available
- May need to move to a higher level of care as dementia progresses

Memory Care Units

These are specifically designed for individuals with dementia. They provide a secure environment to prevent wandering and have staff trained in dementia care. Memory care units often have features like circular hallways to reduce anxiety in residents who wander, and they typically offer activities specifically designed for individuals with cognitive impairment.

Pros:

- Specialized care for dementia patients
- Secure environment to prevent wandering
- Staff trained in dementia care
- Activities designed for cognitive stimulation

Cons:

- More expensive than regular assisted living
- Less privacy than other options
- It may feel restrictive for some individuals

Nursing Homes

These facilities offer 24/7 skilled nursing care and medical supervision, which can be crucial for individuals with advanced dementia and complex medical needs. While the environment might be more clinical, nursing homes can provide a level of medical care that's often necessary in the later stages of dementia.

Pros:

- Round-the-clock medical care
- Can handle complex medical needs
- Often covered by Medicaid after personal funds are

exhausted

Cons:

- More institutional feel
- Less privacy
- It can be expensive if paying out-of-pocket

Continuing Care Retirement Communities (CCRCs)

These communities offer a range of options from independent living to skilled nursing, allowing residents to stay in one community as their needs change.

CCRCs can be a good option for couples where one person needs more care than the other, as it allows them to remain close while each receives appropriate levels of support.

Pros:

- Allows aging in place within the same community
- Good for couples with different care needs
- Often offers a wide range of amenities and activities

Cons:

- Usually requires a large upfront payment
- Can be expensive
- Quality of care may vary between levels

Making the Transition

Once the decision to move to long-term care has been made, the process of transitioning can be emotionally challenging for everyone involved. Here are some strategies to make the transition smoother:

Involve Your Loved One: Include the person with dementia in the decision-making process as much as possible. Visit potential facilities together and discuss their preferences and concerns. Even if they may not fully understand the situation, involving them can help maintain their sense of dignity and control.

Create Familiarity: Bringing personal items from home, such as family photos, favorite blankets, or cherished mementos, can help make the new space feel more comfortable. Creating a memory box outside the person's room with personal mementos and photos can help them identify their room and provide conversation starters for staff.

Prepare the Staff: Provide detailed information about your loved one's needs, preferences, and routines. Share details about their life history, their likes and dislikes, and strategies that have worked well in managing any challenging behaviors. The more the staff knows, the better they can provide individualized care.

Plan the Moving Day: Choose a time of day when your loved one is typically at their best. Consider having a family member or friend take them on an outing while the actual moving happens to minimize stress.

<u>Manage Your Emotions</u>: Feelings of guilt, sadness, and relief are common and expected. Acknowledge these feelings and seek support if needed. Remember that choosing long-term care is often the most loving decision you can make for your loved one's well-being.

The Financial Aspect

The financial aspect of long-term care for a loved one with dementia can be overwhelming, but understanding your options is crucial for effective planning. Long-term care insurance, if purchased before the diagnosis, can be a valuable resource, potentially covering a significant portion of the costs. However, it's essential to review the policy carefully to understand its coverage and limitations.

Many families mistakenly believe that Medicare will cover long-term care costs. Still, it's important to note that Medicare typically only covers short-term skilled nursing care, not long-term residential care. This limitation often comes as a surprise and underscores the need for comprehensive financial planning.

For many families, Medicaid becomes a critical resource for funding long-term care. However, qualifying for Medicaid requires meeting specific income and asset requirements, which often involves a complex process of spending down assets. This process should be navigated carefully, ideally with the guidance of an elder law attorney or financial advisor experienced in Medicaid planning.

Veterans and their spouses may have access to additional resources through Veterans Benefits, which can help cover the cost of care. These benefits are often overlooked, so it's worth investigating if your loved one has a history of military service.

Personal assets, including savings, investments, or proceeds from selling a home, are frequently used to fund long-term care. However, deciding how best to utilize these resources can be complex. Consulting with a financial advisor can provide valuable insights into the most effective strategies for managing these assets while ensuring long-term financial stability.

It's also worth noting that some long-term care expenses may be tax-deductible. While this won't offset the total cost of care, it can provide some financial relief. Consulting with a tax professional can help you understand which expenses qualify and how to properly document them for tax purposes.

Lastly, it's important to consider the long-term financial impact on the entire family. Long-term care costs can quickly deplete savings and affect the financial security of spouses or other dependents. Creating a comprehensive financial plan that addresses both immediate care needs and long-term family financial stability is crucial.

Remember, navigating the financial aspects of long-term care is complex and often requires professional guidance. Don't hesitate to seek help from financial advisors, elder law attorneys, or care managers who specialize in these issues. With proper planning and understanding of available resources, you can make informed decisions that provide the best possible care for your loved one while protecting your family's financial future.

Ensuring Quality Care

Once your loved one has transitioned to a long-term care facility, your role evolves from primary caregiver to advocate and care partner. This shift, while potentially relieving some of the physical demands of caregiving, brings new responsibilities to ensure your loved one receives the highest quality of care possible.

Actively participating in care planning meetings at the facility is crucial. These meetings provide an invaluable opportunity for you to share insights into your loved one's history, preferences, and unique needs. Your intimate knowledge of their likes, dislikes, and daily routines can help staff provide more personalized and effective care, enhancing your loved one's comfort and quality of life.

Regular visits to the facility serve multiple purposes. They allow you to observe the care your loved one is receiving firsthand and maintain your emotional connection with them. Try to vary the timing of your visits to get a comprehensive picture of their daily care routine. These visits not only benefit your loved one but also demonstrate to the staff that you are actively involved in your loved one's care.

Building strong, respectful relationships with the care staff is essential. Regular communication can lead to better care for your loved one and provide you with peace of mind. Share your observations and concerns, but also remember to acknowledge and appreciate good care when you see it. This positive reinforcement can motivate staff and foster a collaborative approach to your loved one's care.

It's important to familiarize yourself with the facility's policies and residents' rights. This knowledge empowers you to advocate effectively for your loved one if you feel these standards aren't being met. Don't hesitate to speak up respectfully if you have concerns about the care provided.

Staying vigilant about changes in your loved one's condition or care is crucial. If you notice anything concerning, such as unexplained bruises, changes in behavior, or lapses in hygiene, bring it to the attention of the staff or management promptly. Your observations can be vital in addressing issues early and maintaining your loved one's well-being.

Maintaining Connections

Establishing a consistent visiting routine provides comfort and continuity for your loved one. Even if they don't always remember the specifics of your visits due to cognitive decline, the emotional impact can be profound and lasting. These regular interactions help preserve your bond and can significantly contribute to their overall quality of life.

During your visits, engage in meaningful activities that resonate with your loved one's interests and abilities. This might include looking through photo albums to stimulate memories, listening to their favorite music, or simply sitting together in comfortable silence. These shared experiences can create moments of joy and connection, even as the disease progresses.

Continuing family traditions and celebrating holidays at the facility helps maintain a sense of normalcy and strengthens family connections. Whether it's decorating their room for a holiday, sharing a special meal, or participating in facility-organized events, these activities can bring comfort and happiness to your loved one.

Between visits, technology can play a vital role in staying connected. Video calls, if appropriate for your loved one's cognitive state, can provide visual and auditory stimulation. Sending photos and messages through the facility's communication system, if available, can help your loved one feel remembered and loved, even when you can't be there in person.

Encouraging visits from other family members and friends can provide diverse social interactions beneficial to your loved one's well-being. Each visitor brings their unique energy and memories, which can stimulate different aspects of your loved one's personality and cognition. Even if your loved one doesn't always recognize visitors, the emotional warmth of these interactions can be profoundly beneficial.

It's important to remember that the goal of long-term care is to provide a safe, comfortable environment where your loved one can receive the care they need while maintaining the highest possible quality of life. While the transition to long-term care can be challenging for both you and your loved one, careful planning and ongoing involvement can ensure they receive the best possible care in their new home.

Your role as a family caregiver doesn't end with the move to a care facility; it evolves. Your love, advocacy, and presence remain vital components of your loved one's care. By maintaining strong connections and actively participating in their care, you continue to play a crucial role in their life, ensuring they feel loved, valued, and supported throughout their journey with dementia.

Caregiver's Corner

Choosing long-term care is one of the deepest expressions of love you can offer, even though it may not feel that way in the moment. This decision, born from deep care and concern, speaks volumes about your commitment to your loved one's well-being. As you step into this new chapter, remember that your role, while changing, remains irreplaceable. Your intimate knowledge of your loved one's needs, your comforting presence, and your unwavering advocacy are precious gifts that no one else can provide. In the face of guilt or doubt, remind yourself that this choice comes from a place of deep love and the desire to ensure the best possible care.

Key Takeaways:

- Recognizing signs that home care is no longer sufficient is crucial for safety and well-being
- Long-term care options include assisted living, memory care units, nursing homes, and CCRCs
- The transition to long-term care requires careful planning and emotional support
- Understanding financial options, including Medicaid and Veterans Benefits, is essential
- Ongoing involvement and advocacy remain vital after the transition to ensure quality care

Quick Tip:

Set up a "Care Circle" group chat or email list with family members and close friends. Use this to share updates, coordinate visits, and discuss care decisions. This can help keep everyone informed and involved, even if they're not local.

Reflection Question:

As you consider the possibility of long-term care, what aspects of your loved one's daily life and routine are most important to maintain? How might these priorities influence your choice of facility or your involvement in their care?

Resource Spotlight:

Visit the National Center for Assisted Living's website for comprehensive resources on choosing a long-term care facility, understanding residents' rights, and ensuring quality care.

Chapter 16

End-Of-Life Care and Difficult Decisions

Maria sat by Evie's bedside, holding her mother's frail hand. The room was quiet except for the soft beeping of monitors and Evie's labored breathing.

It had been three months since Evie moved into the facility, and her decline had been swift and stark. The vibrant, joke-cracking woman Maria knew had become increasingly withdrawn and confused.

"Mom?" Maria said softly, gently squeezing Evie's hand. "It's me, Maria. I'm here."

Evie's eyes fluttered open, unfocused at first, then slowly settling on Maria's face. A faint smile crossed her lips. "Maria... my girl."

Maria felt a lump in her throat. These moments of clarity were becoming rarer. "That's right, Mom. I'm here. How are you feeling today?"

Evie's brow furrowed. "Tired... so tired. Where... where am I?"

"You're in your room at Sunnyside, Mom. Remember? The place with the nice garden you like?"

Confusion clouded Evie's face, then cleared slightly. "Oh... yes. The flowers..."

Maria nodded encouragingly. "That's right. The flowers you love to look at."

They sat in silence for a while, Maria gently stroking her mother's hand. She watched as Evie's eyes darted around the room, sometimes focusing on things that weren't there.

Suddenly, Evie gripped Maria's hand tightly. "Don't... don't forget the ice cream," she said urgently.

Maria felt tears welling up. Even now, her mother's spirit peeked through. "I won't forget, Mom. I promise."

As the afternoon wore on, Maria read to her mother, talked about happy memories, and simply sat in companionable silence. Nurses came and went, checking vitals and administering medication.

Maria leaned in close to her mother. "I love you, Mom. I'll be right here."

Evie's eyes, which had been closed, opened slightly. For a moment, they were clear and focused. "Love you... my Maria... always."

Maria could sense that the time she had remaining with her Mother was quickly running out, but she also knew that she would treasure every moment, every flash of recognition, every glimpse of the mother she knew and loved.

Even in the face of stark decline, their love remained constant, and Maria vowed to be there until the very end.

The journey through dementia is often described as a series of goodbyes, but perhaps none is more profound than the final farewell. As we approach the end-of-life stage in dementia care, we enter a landscape filled with complex emotions, challenging decisions, and opportunities for deep connection. This chapter aims to guide you through this challenging terrain with compassion, practical advice, and a focus on dignity and quality of life.

The Emotional Landscape

The transition to end-of-life care in dementia is often gradual, yet it can still feel sudden and overwhelming. You may find yourself grappling with a mix of emotions: grief for the person who is slipping away, guilt over feelings of relief, anxiety about the decisions ahead, or even anger at the relentless progression of the disease. All of these feelings are normal and valid.

It's important to acknowledge that anticipatory grief – mourning losses before they occur – is common in dementia care. You may have been grieving throughout the disease's progression, mourning the loss of shared memories, familiar routines, or the relationship you once had. This ongoing grief can complicate the emotions surrounding end-of-life care.

Reflective question: What emotions are you experiencing as you consider this stage of the journey? How can you acknowledge and honor these feelings?

Recognizing the Transition

The shift towards end-of-life care often begins with subtle changes. You might notice increased difficulty with swallowing, more frequent infections, or a significant decline in responsiveness. Weight loss, decreased interest in surroundings, and changes in sleep patterns can also signal a transition to the final stage of dementia.

These signs don't necessarily mean the end is imminent, but they do suggest it's time to start thinking about end-of-life care options. This realization can be frightening, but it also offers an opportunity to ensure that your loved one's final days align with their wishes and values. It's a time to focus on comfort, dignity, and quality of life rather than curative treatments.

The progression of dementia in its final stages can vary significantly from person to person. Some individuals may decline rapidly, while others may linger in the late stage for years. This uncertainty can add to the emotional challenge of this period, making it crucial to focus on quality of life in the present moment rather than trying to predict the future.

Opening the Conversation

One of the most challenging aspects of this journey is initiating conversations about end-of-life care. It's natural to want to avoid these discussions, but having them early can provide immense comfort and guidance later on.

Choose a quiet moment when you're both feeling calm. Start by expressing your love and concern. You might say, "I want to make sure we're doing everything we can to honor your wishes. Can we talk about what's important to you for the future?"

Listen more than you speak. Your loved one may have fears or wishes you haven't considered. If they're able to participate in the conversation, encourage them to share their thoughts on quality of life, preferred place of care, and any spiritual or emotional needs.

Remember that these conversations don't have to happen all at once. They can be ongoing dialogues, revisited and refined as circumstances change. It's also okay to acknowledge uncertainty. You might not have all the answers, and that's normal.

If your loved one is no longer able to communicate their wishes, you may need to make decisions based on what you know of their values and preferences. This can be a heavy responsibility, but remember that you're acting out of love and with their best interests at heart.

Reflective question: What aspects of end-of-life care are most important to you and your loved one? How can you ensure these priorities are respected?

Understanding Care Options

As dementia progresses, the focus of care often shifts from curative treatments to comfort care. This is where palliative care and hospice services come into play.

Palliative care focuses on providing relief from symptoms and stress at any stage of illness. It can be provided alongside other treatments and aims to improve quality of life for both the patient and family. A palliative care team might help manage pain, anxiety, or other symptoms, assist with treatment decisions, and provide emotional support.

Hospice care is a form of palliative care specifically for individuals nearing the end of life, typically when life expectancy is six months or less. Hospice provides comprehensive comfort care as well as support for families. Contrary to common belief, choosing hospice doesn't mean giving up. Instead, it's about focusing on quality of life and comfort in one's final days.

Both palliative and hospice care can be provided in various settings, including at home, nursing facilities, or hospitals. The choice depends on your loved one's needs, your capabilities as a caregiver, and your family's preferences.

It's important to note that hospice care for individuals with dementia may look different from hospice care for those with other terminal illnesses. The unpredictable nature of dementia's progression can make it challenging to determine when someone is eligible for hospice. However, many hospice programs have developed specific criteria for dementia patients, recognizing the unique needs of this population.

Navigating Medical Decisions

As dementia advances, you may face difficult decisions about medical interventions. These might include:

1. **Artificial nutrition and hydration:** In advanced dementia, the ability to eat and drink often diminishes. While it might seem intuitive to use feeding tubes, studies have shown they generally don't prolong life or improve quality of life in end-stage dementia. Instead, they can lead to complications and discomfort. Careful hand-feeding, offering small amounts of food and liquids for comfort, is often a more compassionate approach.
2. **Antibiotic use:** When considering antibiotics for infections, it's important to weigh the benefits against potential discomfort. The goal in end-stage dementia is usually comfort rather than cure. Sometimes,

antibiotics might be used for symptom relief, even if not for curing the infection.

3. **Cardiopulmonary resuscitation (CPR):** CPR is often unsuccessful in individuals with end-stage dementia and can cause additional suffering. Many families opt for a Do Not Resuscitate (DNR) order, focusing instead on comfort care. It's important to understand that a DNR doesn't mean no care will be provided – it simply means that if the heart or breathing stops, natural death will be allowed to occur.

4. **Hospitalization:** Hospitals can be disorienting and distressing for individuals with dementia. When possible, managing care in a familiar environment is often preferable. However, there may be times when hospitalization is necessary for acute symptom management.

These decisions are deeply personal and should reflect your loved one's values and wishes. If they've completed advance directives, these can provide invaluable guidance. If not, try to consider what they would want based on their expressed values and preferences.

It's okay to ask for help in making these decisions. Your healthcare team, including palliative care specialists if involved, can provide valuable insights into the potential benefits and burdens of different interventions.

Providing Comfort and Dignity

In late-stage dementia, the focus shifts to maximizing comfort and maintaining dignity. This involves attention to physical comfort, pain management, and sensory stimulation.

Physical comfort goes beyond pain management. It includes regular repositioning to prevent pressure sores, gentle range-of-motion exercises, and creating a soothing environment. Pay attention to room temperature, use soft and comfortable bedding, and minimize disruptive noises. Even small details, like moistening dry lips or providing gentle massage, can significantly enhance comfort.

Pain can be difficult to assess in individuals who can't communicate verbally. Watch for signs like facial grimacing, increased agitation, or changes in breathing patterns. Don't hesitate to ask for help from healthcare providers in assessing and managing pain. There are specialized pain assessment tools designed for individuals with dementia that can be incredibly helpful in this process.

Even in late-stage dementia, sensory experiences can provide comfort and connection. Soft music, gentle touch, familiar scents, or simply sitting in a sunny spot can be soothing. Continue to speak to your loved one, even if they can't respond. Your voice and presence can be a source of comfort. Reading aloud, sharing memories, or simply describing the world around them can provide meaningful stimulation.

Maintaining dignity is crucial. Always speak to your loved one, not just about them. Explain what you're doing during care activities, maintain privacy during personal care, and continue to use their name and preferred forms of address. Respect their individual style by continuing to groom them in the way they preferred when they were able to express their wishes.

Supporting Yourself as a Caregiver

Caring for someone with end-stage dementia is emotionally and physically demanding. It's crucial to take care of yourself during this time. Caregiver burnout is a real risk, and recognizing its signs – exhaustion, irritability, withdrawal from social activities – is essential.

Accept help when it's offered. Whether it's assistance with caregiving tasks, help with errands, or simply a listening ear, support from others can be invaluable. Consider creating a schedule where friends and family can sign up for specific tasks or visiting times. This not only provides you with support but also allows others to feel involved and helpful.

Make time for self-care. This might mean taking short breaks, maintaining connections with friends, or engaging in activities that bring you peace or joy. Remember, taking care of yourself isn't selfish – it's necessary to sustain the energy and emotional reserves needed for caregiving. Even small acts of self-care, like a daily walk or a few minutes of meditation, can make a significant difference.

Seek emotional support. This could be through counseling, support groups, or conversations with trusted friends. Sharing your feelings can help you process your emotions and reduce feelings of isolation. Many hospice programs offer support groups specifically for caregivers of individuals with dementia. These can be invaluable resources for both practical advice and emotional support.

Reflective question: What self-care practices can you incorporate into your routine? Who can you reach out to for support?

Preparing for the End

As the end of life approaches, you may notice changes such as decreased responsiveness, changes in breathing patterns, or a decrease in body temperature. These are natural parts of the dying process. Other signs might include mottled skin, especially on the hands and feet, or long pauses between breaths.

During this time, the focus is on comfort. Medication may be given to manage pain or difficulty breathing. Even if your loved one seems unresponsive, continue to speak to them, hold their hand, or simply sit with them. Your presence can be deeply comforting. Many people find that hearing is one of the last senses to go, so your loved one may be able to hear you even if they can't respond.

This is also a time to consider practical matters like funeral arrangements if you haven't already. Many hospice programs offer assistance with these tasks. Don't be afraid to discuss these matters with your hospice team – they are experienced in handling these sensitive issues with compassion and respect.

The end-of-life journey in dementia is undoubtedly challenging, but it can also be a time of profound love, connection, and meaning. By focusing on comfort, dignity, and quality of life, you can help ensure that your loved one's final chapter is as peaceful and comfortable as possible.

Caregiver's Corner

As you navigate this final, sacred chapter of your journey together, know that your presence is a profound source of comfort and love. The path you're walking is immeasurably difficult, filled with moments of both heartache and deep connection. In those times when you feel overwhelmed or uncertain, remember that your gentle touch, your familiar voice, and your unwavering commitment are the greatest gifts you can offer. Each act of care, no matter how small it may seem, is a powerful expression of your enduring bond. Your compassion lights the way through this challenging passage, surrounding your loved one with dignity and love until the very end.

Key Takeaways:

- End-of-life care in dementia focuses on comfort, dignity, and quality of life

- Recognizing signs of transition to end-stage dementia is crucial for appropriate care
- Open conversations about end-of-life wishes are essential, even if challenging
- Palliative care and hospice services offer valuable support for both patient and family
- Self-care for caregivers is essential during this emotionally demanding time

Quick Tip:

Consider placing a small notebook and pen by your loved one's bedside. When you or visitors spend time with them, jot down a brief note - a cherished memory, a word of comfort, or simply an "I love you." These gentle reminders of connection can be soothing to read aloud, even if your loved one seems unresponsive. Later, this collection of thoughts may become a treasured keepsake, a testament to the enduring bonds of love and care.

Reflection Question:

What aspects of your relationship with your loved one have remained constant throughout this journey, even as dementia has progressed? How can you draw strength from these enduring connections in this final stage?

Resource Spotlight:

Explore the Alzheimer's Association's End-of-Life Care page (alz.org/help-support/caregiving/end-of-life-care) for comprehensive information on late-stage care, making difficult decisions, and finding support during this challenging time.

Chapter 17
Coping With Loss & Grief

The halls of Sunnyside Care Facility seemed unusually quiet as Maria made her way to her mother's room. It had been three days since Evie passed away, and Maria was here to collect her belongings.

The room still held echoes of her mother's presence. The colorful quilt on the bed. The framed family photos on the nightstand. Maria's hands trembled slightly as she began to pack things into boxes.

As she reached for the small stack of books on the shelf, a worn copy of "Pride and Prejudice" caught her eye. It had been Evie's favorite, a constant companion during her stay at Sunnyside.

Maria picked up the book, running her fingers over its tattered spine. Suddenly, it slipped from her grasp, falling to the floor with a thud. The book lay open, and there, pressed between its pages, was a small, light blue, delicate flower—a forget-me-not.

Maria's breath caught in her throat as she knelt to retrieve the book and the flower. She remembered giving it to her mother what felt like a lifetime ago, in those early days after the diagnosis. She had no idea Evie had kept it all this time.

Tears welled up in Maria's eyes as she gently touched the pressed petals. Even in her final days, when so much else had faded away, Evie had held onto this symbol of their love and connection.

"Oh, Mom," Maria whispered, her voice thick with emotion.

She carefully closed the book, keeping the flower safe within its pages. As she held it close to her chest, a flood of memories washed over her – her mother's laughter, her relentless jokes, her unwavering love.

Maria sat on the edge of the bed, allowing herself to feel the full weight of her grief. But amidst the sadness, there was also a profound sense of gratitude. For the time they had together, for the love they shared, for every moment—even the difficult ones.

As she finished packing, Maria placed the book with the forget-me-not on top of the box. It would have a special place in her home, a constant reminder of her mother's enduring spirit.

Leaving the room, Maria paused at the doorway, taking one last look. She could almost hear her mother's voice: "Don't forget the ice cream, dear."

Through her tears, Maria smiled. "I won't forget, Mom. I promise."

As she walked out of Sunnyside, Maria felt a mix of sorrow and peace. The journey had been long and challenging, but also filled with the deepest love, the most genuine laughter, and countless precious moments she would cherish forever.

And in her hands, she carried a book with a little blue flower–reminding her that some bonds truly do last forever.

The journey of dementia caregiving is often described as a long goodbye, a gradual loss stretched over months or years. When your loved one finally passes, you may find yourself facing a complex array of emotions that don't fit neatly into the traditional understanding of grief. This chapter aims to guide you through the immediate aftermath of loss, acknowledging the unique challenges that come with grieving after dementia caregiving.

Unlike sudden loss, where shock often dominates the initial response, your grief may feel like the culmination of a thousand small goodbyes. You've been grieving incrementally throughout the progression of the disease, and now you face the finality of physical loss. This layered grief can be confusing and overwhelming, but understanding its unique nature is the first step in navigating this challenging time.

The First Days After

In the days following your loved one's passing, you may feel as though you've been thrust into a whirlwind of emotions and responsibilities. Practical matters demand attention even as you grapple with your loss. Funeral arrangements, legal issues, and notifying friends and family can feel overwhelming. Remember, it's okay to ask for help during this time. Delegate tasks to willing family members or friends if possible.

Creating a checklist of necessary tasks can help you feel more in control during this chaotic time. Prioritize the most urgent matters, such as notifying immediate family and close friends, contacting a funeral home, and securing important documents. Don't hesitate to ask for assistance with these tasks – many people want to help but aren't sure how.

You may find yourself struggling with the sudden void in your daily routine. The absence of caregiving responsibilities can feel disorienting. The constant vigilance, the familiar routines – all have suddenly ceased. This abrupt change can leave you feeling adrift. It's normal to feel lost or unsure of how to fill your days initially.

During this time, allow yourself to feel whatever emotions arise. You might experience waves of intense sadness, numbness, or even a sense of unreality. These are all normal reactions to loss, especially following the intense experience of dementia caregiving. Some caregivers report feeling a sense of unreality, as if they're waiting for their loved one to return home. This is a normal response to the sudden absence of caregiving duties.

Understanding Your Grief

Grief after dementia caregiving often comes with a complex interplay of emotions. You may feel a sense of relief that your loved one's suffering has ended, quickly followed by guilt for feeling relieved. This emotional tug-of-war is common and doesn't diminish the love and care you provided. It's a natural response to the end of a long and challenging journey.

You may find yourself in the unusual position of grieving for someone you've already been grieving for a long time. The gradual losses that came with dementia – the loss of shared memories, of familiar interactions, of the person you once knew – may have initiated a grieving process long before the physical death. Now, you're faced with the finality of the loss, which can reawaken or intensify grief.

This is also a time when unresolved feelings from the caregiving journey may surface. Regrets, unspoken words, or moments of frustration during caregiving might replay in your mind. You might find yourself revisiting difficult decisions you had to make during the caregiving process. Remember to be gentle with yourself. You navigated an incredibly challenging journey with love and dedication, often making difficult choices with limited information and resources.

It's important to acknowledge that your grief may not follow the "typical" stages often described in grief literature. Your experience may be more cyclical, with emotions ebbing and flowing unpredictably. This is normal, especially given the prolonged nature of loss in dementia.

Physical and Emotional Reactions to Loss

Grief isn't just an emotional experience; it can have profound physical manifestations as well. You might experience fatigue, changes in appetite, difficulty sleeping, or even physical aches and pains. These are normal responses to the stress of loss and the physical toll of long-term caregiving.

The body often holds the stress and strain of caregiving, and with the immediate pressure lifted, you may find yourself feeling unexpectedly exhausted or even becoming ill. This is your body's way of processing the accumulated stress and grief. Listen to your body during this time and allow yourself extra rest and care.

Emotionally, you may find yourself on a rollercoaster. Moments of intense sadness might be interspersed with periods of numbness or even unexpected laughter as you remember good times. You might feel anger – at the disease, at the unfairness of the situation, or even irrationally at your loved one for leaving. All of these feelings are valid parts of the grieving process.

Some caregivers report feeling a sense of disorientation or loss of purpose after their loved one's passing. If caregiving has been your primary focus for months or years, you may struggle with questions of identity and purpose. This is a normal part of the transition and an opportunity for personal growth and rediscovery.

Navigating Relationships After Loss

As you grapple with your loss, you may find that some relationships feel strained. Friends and family who haven't experienced dementia caregiving might struggle to understand the complexity of your grief. They may expect you to feel relieved or to "move on" quickly, not realizing the depth of your loss and the adjustment you're facing.

It's okay to set boundaries with well-meaning but insensitive comments or advice. You might need to explain that while the caregiving journey has ended, your grief is complex and ongoing. Educating others about the unique nature of grief after dementia can help foster understanding and support.

Seek out others who have been through similar experiences. Support groups for former dementia caregivers can provide a space where you feel truly understood. These connections can be invaluable as you navigate your grief. Sharing your experiences with others who've walked a similar path can be deeply validating and healing.

You might also find that some relationships have changed or faded during your caregiving journey. This is a time to reassess and possibly rebuild connections that are important to you. Reach out to friends you may have lost touch with, but be patient with yourself if socializing feels challenging at first.

Self-Care in Early Grief

In the midst of grief, taking care of yourself might feel impossible or unimportant. However, basic self-care is crucial during this time. Try to maintain regular sleep patterns, eat nutritious meals, and engage in gentle exercise. These basic acts of self-care can help you weather the intense emotions and stress of early grief.

Create a simple self-care routine that feels manageable. This might include a short daily walk, a few minutes of meditation or deep breathing, or setting aside time to read or listen to music. Small, consistent acts of self-care can provide a sense of stability during this tumultuous time.

Allow yourself time and space to grieve. There's no timeline for grief, and healing isn't a linear process. Some days will be more challenging than others, and that's okay. Be patient with yourself as you adjust to this new reality. Permit yourself to say no to obligations that feel overwhelming and to take breaks when you need them.

Remember that self-care also includes emotional and mental care. This might mean journaling to process your feelings, speaking with a counselor, or engaging in activities that bring you comfort or joy. Don't feel guilty for moments of happiness or distraction – they're a natural and healthy part of the grieving process.

When to Seek Professional Help

While grief is a normal response to loss, sometimes it can become overwhelming. If you find yourself unable to function in daily life, experiencing persistent depression or anxiety, or having thoughts of self-harm, it's important to seek professional help.

Signs that you might benefit from professional support include:

- Persistent feelings of guilt or self-blame
- Inability to focus on anything but your loved one's death
- Excessive irritability or anger
- Neglecting personal hygiene or responsibilities
- Inability to enjoy life or imagine a positive future
- Substance abuse to cope with grief

There are various types of support available, including grief counselors, therapists specializing in bereavement, and support groups. Don't hesitate to reach out if you feel you need additional support. Seeking help is a sign of strength, not weakness.

Honoring Your Loved One's Memory

As you begin to emerge from the initial fog of grief, you might want to find ways to honor your loved one's memory. This could involve creating a memory book, participating in fundraising for dementia research, or simply sharing stories about your loved one with friends and family.

Consider establishing a small ritual or tradition to help you feel connected to your loved one. This might be lighting a candle on special days, continuing a hobby they enjoyed, or visiting a place that was meaningful to them. These acts can provide comfort and a sense of continued connection.

Reflect on the lessons learned from your caregiving journey. The patience, compassion, and resilience you've developed are profound gifts that can enrich your life and the lives of others. Consider how you might use these qualities moving forward, perhaps in volunteering or supporting other caregivers.

The Path Ahead

As this chapter closes, you stand at the beginning of a new journey – one of healing and rediscovery. The path ahead may seem unclear, but remember that you've already demonstrated incredible strength and resilience through your caregiving journey.

Healing takes time, and it's not a linear process. There will be good days and difficult days. Be patient with yourself. Allow yourself to grieve, to remember, and gradually, to look toward the future. Each small step forward is an achievement, even if it doesn't feel like it in the moment.

Remember, the love you shared with your loved one, the care you provided, and the strength you discovered along the way are now part of who you are. These experiences have shaped you, giving you a depth of understanding and compassion that is truly unique.

As you take these first steps forward, carry with you the knowledge that you have the inner resources to face whatever lies ahead. Your capacity for love and care, so evident in your caregiving journey, will continue to be a source of strength as you navigate this new chapter of your life.

Your journey of caregiving has ended, but your journey of healing and growth is just beginning. Take it one day at a time, be kind to yourself, and know that brighter days lie ahead. The road may not be easy, but you have the strength to walk it, carrying with you the love and memories that will always be a part of you.

Caregiver's Corner

Your journey of love and care has been profound, and now you face a new chapter of healing. The grief you feel is a testament to the depth of your bond. Be patient and gentle with yourself as you navigate this path. Remember, your capacity for love and resilience, so evident in your caregiving, will light the way forward.

Key Takeaways:

- Grief after dementia caregiving is complex and may not follow typical patterns
- Physical and emotional reactions to loss can be intense and varied
- Self-care is crucial during the grieving process
- Seeking support from those who understand your journey can be invaluable
- Honoring your loved one's memory can be a healing part of the grieving process

Quick Tip:

Set a daily "grief check-in" time. Take five minutes each day to pause and acknowledge your feelings. This brief moment of mindfulness can help you process your emotions gradually and prevent them from becoming overwhelming. There's no right or wrong way to feel during this check-in; simply allowing yourself to recognize and sit with your emotions can be a powerful tool in your healing journey.

Reflection Question:

What strengths or qualities did you discover in yourself during your caregiving journey? How might these attributes help you as you navigate this new phase of life?

Resource Spotlight:

Explore The Compassionate Friends website (compassionatefriends.org) for resources specifically tailored to those grieving after a long-term caregiving experience, including online support groups and helpful articles.

Chapter 18

Hope, Growth, and the Path Forward

A year had passed since Evie's passing, and Maria found herself once again walking through the doors of the community center. The familiar sounds of chatter and laughter greeted her, bringing a bittersweet smile to her face.

As she entered the room where the caregiver support group met, she was struck by how much had changed and how much remained the same. Familiar faces nodded in greeting, while new ones looked on with a mix of curiosity and apprehension.

Maria's eyes were drawn to a man sitting alone in the corner, his face etched with worry and exhaustion—a look she knew all too well. She approached him gently.

"First time here?" she asked, offering a warm smile.

The man nodded, running a hand through his hair. "Yeah, I'm Andy. Sorry. I'm a bit of a mess right now. My dad was just diagnosed with dementia last month. I... I don't know what I'm doing."

Maria sat down beside him. "I'm Maria. I was in your shoes not too long ago. My mom had dementia."

Andy's eyes widened. "Had?"

Maria nodded, feeling a familiar pang in her heart. "She passed away last year. We were on this journey together for five years."

"Five years," Andy repeated, his voice barely above a whisper. "I don't know if I can do this for five weeks, let alone five years."

Maria reached out and patted his hand. "You can, and you will. It won't be easy, but I promise you—it will be worth it."

Andy looked at her skeptically. "Worth it? How can watching someone you love slip away be worth it?"

Maria took a deep breath, thinking back on her journey with Evie. "Because for every difficult moment, there will be moments of joy, laughter, and love that you'll cherish forever. This journey will teach you strength you never knew you had, patience you never thought possible, and a depth of love you couldn't imagine."

She reached into her purse and pulled out the worn copy of Pride and Prejudice, carefully opening it to reveal the pressed forget-me-not. "My mom kept this flower I gave her, right until the end. It reminded her of our love, even when she couldn't remember much else."

Andy's eyes misted over as he looked at the flower.

Maria continued, her voice now gentle but firm. "There will be hard days, Andy. Days when you'll want to give up. But there will also be beautiful moments—a shared laugh, a moment of clarity, a simple touch that says more than words ever could. Those moments will rejuvenate you and make it all worthwhile."

She closed the book carefully. "This journey will change you. You'll learn to find joy in the smallest things, to live in the present moment, and to appreciate every second you have with your dad."

Andy wiped his eyes. "How do you do it? How do you stay strong?"

Maria smiled. "You take it one day at a time. You lean on others when you need to. You laugh when you can, cry when you must, and always, always hold onto love. That's what will guide you through the darkest days."

She gestured around the room to other caregivers, both current and past. "And remember, you're not alone. We're all here, ready to support you, just as others supported me when I needed help."

Maria saw a spark of hope in Andy's eyes that wasn't there before. Her journey with Evie had ended, but in sharing her experience and offering support to others, that journey continued to have enduring value and lasting meaning.

In her mind, she could hear Evie's voice: "That's my girl. Always helping others."

Maria smiled. This was her path now—to be a beacon of hope for others, just as Evie had always been for her. And in doing so, her mother's legacy of love, laughter, and resilience would live on.

As the sun sets on your journey as a dementia caregiver, you stand at the threshold of a new dawn. The path you've walked has been long and arduous, filled with moments of heartache and triumph, despair and unexpected joy. Now, as you turn the page to a new chapter in your life, it's time to reflect on the profound transformation you've undergone and the boundless possibilities that lie ahead.

The Crucible of Caregiving

Caregiving is not merely a role; it's a crucible that reshapes the very essence of who you are. In the face of dementia's relentless progression, you've been forged anew, emerging stronger, more compassionate, and profoundly wiser.

Think back to who you were before this journey began. Could you have imagined the depths of love and resilience you'd discover within yourself? The patience you'd cultivate? The strength you'd find in your most vulnerable moments?

You've learned to find beauty in the smallest gestures—a fleeting smile, a moment of recognition, the warmth of a hand in yours. You've become fluent in the language of unspoken love, communicating through touch, presence, and unwavering commitment when words fail.

In the crucible of caregiving, you've developed an emotional intelligence and empathy that transcends ordinary experience. You've seen the human spirit at its most fragile and its most indomitable. This profound understanding of the human condition is a gift, albeit one earned at great cost.

Transforming Pain into Purpose

As you stand at this juncture, you may feel a complex mix of emotions—relief tinged with guilt, sadness intertwined with a tentative sense of freedom. Know that every feeling is valid, a testament to the depth of your caregiving experience.

Now is the time to alchemize the pain and challenges of your journey into a renewed sense of purpose. The wisdom you've gained is a light that can illuminate the path for others. Your hard-earned insights have the power to comfort, guide, and inspire.

Consider opportunities for channeling your experience to positive action:

Mentorship: Your journey has equipped you with invaluable knowledge. By mentoring new caregivers, you can ease their burden, offering the understanding and guidance you once longed for.

Advocacy: Your voice, strengthened by experience, can be a powerful force for change. Advocate for better support systems, increased research funding, or improved care facilities. Your firsthand knowledge lends authenticity and urgency to the cause.

Creative Expression: Channel your experiences into art, writing, or music. Your creative expressions can touch hearts, raise awareness, and help process your own emotions.

Nurturing Your Renewed Self

As you've poured yourself into caregiving, you may have neglected your own needs. Now is the time to turn that nurturing energy inward. Self-care isn't a luxury; it's an essential part of your healing and growth.

Begin by acknowledging the toll caregiving has taken on you, both physically and emotionally. Permit yourself to rest, to grieve, to simply be. Your body and soul need time to recover from the marathon you've run.

Rediscover the rhythms of your own life. What activities once brought you joy? What dreams did you set aside? It's time to reacquaint yourself with your passions and aspirations.

Seek support for your healing journey. Consider counseling or therapy to process your experiences. Join support groups for former caregivers who understand the unique challenges of this transition.

Remember, caring for yourself honors the love and dedication you've shown throughout your caregiving journey. You've proven the depths of your capacity to care; now, include yourself in that circle of compassion.

Embracing the Future

As you step into this new chapter, you do so not just as a survivor, but as someone poised to thrive. The strength you've developed, the compassion you've cultivated, and the wisdom you've gained are not burdens to carry, but gifts to cherish and share.

Your experiences have given you a unique perspective on what truly matters in life. You've seen firsthand the fragility of memory and the enduring power of love. Let this wisdom guide you as you reshape your life.

Set new goals that align with your evolved self. Perhaps you'll pursue education in a field related to caregiving or healthcare. Maybe you'll travel to places you and your loved one dreamed of visiting. Or you might dedicate time to strengthening relationships that may have been strained during your caregiving years.

Embrace new beginnings while honoring your journey. You don't need to move on from your experiences, but rather move forward with them, allowing them to enrich your life and the lives of those around you.

A Torch in the Darkness

As you navigate this transition, remember that your caregiving journey has left an indelible mark on the world. In the face of a disease that steals memories, you became a keeper of stories, a guardian of dignity, a beacon of unwavering love.

Your acts of care, no matter how small they may have seemed in the moment, rippled out into the world, touching lives in ways you may never fully know. You stood as a testament to the heights of human compassion and the depths of human resilience.

The love you've shown, the strength you've embodied, and the dignity you've upheld in the face of tremendous challenges – these are your legacy. They live on, not just in memories, but in the very fabric of who you've become.

Embracing Your New Reality

As this chapter of intense caregiving closes, you stand at a threshold. The journey you've traversed has changed you, irrevocably and profoundly. Like a soldier returning from a long campaign, you may find yourself viewing the world through different eyes. The battles you've fought, the losses you've endured, and the love you've given so selflessly have left their mark.

You may feel a complex mixture of relief and disorientation. The weight of constant caregiving has lifted, yet its absence might leave you feeling adrift. This is normal. The hyper-vigilance, the constant concern, the daily routines that have structured your life for so long – these don't disappear overnight. It's okay to feel lost, to grieve not just for your loved one, but for the person you were before this journey began.

Recognize that you are emerging from an experience that has fundamentally altered you. You've developed strengths you never knew you had, faced fears you never imagined, and loved more deeply than you thought possible. These changes aren't simply positive or negative—they're a complex tapestry of growth, loss, resilience, and wisdom.

You may find that you relate to the world differently now. Small problems that once seemed significant may pale in comparison to what you've faced. You might feel out of step with friends who haven't shared similar experiences. Your priorities have likely shifted, and your perspective on life and death has profoundly altered.

But know this: the depth of your experience, while at times isolating, also equips you with a unique capacity for empathy, hard-earned wisdom, and a profound appreciation for life's fragile beauty. These are gifts of the highest degree, albeit ones that have come at a significant cost.

As you move forward, be patient with yourself. Healing and rediscovery take time. There's no need to rush into a new purpose or to immediately make sense of all you've been through. Allow yourself space to process, to rest, to simply be.

When you're ready, know that your experiences—both the painful and the transcendent—have equipped you with insights and strengths that the world desperately needs. Your capacity for compassion, your understanding of human frailty and resilience, and your ability to find meaning in small moments are powerful forces for good.

You've been through a war of sorts, a battle against time, against loss, against the relentless progression of disease. You may bear scars from this battle, but you also carry with you a hard-won wisdom and depth of spirit.

The path ahead may not be clear, and that's okay. You've proven your ability to navigate uncertainty with grace and courage. Trust in the strengths you've developed. Lean on the support of those who understand your journey. Be kind to yourself as you adjust to this new chapter of life.

The road forward may not be easy, but you've proven your ability to face incredible challenges. You are stronger than you know, more resilient than you realize, and more capable than you might believe. Trust in your journey, in your growth, and in your innate capacity to find meaning and purpose, even in the aftermath of profound challenge.

Your story isn't over. You, with all your battle-earned wisdom and deep capacity for love, are ready for whatever comes next. Step forward, not with blind optimism, but with the quiet strength of one who has faced the storm and emerged, changed but undefeated.

The world awaits the unique gifts that only you, shaped by this life-changing journey, can offer. Your path forward may not be easy, but you have everything you need within you to face it. Trust yourself, be patient with your healing, and know that your experiences, however difficult, have value beyond measure.

Chapter 19

Caregiver Resources

This resource page is designed to connect you with valuable support, information, and services that can assist you throughout your caregiving experience. Whether you're seeking general information about dementia, looking for support groups, exploring long-term care options, or needing guidance on legal and financial matters, the organizations listed below offer a wealth of resources to help. Remember, every caregiving journey is unique, and you may find some resources more helpful than others at different stages. We encourage you to explore these offerings and reach out to those that resonate with your current needs. Your well-being as a caregiver is crucial, and seeking support is a sign of strength and commitment to providing the best care possible for your loved one.

General Information and Support:

• Alzheimer's Association (alz.org) ○ 24/7 Helpline: 1-800-272-3900

• National Institute on Aging - Alzheimer's and related Dementias Education and Referral Center (nia.nih.gov/health/alzheimers)

• Alzheimer's Foundation of America (alzfdn.org)

• Dementia Care Central (dementiacarecentral.com)

• Mayo Clinic - Dementia (mayoclinic.org/diseases-conditions/dementia/symptoms-causes/syc-20352013)

• Alzheimer's Disease International (alzint.org)

Specific Types of Dementia:

- Lewy Body Dementia Association (lbda.org)

- Association for Frontotemporal Degeneration (theaftd.org)

- Vascular Dementia Organization (vascular-dementia.org)

- Creutzfeldt-Jakob Disease Foundation (cjdfoundation.org)

- Huntington's Disease Society of America (hdsa.org)

Caregiver Support Organizations:

- Family Caregiver Alliance (caregiver.org)

- National Alliance for Caregiving (caregiving.org)

- Caregiver Action Network (caregiveraction.org)

- Well Spouse Association (wellspouse.org)

- Rosalynn Carter Institute for Caregiving (rosalynncarter.org)

- National Family Caregivers Association (nfcacares.org)

Practical Caregiving Resources:

- AARP Caregiving Resource Center (aarp.org/caregiving)

- National Adult Day Services Association (nadsa.org)

- Memory Cafe Directory (memorycafedirectory.com)

- Eldercare Locator (eldercare.acl.gov)

- Meals on Wheels America (mealsonwheelsamerica.org)

- National Respite Network (archrespite.org)

Long-Term Care Information:

- National Center for Assisted Living (ahcancal.org/ncal)

- National Association of Area Agencies on Aging (n4a.org)

- LeadingAge (leadingage.org)

- The Green House Project (thegreenhouseproject.org)

- Pioneer Network (pioneernetwork.net)

Financial and Legal Resources:

- Veterans Affairs Caregiver Support (caregiver.va.gov)

- National Academy of Elder Law Attorneys (naela.org)

- Benefits.gov - Caregivers (benefits.gov/categories/Caregivers)

- Medicare.gov (medicare.gov)

- Social Security Administration (ssa.gov)

- National Resource Center on LGBT Aging (lgbtagingcenter.org)

Grief and Bereavement Support:

- The Compassionate Friends (compassionatefriends.org)

- GriefShare (griefshare.org)

- National Hospice and Palliative Care Organization (nhpco.org)

- Hospice Foundation of America (hospicefoundation.org)

- Center for Complicated Grief (complicatedgrief.columbia.edu)

Cognitive Health and Activities:

- BrainHQ (brainhq.com)

- National Institute on Aging's "Go4Life" program (go4life.nia.gov)

- Lumosity (lumosity.com)

- Dementia Activities (dementiaactivities.com)

- Music & Memory (musicandmemory.org)

- TimeSlips Creative Storytelling (timeslips.org)

International Resources:

- Alzheimer's Society (alzheimers.org.uk) - UK

- Alzheimer Society of Canada (alzheimer.ca)

- Dementia Australia (dementia.org.au)

- Alzheimer Europe (alzheimer-europe.org)

- Alzheimer's Disease International (alz.co.uk)

- World Health Organization - Dementia (who.int/health-topics/dementia)

Research and Clinical Trials:

- Alzheimer's Prevention Registry (endalznow.org)

- ClinicalTrials.gov (clinicaltrials.gov)

- National Institute on Aging - Alzheimer's Disease Research Centers (nia.nih.gov/health/alzheimers-disease-research-centers)

- Alzheimer's Association TrialMatch (alz.org/alzheimers-dementia/research_progress/clinical-trials/trialmatch)

Remember to consult with healthcare professionals for personalized advice and support in your caregiving journey. Each of these organizations offers unique resources and support that can be valuable at different stages of the caregiving journey.

Dear Caregiver

Letters of Hope and Wisdom From Experienced Caregivers of Alzheimer's and Other Dementias | Real-Life Stories to Encourage, Support, and Guide Your Journey

Introduction

This book is ugly.

It's raw and unpolished — *and that's entirely the point.*

It's not going to give you 10 easy steps to make everything better, because dementia care doesn't work like that.

What this book will give you, however, is far more powerful...

Hope.

I'm Ben Clardy, the "author" of this book. I didn't write it, but only collected and assembled the stories it contains. The real Authors are the experienced caregivers who put pen to paper, bearing their souls and sharing their individual journeys for the benefit of others.

Imagine sitting across from someone who has walked the same challenging path you're on. Their eyes meet yours, filled with understanding, as they begin to share their story. *This book is that conversation* — multiplied by dozens of voices, each with its own unique tale of struggle, triumph, and unwavering love. It's an extraordinarily powerful resource but, *I have to warn you...*

The stories contained in this book are as honest as it gets. Aside from some basic formatting and addressing any apparent errors, I've left them untouched. As a result, some contain harsh language and describe very difficult situations. Despite this, I felt compelled to preserve the purity of their message rather than alter them to be *"easier to read"*. Interestingly, even the most difficult stories manage to naturally conclude with a positive message, which helps to prove that there is always light beyond the darkness.

There's no denying that some of the stories are painful to read, but others are so unbelievably funny that you may laugh until you cry. This vast diversity of emotion helps to illustrate how unpredictable and dynamic the role of caregiving can be. It's encouraging how we, as humans, always have the option of choosing a perspective of hope, positivity, and humor — even against all odds. As you'll soon see, this remarkable trait is demonstrated time and time again on the pages that follow.

When I reached out to caregivers asking if they would like to include their story in this book, I provided them with the following simple guidelines:

- **Synopsis:** First names and ages of the caregiver and their loved one, type of dementia diagnosed, length of time providing care, and any details concerning additional support.
- **Story:** Their unique, personal account, written in their own words — unfiltered, and straight from the heart. Begin the story with the words, *"Dear Caregiver"*.
- **Advice:** The single most valuable piece of advice they can provide to benefit their fellow caregivers.
- **Encouragement:** Any words of guidance or encouragement they would like to share to help fellow caregivers.
- **Photo:** A single photo can be provided, if desired, but is not required if they'd prefer to remain anonymous.
- **Word Count:** Between 800-1200 words.

As you delve into these stories, remember that each one is speaking to *YOU, dear caregiver*. Their insights, wisdom, and encouragement are significant and highly relevant for those walking this challenging path of dementia caregiving.

Whether you choose to read this book cover to cover or dip into it as needed, my hope is that these stories will serve as a source of comfort, guidance, and inspiration that will prove deeply beneficial to you on your caregiving journey.

As you turn the page, imagine that you're sitting down with a fellow caregiver at the end of a long, hard day. They look you in the eye and say, *"Let me tell you about the time..."*

And just like that, the conversation begins.

Chapter 1
Mom, Unfiltered

Synopsis:

- **Caregiver:** Cindy, 46
- **Loved one:** Jen, 68
- **Relationship:** Mother/daughter
- **Dementia type:** Frontotemporal
- **Duration of care:** 2 years
- **Living situation:** Mother lives with Cindy
- **Support system:** Cindy and her husband

Story:

Dear Caregiver,

Welcome to my life: daughter, caregiver, and Mom's personal censor.

It started small. A remark here about someone's outfit, a too-loud observation about a neighbor's weight. But lately, it's like living with a combination of a six-year-old and a drunk frat boy.

Two years ago, when Mom was diagnosed, I thought I was prepared. Memory issues? Check. Confusion? Check. But no one warned me about the flood of unfiltered comments that would start pouring out of my once-proper mother's mouth.

The latest incident was at the grocery store.

We were on the cereal aisle, I think. My head snapped up from the shopping list. There was Mom, pointing and cackling at a man 10 feet away who was built like a linebacker. I felt the heat rush to my face as I grabbed her arm, steering her away.

I told her, "We don't say things like that."

She said, "Why? He's enormous!"

It's something to do with her sense of empathy. It comes and goes, but when it goes, it's just gone. Like way gone.

So we carried on with our shopping, and I thought we were in the clear. Oh, silly me. Eventually, our paths crossed with the same guy again, and Mom stage-whispered, "See? His pants aren't even pulled up!" I swear, at that moment, I would've traded my soul for the ability to turn invisible. What you have to understand is that she's speaking these things at full volume, without a hint of subtlety.

The "big guy" heard her, of course. Our eyes met. I suppose the expression of shock and disbelief on my face was enough to communicate to the linebacker that I was beyond embarrassed. He must have known that Mom couldn't really help it. Thank GOD we had a kind of non-verbal understanding.

But the grand finale? Out of nowhere, Mom announces, "He was probably trying to find someone to do."

Luckily the man didn't hear that one. I nearly choked on my own spit. This from the woman who once washed my mouth out with soap for saying "crap" at the dinner table!

Some days, I laugh. Some days, I cry. Most days, I do a combination of both. It all depends.

I've become an expert at the apologetic smile, the quick exit, the distraction technique. "Oh look, Mom! A sale on cornflakes!"

My friends don't get it. They say, "Just don't take her out." As if it's that simple. As if keeping her locked away is the solution. As if I could bear to rob her of the simple joy of choosing her own cereal or feeling the sun on her face.

So we venture out, this unfiltered version of my mother and I. We brave the stares, the awkward silences, the occasional angry retort. And in between the mortifying moments, we find new ways to connect.

Like when she gleefully points out all the dogs we see, cooing over them like a kid at Christmas. Or when she spontaneously hugs the cashier, thanking them for their service with such genuine warmth that even the grumpiest employees crack a smile.

It's a tightrope walk, this new life of ours. Balancing her need for independence with my need to not die of embarrassment. Cherishing the good moments while bracing for the next full-volume verbal grenade.

But here's the kicker: as unfiltered as she's become, she's also more openly affectionate than ever. The mom who once showed love through acts of service now tells me she loves me a dozen times a day. She hugs freely, laughs easily (even if sometimes inappropriately), and seems to find joy in the smallest things.

So yeah, my mom now sometimes talks like she's auditioning for a R-rated movie. But she's still mom. And I'm learning that sometimes, the most loving thing I can do is to let her be exactly who she is in this moment — filter or no filter.

Key Advice:

I started carrying little cards explaining Mom's condition. Basically, just a business card that says:

"My Mother has dementia, a condition that affects behavior and impulse control. We appreciate your understanding and patience."

Now, when Mom makes an inappropriate comment, I discreetly hand a card to anyone within earshot. It's incredible how quickly tension dissipates when people understand what's going on.

It's a small thing, but in this topsy-turvy world of dementia care, sometimes small things make all the difference.

Words of Encouragement:

It's okay to feel embarrassed. It's OK to want to hide under a rock sometimes. It's even OK to laugh when the situation is so absurd you don't know what else to do.

You're not failing if you can't control every word that comes out of your loved one's mouth.

Remember, in a world that often values propriety over authenticity, you're witnessing raw, unfiltered humanity. It's messy. It's uncomfortable. But it's also real. And there's a strange beauty in that realness, if you look for it.

So hang in there. You're doing holy work, even when it doesn't feel like it. Especially when it doesn't feel like it.

Chapter 2
The Long Goodbye

Synopsis:

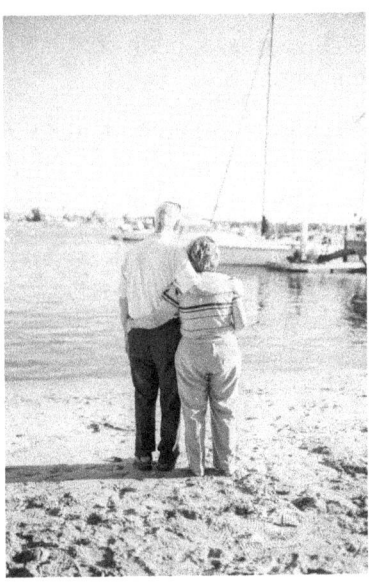

- **Caregiver:** Emma, 53
- **Loved one:** Her Father, Robert, 77
- **Relationship:** Daughter / Father
- **Dementia type:** Alzheimer's
- **Duration of care:** 11 years
- **Living situation:** Family home, assisted living, finally full-time care facility
- **Support system:** Emma, her Mother, Sarah, and her 2 Sisters

Story:

When you asked me to share our family's journey with dementia, I hesitated. It's been a very long road. 11 years to be exact. What made me decide to write this was a feeling of conviction. If our story can help even one person, then it's a story worth telling.

It started back in 2012. My Dad's name is Robert, but everyone called him Bob. He was only 66 when he was diagnosed. He'd always been sharp as a tack, a retired accountant who could do complex math in his head. We started noticing little things. He'd forget appointments, struggle with simple calculations, misplace his keys.

At first, we brushed it off as normal aging. But Mom (Sarah) knew something wasn't right. She convinced Dad to see a doctor, and in early 2013, we got the diagnosis we'd been dreading: Alzheimer's disease.

I remember the day Mom called to tell me. I was at work, and even though we'd all suspected something was wrong, hearing those words felt like a punch to the gut.

The next few years were a blur of doctor's appointments, research, and life adjustments. We learned everything we could about the disease, but nothing really prepares you for watching your loved one slowly slip away.

By 2016, Dad's decline was becoming more noticeable. He started wandering at night, sometimes managing to let himself out of the house. That's when we made the heartbreaking decision to move Mom and Dad out of our childhood home and into an assisted living facility with better security.

It was hard saying goodbye to that house. So many memories, so many milestones celebrated within those walls. But we knew it was necessary for Dad's safety.

The move brought new challenges. Dad's incontinence worsened, which was especially hard on Mom. No one's ever really prepared to handle that kind of care for their spouse. There were a few scary incidents where Dad managed to get out despite the facility's security. It was beyond difficult on so many levels.

We set up a routine where Dad would go to day care a few times a week. It gave Mom some respite, and Dad seemed to enjoy the activities and socializing. The staff always commented on what a sweet man he was, even as his condition worsened.

Dear Caregiver

In December 2020, Dad caught pneumonia and ended up in the hospital. We thought we might lose him then, but he pulled through. However, that hospital stay seemed to accelerate his decline.

After that, we moved Dad into a full-time care facility. It was one of the hardest decisions we've ever had to make, but we knew Mom couldn't provide the level of care he needed anymore. The guilt was overwhelming, but we reassured her it was the right choice.

The COVID-19 pandemic made everything so much harder. Visits were restricted, and Dad's condition deteriorated rapidly without the stimulation and familiar faces. It felt like the disease was robbing us of what little precious time we had remaining with him.

Dad passed away peacefully in his sleep, just shy of his 77th birthday. The last few years had been so difficult that there was a sense of relief mixed in with our grief. Relief that he was no longer suffering, no longer confused and afraid.

As we share memories and look back at old photos, I'm struck by how much of Dad had already been gone for years. The sharp wit, the booming laugh, the man who taught me to ride a bike and walked me down the aisle. In retrospect, we'd been grieving his loss in pieces for over a decade.

Even now, we're still figuring out how to move forward. Some days, the grief is overwhelming. Other days, we find ourselves laughing at a funny memory of Dad in his prime. It's a strange, bittersweet time.

Mom is slowly finding her footing as a widow after 52 years of marriage. She's thinking about volunteering at the local Alzheimer's Association, wanting to support other families going through what we did.

As for me and my sisters, we're learning to live in a world without Dad. It's hard, but we're also grateful for the 11 years we had to say goodbye, even if they weren't the years we would have chosen.

If there's one thing I've learned from this journey, it's that love persists even when memories fade. Dad might not have remembered our names towards the end, but he always lit up when we walked into the room. That connection, that love — it never truly goes away.

Thank you for letting me share our story. It feels good to have put it down on paper. Therapeutic, even. I hope it helps someone out there feel a little less alone in their own journey.

All the best,

Emma

Key Advice:

Trust your instincts when you notice changes in your loved one. Early diagnosis can make a huge difference. Be prepared for the road to be unpredictable. Everyone's experience with dementia is unique. Create a support network early on. You'll need it. Find moments of joy and connection where you can, even as the disease progresses.

Words of Encouragement:

The road ahead is tough, but you're not alone. Cherish the good moments, forgive yourself for the bad ones, and remember that your love makes a difference, even when it doesn't feel like it. There is life and hope after dementia. Hold onto that.

Chapter 3

The Great Bathroom Barricade

Synopsis:

- **Caregiver:** Jess, 39
- **Loved one:** Mildred, 75
- **Relationship:** Daughter-In-Law / Mother-In-Law
- **Dementia type:** Alzheimer's and Parkinson's
- **Duration of care:** 2 years
- **Living situation:** Mildred lives with Jess and her husband Leonard
- **Support system:** Jess, her husband Leonard, and occasional help from a neighbor

Ben Clardy

Story:

Dear Caregiver,

I have a story for you, but first, some context.

We live in this charming 1940s house. Tons of character, original hardware, the works. Sounds quaint, right? Well, it is until you realize that charm comes with some serious drawbacks — like bathroom doors that can only be unlocked from the inside, for instance. An oversight we've since remedied, I assure you.

It was a Friday. I remember because Leonard was bringing home pizza for dinner. Mildred, my mother-in-law with Alzheimer's and Parkinson's, announced she needed the bathroom. Nothing unusual there.

Twenty minutes passed. Then thirty. Starting to become concerned, I go to check on her.

I knock on the door. "Mildred? You okay in there?"

A brief silence, and then, "Who's there? Go away!"

My heart sank. She'd forgotten who I was, again. And worse, she'd locked the door.

I tried explaining to her who I was. I also tried talking her through unlocking the door from the inside, but no luck. I assumed she was ignoring me or avoiding me, but I soon realized that she was busy implementing defensive countermeasures.

I heard an unusual sound. Something heavy on the the other side of the door, scraping slowly along the floor, followed by a thud.

"Mildred? What are you doing?"

"Keeping you out!" came the muffled reply.

She'd barricaded the door. I later found out she'd managed to wedge our small accent table under the doorknob.

I ran downstairs to get Leonard's toolbox, determined to take the lock apart from the outside. Bad move. The sound of the screwdriver clicking and clanking on the lock only freaked Mildred out more.

Mildred started banging on the walls and yelling for help.

Next I heard a squeak, squeak, squeak sound. It was the faucet turning on.

"Mildred, did you turn on the tub?"

"GO AWAY"!

Oh, lord.

I raced back downstairs to shut off the water main, but not before a small river started flowing under the bathroom door.

That's about the time when Leonard arrived home with the pizzas.

"Honey, why is the floor wet?"

I thrust the phone at him. "Call for help. Your mother's flooded the bathroom and barricaded herself inside."

The next hour was chaos. Police arrived, followed shortly after by firefighters. The whole neighborhood was flashing with blue, red, and yellow lights. They assessed the situation, and decided to take the door off its hinges.

A few minutes later and the door was loose.

As the door was pulled away, there stood Mildred.

She was completely naked and covered in soap — standing in the flooded bathroom, wielding the toilet plunger like a weapon.

I imagine that must sound funny as you read it, but in the moment, it was heartbreaking. Mildred looked so scared, so confused. Shaking uncontrollably.

I slowly approached her with a bathrobe. Told her who I was. When she saw me, she settled down.

Recognition dawned in her eyes. "Jess, what happened?"

As I helped her into the robe, I explained as gently as I could. The fear, the confusion, the flood, the firefighters, the police officers — all of it.

The firefighters and police were incredibly kind, averting their eyes and helping to clean up the water.

When the scene settled down, we all sat down to eat cold pizza, laughing nervously about the event.

Now, we can look back and see the humor in it. Even Mildred chuckles when we reminisce. It was during a retelling of the story that she dropped the final bombshell.

I asked her why she was naked and soapy if she only went in there to use the bathroom.

Her reply:

"Can't catch me all soaped up."

In case you don't quite follow that — it turns out that getting completely nude and soapy was part of her improvised defensive strategy against her imaginary attackers. Sounds crazy, I know — but doesn't it also kind of make sense?

Providing care for someone with dementia is a constant balance of ensuring safety and preserving dignity. Some days we get it right. Other days we end up with a flooded bathroom and a naked, soapy, plunger-wielding mother-in-law.

So here's to all of us out there, navigating these weird times.

May your locks always open, your floors remain dry, and your sense of humor ALWAYS stay intact.

Sending good vibes.

Jess

Key Advice:

Look at every room through the eyes of someone with cognitive impairment. Replace inside-locking doors with simple push/pull mechanisms. Install flood sensors in bathrooms and kitchens. Gas detectors near the stove. Your forethought into these matters is time well spent.

Words of Encouragement:

You won't catch every potential problem, but each one you do address is a victory. Keep thinking ahead, keep adapting, and don't forget to give yourself credit for the crises you prevent.

Chapter 4
Someone Is Watching

Synopsis:

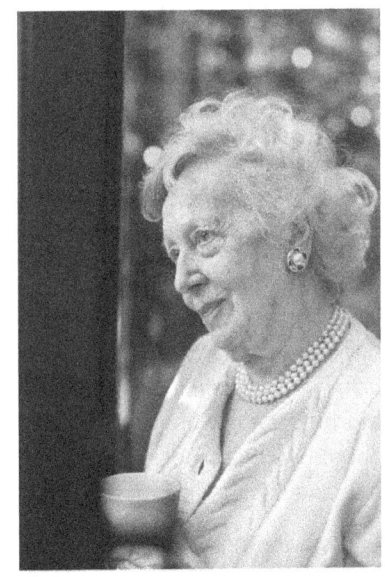

- **Caregiver:** Sarah, 64
- **Loved one:** Mother, 82
- **Relationship:** Mother / Daughter
- **Dementia type:** Lewy Body
- **Duration of care:** 5 years
- **Living situation:** Mother lives alone, Sarah nearby
- **Support system:** Sarah and her sister

Story:

Dear Fellow Caregiver,

I never thought I'd be pouring my heart out like this, but here I am, sharing the rollercoaster ride that's been my life for the past five years. Mom's got Lewy body dementia. It took us way too long to get that diagnosis, and I hope by sharing our story, I can save you some of the heartache we went through.

It all started when Mom was 77. She'd call me in the middle of the night, feeling very anxious about being watched. At first, I brushed it off. Mom had always been a bit of a worrier. But then the paranoia ramped up. She started taping her blinds shut and hanging sheets over windows. She was meticulous in eliminating all gaps where someone might be able to peek through.

We thought we'd struck gold when her best friend, Linda, moved in with her. For a while, things seemed better. We'd navigate around Mom's paranoid comments, redirecting conversations like pros. But then... oh boy. Mom accused Linda of stealing her jewelry. These women had been thick as thieves (pardon the pun) for decades, and suddenly Mom's convinced Linda's some kind of cat burglar.

Things blew up. Mom kicked Linda out, and we were back to square one. Worse, actually, because now Mom was alone and convinced her ex-best friend was breaking in at night to move things around and "make her look crazy."

Here's where it gets really tough. We installed a camera. What we saw... well, it broke my heart. Mom doesn't sleep much at all. She paces all night, moving from window to window, rearranging stuff, then forgetting she's done it. One morning, she swore someone had placed a broom in her bed while she slept. Turns out, she'd been clutching it all night. I can only imagine it as a weapon to use against the intruder.

Getting the Lewy body dementia diagnosis was a battle. We must've seen a dozen doctors. They'd run tests, say everything was clear, try to push anxiety meds. But we knew it was more than that. Finally, we found a neurologist who listened, who saw past Mom's "good days" and recognized the pattern.

This journey's been tough as hell. But we're figuring it out, day by day. We've learned to validate Mom's feelings without feeding into the delusions. Instead of saying, "No, Mom, no one's watching the house," we'll ask, "What makes you think someone's watching?" It doesn't always work, but when it does, it's a little victory.

We've become tech wizards out of necessity. That camera's been a godsend and a curse. It helps us keep Mom safe, but wow, watching those nighttime wanderings... it's rough.

A typical day? Ha! There's no such thing anymore. It usually starts with a pre-dawn phone call from Mom about another "intrusion." I listen, validate, reassure. Then I check the camera footage. Mid-morning, I'm at her place with groceries and forced cheer, helping her tidy up (often undoing her nighttime "redecorating"). We look at old photos, listen to her favorite tunes — anything to keep her mind off the fears.

Afternoons are the worst. As the day wears on, Mom's paranoia kicks into high gear. I get frantic calls about suspicious cars or noises in the attic. More than once I've rushed over to find her huddled in a corner with that darn broomstick.

But you know what? It's not all doom and gloom. This whole mess has brought my sister and me closer. We're in this together, tag-teaming Mom's care. And I've discovered I'm tougher than I ever knew. There are even moments of joy — Mom's smile when she recognizes an old photo, the peace on her face during those rare moments of rest.

Things are going... okay. Despite her weird episodes, she loves her independence. Still, I recognize that we're right on the line of having to make some new changes concerning her living situation.

Taking it one day at a time.

Sarah

Key Advice:

Dealing with Mom's paranoia nearly drove me up the wall at first. I'd argue with her, try to prove she was wrong about the "intruders" or the "spying cars." Big mistake. It only made her more agitated and convinced I was in on some grand conspiracy.

Then, one day, out of sheer exhaustion, I tried something different. Instead of saying, "No, Mom, there's no one watching the house," I asked, "What makes you think someone's watching?" And you know what? It was like a light switch flipped.

This simple shift in approach, validating her feelings without feeding into the delusions, has been a game-changer. It doesn't always work, mind you. There are still plenty of tough days. But when it does work, it's like magic.

Words of Encouragement:

[None provided]

Chapter 5
Seafood Surprise

Synopsis:

- **Caregiver:** Mitsie, 76
- **Loved one:** Frank, 77
- **Relationship:** Wife / Husband
- **Dementia type:** Alzheimer's
- **Duration of care:** 3 years
- **Living situation:** Couple lives together in their home
- **Support system:** Mitsie, 2 adult kids, and a neighbor who helps out

Story:

Dear Caregiver,

I never thought I'd be so grateful for a sense of humor, but these days, it's what keeps me going.

It started with the doorbell. Frank, my husband of 53 years, with Alzheimer's, heads to the front door. By the time I got to the door, our porch was piled high with boxes.

Turns out, while I was sleeping, Frank had gone on a little online shopping spree. To the tune of about $1,200 — in shrimp.

Now, don't get me wrong. I do love seafood. But this? This was ridiculous. Our kitchen looked like we were planning to cater a wedding.

One of Frank's oddities is that he's a bit of a shopper, but get this — we'd already hidden his credit cards! After he'd bought a bunch of random stuff online a few months back, we thought we had this under control. Nope. Somehow, Frank remembered his login for some fancy seafood website.

After the shrimp incident, we went full lockdown. No phone, no computer, no tablet. Our house turned into a tech-free zone faster than you can say "cocktail sauce."

Problem solved, right?

Yes and no.

Now I've got a husband who thinks he's starring in his own episode of CSI: Lost Phone. He's looked everywhere. And I mean EVERYWHERE.

It breaks my heart.

I feel like the meanest wife ever, but what else can I do? We're holding it together financially, but we can't afford more random shr...

Oh my goodness, I almost wrote *"shrimpments"*.

We can't afford any more random shipments from his random shopping sprees. It's so ridiculous that I can't believe what I'm typing.

I know it might sound like I'm making light of our situation, and maybe I am. But honestly? Sometimes laughter is the only thing that keeps me from crying. This journey with Alzheimer's — it's hard. Harder than anything I've ever done.

There are days when I look at Frank and I hardly recognize the man I married. But then there are moments, those precious moments. Like when we're sitting on the porch, watching the sunset, and Frank turns to me with that twinkle in his eye — the one I fell in love with all those years ago. Or when he remembers the punchline to an old joke we've shared a thousand times. Those moments? They're incredible. You don't realize how special they are until you realize that they're running out.

So yeah, I joke. I tease. I laugh at the absurdity. Because if I didn't, I'm not sure I could get through this. But underneath the laughter, there's love. So much love. For the man Frank was, for the man he is now, and for whatever comes next.

This is our story.

Mitsie

Key Advice:

Create a daily routine and stick to it.

I realized we needed some structure in our lives. So I made a schedule and put it all over the house. On the fridge, by Frank's bedside, and even in the bathroom.

We wake up at the same time every day. Breakfast at 8, walk around the block at 9, puzzles or crafts at 10, and so on. Even our meals are on a rotation.

At first, Frank fought it. Change isn't easy for him these days. But after a while, I noticed something remarkable. He was calmer. Less anxious. The constant questions about what's happening next or where his phone is has decreased dramatically.

The routine gives Frank a sense of control and predictability in a world that's becoming increasingly confusing for him. And for me? Well, it's one less thing to worry about. I know what's coming next, and so does he.

It's not foolproof. We still have our off days. But this simple change has brought more peace to our home than I ever thought possible. And on good days, Frank even reminds me what's next on the schedule. Those moments are pure gold.

Words of Encouragement:

It's okay to cry in the shower, to get frustrated, to wish things were different. Those feelings don't make you a bad caregiver. They make you human.

Remember to actively look for the moments of joy, even in the midst of the hard stuff. They might be small, but they're there. A shared laugh over a silly joke. A moment of recognition in their eyes. The peace of holding hands while watching TV. Cherish these moments.

Chapter 6
A Patient Enemy

Synopsis:

- **Caregiver:** Olivia, 35
- **Loved one:** Mother, Patricia 64
- **Relationship:** Daughter / Mother
- **Dementia type:** Early Onset Alzheimer's
- **Duration of care:** 11 years
- **Living situation:** Family home and care facility
- **Support system:** Olivia and her Brother

Story:

Dear Caregiver,

Mom was only 50 when the clues of Alzheimer's first crept into our lives. It started with little things. Misplaced things, forgotten appointments, the same story told twice in one conversation. At first, we brushed it off. After all, everyone gets a little forgetful eventually.

I remember the day I first realized something might really be wrong. Mom and I were baking cookies, something we'd done together since I was little. She'd always been the queen of the kitchen, able to whip up gourmet meals without breaking a sweat. But that day, she kept forgetting ingredients, asking me the same questions over and over. When she put salt in the cookie dough instead of sugar, I saw the flash of fear in her eyes.

Mom knew. She'd seen this before with her own mother. One day, she sat me down and said, "Livvy, I think it's happening to me too." I remember laughing it off, telling her she was too young, that she was just stressed.

Three years later, we sat in a neurologist's office, holding hands as he confirmed our worst fears: early-onset Alzheimer's. Mom was 53. I was 24, fresh out of college and suddenly facing a future I'd never imagined. I remember walking out of that office feeling like I was in a different reality. Everything looked the same, but it also felt entirely different.

The next few years were a whirlwind of adjustments. We became experts in adapting, turned the house into a labyrinth of Post-It notes, and learned to navigate the complex world of healthcare and insurance. Mom, ever the fighter, approached her diagnosis like a battle to be won. "We'll outsmart it," she'd say with a wink. Her determination was both inspiring and heartbreaking.

We developed a system of alarms and reminders. Her phone would ping for medication times, appointments, and even meals. We labeled everything in the house — drawers, cupboards, even the TV remote. Mom would laugh and call it her "treasure hunt." Her ability to find humor in our situation was admirable.

For a long time, we thought we were winning. We found workarounds for every new challenge. When Mom forgot how to use the stove, we got her meals delivered. When she couldn't remember to take her pills, we got her a dispenser with alarms. We had good days — days when Mom was almost her old self, cracking jokes and fussing over my hair. Those days gave us hope, made us think we could beat this thing.

Dementia is a patient enemy. It waits, it watches, and takes little pieces away so slowly that it's difficult to see until something obvious happens. The day I realized Mom no longer recognized me was the day I understood the true cruelty of this disease. It was a spring morning, and I'd brought her favorite flowers — daffodils. She smiled when I walked in, but it was the polite smile she gave to strangers. She said, "Are you new?" In that moment, I felt my heart shatter into a million pieces. I'll always remember those 3 words.

From then on, our relationship entered a new phase. Some days, she knew me as her daughter. Other days, I was a kind stranger. And some days, she thought I was her sister or her mother. I learned to go with the flow, to be whoever she needed me to be in that moment. It was a strange dance, but it allowed us to maintain a connection, even as the disease progressed.

Eventually, we had to make the decision to move Mom into a care facility. She was 60, surrounded by residents decades older. Watching her confusion as I left her there... it's a moment that still haunts me. I cried the whole way home, feeling like I'd abandoned her. But I knew it was the right decision. She needed round-the-clock care that I couldn't provide.

The last four years were a slow descent into a world where communication became increasingly difficult and moments of clarity were rare and precious. As the disease progressed, Mom lost her ability to speak, and then to walk. But even then, as her body failed her, there were beautiful moments when I saw her shine through.

It was in the way her eyes would light up when I walked into the room, even if she didn't know my name. It was in how she would still hum along to her favorite songs. She always had a soft spot for Fleetwood Mac. It was in the gentle way she would pat the hand of a distressed fellow resident, even from her bed. Her inherent kindness never faded, even when she couldn't express it in words.

I remember one day, near the end, when I was sitting with her, feeling particularly low. I was holding her hand, telling her about my day, not sure if she could understand or even hear me. Suddenly, she turned to me and said, clear as day, "Don't worry, sweetie. Everything will be okay." It was the first coherent sentence she'd spoken in months. I burst into tears, overwhelmed by this moment of connection. It was a precious gift I'll cherish forever.

Mom passed away last month, just shy of her 64th birthday. In her final moments, as I held her hand and told her how much I loved her, she squeezed my fingers. One last moment of connection, of love. Even at the very end, she was still comforting me, still being my mom.

This journey has taught me so much. About resilience, about the power of love, about finding joy in the smallest moments. But most of all, it's taught me that even when memories fade, when words fail, when the mind and body betray us — love remains. It's in the small gestures, the fleeting smiles, the squeeze of a hand. Love finds a way to express itself, even in the face of this cruel disease.

I've learned to celebrate small victories. A smile, a moment of recognition, a peaceful day. I've learned that grief doesn't wait for death; it comes in waves throughout the journey of Alzheimer's. But I've also learned that joy can coexist with grief, that beautiful moments can be found even in the darkest times.

Thank you for letting me share our story. I hope it brings some comfort to others walking this path.

With deepest gratitude,

Olivia

Key Advice:

Trust your instincts. If you suspect something's wrong, seek help early. Every moment of clarity is precious. Cherish them. Adapt and be creative in problem-solving; what works today might not work tomorrow, and that's okay. Most importantly, remember that your loved one is still there, even when it's hard to see them. Connection can happen in ways beyond words or recognition.

Words of Encouragement:

Your loved one might forget your name, but they never forget the feeling of being loved. Keep going, keep loving, and know that what you're doing matters so much more than you can imagine.

Chapter 7
My Dolphin Sister

Synopsis:

- **Caregiver:** Debbie, 55
- **Loved one:** Gladys, 80
- **Relationship:** Daughter / Mother
- **Dementia type:** Alzheimer's
- **Duration of care:** 3 years
- **Living situation:** Gladys lives with Debbie
- **Support system:** Debbie, her husband Rick, and Debbie's sister Karen

Story:

Dear Caregiver,

I know you've likely been on a long and weary road. I can certainly relate, but I have one particular story that I'm certain will put a smile on your face.

I'm Debbie. Mom's name is Gladys. She's been living with Alzheimer's for most of a decade, I suppose, but it's been getting worse fairly rapidly.

The agitation, the sundowning — those parts of it were really wearing us all down, so we had been looking for solutions. We'd tried everything the doctors suggested, but nothing seemed to help much. That's when our neighbor mentioned that his wife takes CBD gummies. He said they were a *"magic bullet"* for her anxiety.

We were skeptical at first. I mean, giving my 80-year-old mother cannabis? But after a few more nights of Mom pacing and asking to "go home" at 2 AM, we were desperate enough to try anything.

We started slow. Giving her little nibbles at a time. A little more and a little more until we settled on a dosage that seemed to help her sleep better without making her goofy. She still takes the gummies to this day, and it's amazing how well they work. She was calmer, slept better, and even seemed more like her old self. It honestly felt like we'd found a small miracle.

Ok so that's the first part. Now, enter my sister, Karen. She offered to stay with Mom for an afternoon while Rick and I attended a friend's retirement party. We left detailed instructions about Mom's care, including the gummies — when to give them, how much, the works. So far so good.

We returned about five hours later to find Karen and Mom on the couch, both looking a bit... off. Karen's eyes were wide and slightly red, and she kept giggling at nothing in particular. Mom seemed unusually happy and well-entertained.

"Karen," I said slowly, "is everything okay?"

She looked at me with a grin. "Mom and I are having a great time. Did you know she used to be a fantastic dancer?"

Mom chimed in, "Karen's been so much fun, dear."

I shot a questioning look at Karen, who just shrugged and said, "Those gummies are pretty relaxing, sis."

It wasn't until later, after we'd put Mom to bed and Karen had gone home, that we had the idea to check the security cameras we'd installed.

Oh boy.

There was Karen, attempting to follow along with a yoga video on TV, while Mom offered enthusiastic if not entirely accurate coaching from her chair.

In another clip, they were both trying to fold laundry, but somehow ended up wearing the towels as capes and parading around the living room.

The funniest bit? Karen and Mom sitting on the floor, making dolphin noises. Karen kept insisting she was "speaking dolphin" while Mom nodded sagely, offering occasional squeaks of her own. It was ridiculous, hilarious, and oddly heartwarming all at once.

As we watched, I didn't know whether to laugh or sigh. On one hand, I was concerned that Karen had irresponsibly eaten too many gummies. On the other, I hadn't seen Mom so happy in ages.

The next day, a sheepish Karen confessed to trying one gummy, which turned into two when she didn't feel anything right away. My sister ended up having 4 times as much as Mom's nighttime dose.

Karen and I had a serious talk about medication safety, but you know what? A part of me was grateful for Karen's minor misadventure. Despite being somewhat upset with my sister, I was also thankful. For one afternoon, it had given me a glimpse of my old Mom — giggly, carefree, free-spirited, and full of mischief.

So here's to those unscripted, unexpected moments in caregiving. Sometimes they come in the form of CBD-induced giggles and impromptu dolphin impersonations. And sometimes, those little mishaps give us moments of joy we didn't know we needed.

To all my fellow caregivers out there: May your days be filled with more laughter than tears, even if that laughter comes from watching security camera footage the next day.

I hope my story brought a smile to your face.

Debbie

Key Advice:

Always secure medications, even the ones that seem harmless. And maybe, just maybe, don't be too quick to judge the occasional moment of silliness. Sometimes, laughter really is the best medicine.

Words of Encouragement:

To my fellow caregivers riding this rollercoaster of emotions: You are the unsung heroes of everyday life. In between the challenges and the heartaches, don't forget to look for those unexpected moments of joy. They might come disguised as misadventures or silly mishaps, but they're there. Remember, in this journey of caregiving, it's okay to laugh, it's okay to cry, and it's definitely okay to do both at the same time.

Chapter 8
Human Expiration Dates

Synopsis:

- **Caregiver:** Dianne, 55
- **Loved one:** Her Father, 75
- **Relationship:** Daughter / Father
- **Dementia type:** Vascular
- **Duration of care:** 5 years
- **Living situation:** Father in memory care facility
- **Support system:** Dianne and her brother

Story:

[What follows is not a letter Dianne provided for this book, but one of her personal journal entries after more than 4 years of very difficult caregiving]

I wish that people came with expiration dates.

God, that sounds awful — but here I am thinking it.

Dad's in memory care. We sold his house to afford it. $2400 more a month for what? A room full of people who can't even talk to him.

He keeps trying to leave. Like, actively trying to die. He walked out and sat in the street so a car would hit him. The man survived TWO quadruple bypasses. He's the one we all thought would go before Mom, but nope. She's been gone 3 years and he's still here, going strong.

I'm the world's worst daughter for even thinking this, but sometimes I find myself praying for a trade. Take dad, who's ready to check out, and give those years to someone who deserves them, you know? The guilt hits me like a truck every time, but the thought keeps coming back.

He hates this. Hates being alive. And I hate seeing him like this. The dad I knew? He's gone. This angry, confused guy in his place?

I'm so scared he's going to outlive his money. Then what? I don't know what I'll do with him. If he had an expiration date, at least I could plan. But this limbo? It's hell.

I feel guilty ALL THE TIME. For my thoughts. For not being able to care for him myself. For feeling relieved when I leave that place. It's eating me alive.

[End journal entry]

[Here is the story she sent me for this book, only a few weeks after her Father passed away]

He's gone. Went in his sleep on a Tuesday.

The relief I felt? Crushed me almost as much as the grief. What kind of daughter feels RELIEVED when her dad dies?

The funeral was a blur. Black clothes. Empty words. "He's in a better place." All that.

It's been three months now. Some days I struggle to get out of bed. Others, I find myself smiling at a memory, then breaking down crying. It comes in waves, you know?

But, something's changing. Slowly. The edges aren't as sharp anymore. I'm starting to remember Dad from before all this happened. The real him. Not the shell at the end.

I'm seeing a therapist. Should've done it years ago. She's helping me see that everything I felt? She says it was okay. Normal, even. Wanting an end to his suffering didn't make me a monster. Feeling relief doesn't erase the love.

I'm learning to forgive myself. For the thoughts. For the times I lost it. For not being perfect. Turns out, there's no such thing as a perfect caregiver. Just people doing their best in impossible situations.

I still have hard days. Lots of them. Most of them. Still cry. Still miss him. But I'm healing, I think. Finding myself again. The me that got lost in it all.

Sometimes, in quiet moments, I swear I can feel him. Not the angry, confused guy from the facility. My Dad. The real one. And I think... I hope... he'd be proud of me for carrying on.

It's a long road ahead. But for the first time in forever, I feel hope. I'm not there yet. But I'm walking towards it. One day at a time.

I hope this helps someone.

Key Advice:

Get a therapist. Don't wait till you're drowning in guilt and grief. Find someone to talk to NOW. I waited far too long to get help. A pro can help you deal with all the messed up feelings that come with this. It's not weak to ask for help.

Words of Encouragement:

To anyone still in the trenches, or trying to climb out:

Your feelings? ALL of them? They're okay. The love, the hate, the guilt, the relief. It's all part of this crap sandwich we've been served. Don't beat yourself up for your thoughts. You're human, doing an impossible job.

Be kind to yourself, yeah? No one gets it unless they've been there. So cut yourself some slack. Rest when you can. Find tiny joys and cling to them.

If you're in the grief phase, know there's no timeline. Good days, bad days, it's all part of it. It's okay to feel relief and sadness at the same time.

You're doing the hardest job there is.

Chapter 9

Mom's Imaginary Boyfriend

Synopsis:

- **Caregiver:** Tanya, 38
- **Loved one:** Maggie, 61
- **Relationship:** Mother / Daughter
- **Dementia type:** Lewy Body
- **Duration of care:** 1 year
- **Living situation:** Mother lives with Tanya
- **Support system:** Tanya & occasional help from her sister

Story:

Dear Caregiver,

You asked for my caregiving story, and honestly, I wasn't sure what to share, but then Mom's new boyfriend showed up. Yep, you read that right. Boyfriend. And trust me, it's not what you think.

Mom's been living with me for about a year now. It wasn't exactly a planned thing. One day, she was living in her own place, having odd memory lapses here and there, but nothing major. The next, she was setting the microwave on fire, trying to heat up a fork. Her dementia has rapidly worsened.

So, skipping a bunch of extraneous details — here we are, cohabitating in my once-peaceful suburban home. It's been... an adjustment, to say the least.

Lately, Mom's been doing some particularly odd things. Here's the story I have for you...

It's 7 AM. I'm barely conscious, fumbling with the coffee maker, praying to the caffeine gods for a swift and potent brew. Then, here comes the sound of my mother's slippered feet shuffling down the hallway.

Mom's on a mission. She bursts into the kitchen, hair askew, nightgown slightly rumpled.

"Tanya, I need coffee in my room. Two cups, please."

I blink at her, my sleep-addled brain struggling to process this request. "Two cups?"

She nods emphatically and then says, "Yes, one for me and one for him."

Him? Last I checked, the only "him" in this house was my cat.

"Who's *'him'*, Mom?"

She looks at me like I've grown a second head. "My boyfriend, of course. Don't be rude, Tanya. He's waiting."

The funny thing, at this particular moment, is that I actually considered if she might have a real-life man in her room, but that notion only lasted a second.

Next, I'm having a minor panic attack about potential coffee stains on my carpet. Because apparently, at some point between yesterday's dinner and this morning's sunrise, my mother has acquired an imaginary boyfriend. A boyfriend who, it seems, shares her enthusiasm for bedroom coffee.

Now, I'd love to tell you that I handled this situation with grace and understanding. That I calmly explained to Mom that there was no boyfriend, gently redirected her attention, and we all lived happily ever after. But that would be a lie, and if there's one thing this caregiving gig has taught me, it's that sometimes honesty is not necessarily the best policy.

So what did I do? I compromised. I grabbed not one but two sippy cups and poured a tiny amount of coffee into each one. Then, with all the fake cheerfulness I could muster at 7 AM sans caffeine, I handed them to Mom and said, "Here you go!"

After that, I just sat there in the kitchen, staring at my own untouched coffee, wondering if I should go check on her. Was she actually drinking the coffee? Was she having a full-on conversation with her imaginary fella? Was I going to walk in on a one-person coffee date?

This is my new normal. Caffeinated, imaginary boyfriends and all.

I don't have any profound wisdom to share. Most days, I'm just trying to keep my head above water. But I've learned a few things along the way:

1. Embrace the absurd. Dementia's going to throw you some curveballs. Imaginary boyfriends? Just another day in paradise. The sooner you learn to roll with the punches, the easier your life will be. Trust me on this one.

2. Adapt your environment. I bought this house for me, but now it's Mom's home too. That means some changes. Spill-proof cups are my new best friends. I've child-proofed more things than I care to admit, and I've developed a sixth sense for potential hazards.

3. Pick your battles. Coffee in the bedroom seemed like a hill to die on at first, but trust me, there are bigger fish to fry. Sometimes, it's easier to just go with the flow. Does it really matter if Mom thinks she has a boyfriend? As long as she's happy and safe, I've learned to let some things slide.

4. Find your sense of humor. I started a "Things Mom's Boyfriend Said" journal. It's weirdly therapeutic. Some days, when things get really tough, I flip through it and can't help but laugh.

5. Take care of yourself. This one's crucial, and it's something I'm still working on. It's easy to get so caught up in caregiving that you forget about your own needs. You know how the saying goes, but my version would be "you can't pour from an empty sippy-cup". Yeah. Find time for yourself, even if it's just five minutes of peace with your morning coffee.

6. Build a support system. Whether it's friends, family, or a support group, having people you can turn to makes all the difference. Sometimes you need to vent, sometimes you need advice, and sometimes you just need someone to remind you that you're doing a good job.

7. Celebrate the small victories. Did Mom remember my name today? Victory! Did we make it through breakfast without any major incidents? Break out the champagne! When you're dealing with dementia, every day brings new challenges. Learning to appreciate the good moments, no matter how small, can help balance out the tough times.

So that's my story. Not exactly the heartwarming tale of caregiving triumph you might have been hoping for, but it's real. It's messy. It's frustrating. Sometimes even funny. It's a journey I never expected to be on, but here I am.

Thanks for letting me share. If nothing else, I hope it gives you a laugh. Because sometimes, in this crazy world of caregiving, that's the best medicine we've got.

Best,

Tanya

Key Advice:

Pick your battles wisely. Find humor where you can; it's a powerful coping tool. Be flexible with your plans and expectations; this situation isn't forever, but it is your current reality.

Words of Encouragement:

Somewhere out there, another caregiver is dealing with their own version of caffeinated imaginary boyfriends. Keep going, keep loving, and keep laughing when you can and go ahead and cry when you can't. As hard as it can be sometimes, this is temporary.

Chapter 10
Of Love, Laughter, & Toothbrushes

Synopsis:

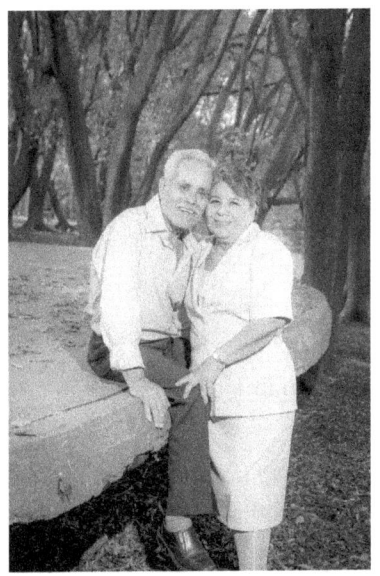

- **Caregiver:** Silas, 73
- **Loved one:** Ellen, 71
- **Relationship:** Husband / Wife
- **Dementia type:** Alzheimer's
- **Duration of care:** 6 years
- **Living situation:** Couple lives in their long-time home
- **Support system:** Silas and their three adult children

Story:

[This story is provided by Tom, Silas and Ellen's eldest Son]

Dear Caregiver,

Mom and Dad had been married for 48 years when Alzheimer's came knocking. Dad took on the role of full-time caregiver like it was the most natural thing in the world. "In sickness and in health." He'd say that with a shrug when we'd express concern about the toll it was taking on him.

As Mom's condition progressed, one of the hardest things to watch was how she started losing recognition of even the most familiar faces. Dad, her husband of nearly five decades, was sometimes a stranger to her. But Dad, bless him, never let it get him down for long.

One night, about five years into Mom's diagnosis, Dad was getting ready for bed. He went to brush his teeth, leaving Mom already tucked in. On his way back to the bedroom, he called out, "I'm coming to bed in just a minute, dear."

Now, you have to picture this: Dad, in his pajamas, toothbrush in hand, probably with a bit of toothpaste still in the corner of his mouth. And there's Mom, looking startled and a bit scandalized.

"I don't think that's appropriate, do you?" she said, in that prim voice she used to use on us kids when we'd done something shocking.

Dad, completely confounded, asked what she meant.

And Mom, bless her heart, said, "Well, I'm a married woman!"

Can you imagine? Forty-eight years of marriage, and suddenly you're being accused of impropriety for getting into your own bed!

When Dad first told us this story, my heart broke a little. The thought of Mom not recognizing her own husband, the man she'd loved for nearly half a century... it stung.

But then I saw the twinkle in Dad's eye as he recounted it, and I realized something important. Dad wasn't dwelling on the pain of not being recognized. Instead, he was finding the humor in the situation. He was choosing to laugh.

That moment became a sort of touchstone for us. Whenever things got really tough — when Mom would have a bad day, or when the weight of caregiving seemed too much for Dad — one of us would inevitably bring up "the toothbrush incident." And we'd laugh. Sometimes through tears, but we'd laugh none-the-less.

Dad's ability to find humor in even the toughest moments was his superpower. It got him through the darkest days of Mom's illness. It helped us, their children, cope with watching our vibrant mother slip away and our strong father shoulder an impossible burden.

Mom passed away last year, but "the toothbrush incident" lives on in our family lore. It's a reminder that even in the midst of a devastating illness, there can be moments of truest joy.

So that's our story.

Thanks for the opportunity to share.

Tom

Key Advice:

Find the humor. It's not about making light of the illness, but about finding moments of joy to sustain you through the hard times. Remember that your loved one is still in there, even when they don't recognize you.

Words of Encouragement:

Try to be like my Dad. He had a saying that was all about not letting the world get you down. *"Like water off a duck's back"*. It just means to let things go and not be bothered and affected easily. Easier said than done, I know, but I think that particular strength served him very well as he cared for my Mother.

Chapter 11
The Reluctant Warrior

Synopsis:

- **Caregiver:** Marcus, 52
- **Loved one:** Father (Wayne), 78
- **Relationship:** Son / Father
- **Dementia type:** Vascular
- **Duration of care:** 3 years
- **Living situation:** Marcus moved into his Father's house
- **Support system:** Marcus, minimal family support

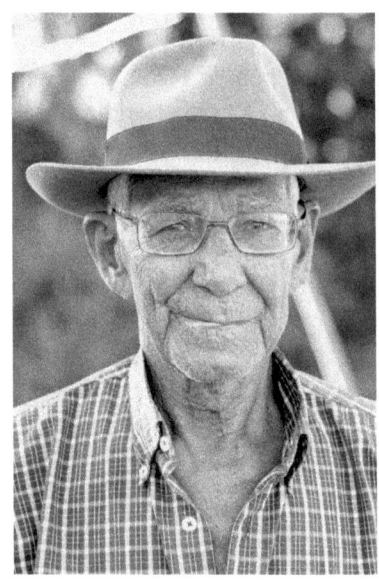

Story:

Dear Caregiver,

Three years ago, I was living my best life. Great job in finance, apartment in the city, dating a model. I was loving life.

My relationship with my father? Nonexistent, and that was just fine by me. Then boom - Dad has a stroke. As part of all that, he came away with a diagnosis of vascular dementia. Suddenly I'm playing nurse to a man who spent most of my childhood telling me I wasn't good enough.

Yeah, I know. "But he's your father, Marcus." Trust me, I've heard it all. The thing is, Dad and I were never close. He was the stern, disapproving type. Nothing I did was ever quite right.

Growing up, it was always, "Why can't you be more like whoever?" What happened to the other points?" So when I got the call about his condition, my first thought wasn't concern. It was resentment.

Why me? Why not my sister in California, or my brother? But they had their excuses, their own lives, and somehow, I ended up being the only option.

Here I am, three years later, living in the suburbs in Dad's old house, my life turned upside down. Some days, I wonder how the hell I ended up here. The faded wallpaper, the worn carpet, the dusty photos of a family that never quite lived up to the smiling façade. I feel like I'm living in a past I thought I'd escaped.

It hasn't been easy. Dad's not the kindly, forgetful old man you see in sappy movies. The dementia has made him more like himself, which isn't a good thing — irritable, demanding, often cruel. There are days when I want to walk out the door and never look back.

But I don't leave. I stay. I help him dress, make sure he eats, deal with his mood swings. Why? Hell if I know. Maybe it's duty. Maybe I'm just stubborn.

The first year was the worst. I had no clue what I was doing. My life went from business deals to bedpans. Dad would have these episodes where he'd get confused and agitated. Once, he accused me of trying to poison him when I gave him his medication. I spent an hour trying to convince him I wasn't some stranger trying to kill him, only for him to forget the entire incident five minutes later.

Another time, he wandered out of the house at 2 AM, convinced he was late for work. I found him two blocks away, talking to a stop sign. As I guided him home, his hand gripping my arm with surprising strength, I realized this was the most physical contact we'd had in decades. A sobering thought.

I've had to learn fast. How to redirect him when he gets fixated on something. How to handle his personal care without making him feel like a child. How to swallow my anger when he lashes out. I've become an expert in things I never wanted to know. Adult diapers, pureed diets, all that.

It's not all bad, surprisingly. One day he looked at me and said, "You're a good son, Marcus." First time he ever said that. Of course, five minutes later he was back to calling me by his brother's name, but still. I'll take what I can get. These moments are like finding water in the desert. Brief, precious, and never enough.

I've had to give up a lot. My job — turns out high-powered executives aren't too understanding when you negotiate remote work so you can care for your old man. My social life — hard to date when you're essentially on call 24/7. My independence — every decision, every move, now revolves around Dad's needs. Some days, the bitterness threatens to swallow me whole. I look at my friends' lives on social media. Promotions, vacations, families of their own, and I feel like I'm watching my life pass me by.

But then I see Dad looking lost and scared, his eyes searching the room for something familiar, and despite all the shit, my heart breaks for him. In those moments, I see past the stern father, past the confused patient, to the vulnerable human being underneath. And I realize that maybe, in some twisted way, this is giving me the chance to know my father in a way I never did before.

This caregiving gig is brutal. It's exhausting, frustrating, and often thankless. I often look in the mirror and I don't recognize the haggard, worn-out man staring back at me. Most people will never understand. How could they?

But I'm learning patience I never knew I had. Learning to find small victories in getting Dad to eat a full meal or having a calm day. Learning that maybe I'm stronger than I thought. I'm learning to forgive both my father and myself. Letting go of the past hurts and focus on the present, because that's all we really have.

I'm also learning to reach out. To the neighbor who brings over casseroles. To the support group where I can vent. To the therapist who's helping me.

I don't know how this story ends. I don't know if Dad and I will ever have the relationship I always wanted. But I'm here, showing up every day, doing the best I can. And some days, that has to be enough.

There are moments in the quiet of the evening, when Dad's asleep and the house is still, that I allow myself to think about the future. What happens when he's gone? Will I regret the career I put on hold, the relationships I let slip away? Or will I find peace in knowing I did everything I could?

I don't have the answers. But I'm starting to realize that maybe the journey is the point. Maybe I'm not just taking care of Dad. I'm learning how to take care of myself, how to be a better person, how to love even when it's hard.

So there it is.

It's not glamorous, but someone has to do it.

Marcus

Key Advice:

Vent. Find your pressure release valve. Whether it's a punching bag, a journal, or screaming into the void. Just figure out how to let off steam without guilt. You're in this for the long haul, so sustainability is absolutely key.

Words of Encouragement:

Cut yourself some slack. You're dealing with a tough situation and a complicated history. The fact that you're still here, still trying? That's courage. It's okay if you don't have warm, fuzzy feelings about this gig. Your actions speak louder than your emotions.

Chapter 12
Plastic Crested Spoonbill

Synopsis:

- **Caregiver:** Zoe, 52
- **Loved one:** Mother, 75 & Father, 78
- **Relationship:** Daughter / Mother / Father
- **Dementia type:** Alzheimer's
- **Duration of care:** 6 years
- **Living situation:** Parents live with Zoe
- **Support system:** Zoe, her partner Alex, and friends

Story:

Dear Caregiver,

Six years ago, my life took an unexpected turn when my Mother was diagnosed with Alzheimer's, followed closely by Dad's Parkinson's.

Mom, a once vivacious art teacher, now lives in a world of shifting memories and a newfound love for birds.

Dad, a former marathon runner, now struggles with the tremors and stiffness. He's gradually becoming more child-like.

Let me paint you a picture of a typical day in our household. It starts with Dad's morning medication routine — a delicate balance of timing and patience. We've turned it into a game show we call "Pill or No Pill," complete with dramatic music and over-the-top announcements. It might take longer, but Dad's laughter makes it worth every second.

Mom, as I mentioned, has developed a deep fascination with birds. To her, our backyard is an exotic aviary.

This morning, she excitedly pointed out a "crested spoonbill" — which was actually a 2-decade-old, faded, pink, plastic flamingo. But you know what? Her eyes lit up with such joy that I found myself asking about the warbler's migratory patterns, bless her.

Mealtimes are an adventure. We've had to get creative with Dad's meals due to his swallowing difficulties. Everything goes into the blender these days, but we have fun coming up with fancy names for our concoctions. Today's lunch? "Pureed Beef Wellington with Creamed Potatoes." Mom, on the other hand, has decided that forks are overrated. We've adapted by serving a lot of finger foods and investing in a good stain remover.

Getting Dad dressed used to be a struggle until we discovered the magic of music. Now, our bedroom transforms into a dance studio most mornings. We put on some classic rock, and suddenly, the tremors seem less pronounced as Dad grooves to the beat while I help him button his shirt. It takes longer, but the smile on his face is priceless.

Mom's artistic side still shines through. She may not remember my name some days, but she can still create beautiful abstract paintings. We've turned our living room into a rotating art gallery. When she asks who the talented artist is, I tell her it's a rising star named "Mom-et." Get it? I don't think Mom does, but she beams with pride every time.

One of our greatest hits is laundry folding. Mom tends to creatively fold things into abstract shapes, and Dad meticulously smooths out wrinkles with shaky hands. I've given up on matched socks. In our house, wearing two different socks is the norm.

There are hard days, of course. Lots of them. Days when Dad's tremors are so bad he can barely hold a spoon, or when Mom doesn't recognize her reflection. But we've learned to dance in the rain, to find joy in small victories and laugh at the absurd.

Dancing through the storm,

Zoe

Key Advice:

Redefine your idea of "normal." In the world of caregiving, flexibility is your greatest asset. Learn to see the world through your loved one's eyes. You might be surprised at the beauty and wonder you find there.

Words of Encouragement:

To my fellow improv artists in the caregiving world: You are doing incredible things, even when it feels like you're just barely keeping your head above water. On the tough days, remember the small victories, the moments of connection, the times when your love broke through the fog of confusion or the barriers of physical limitations. I know you probably don't believe it, but you've got this!

Chapter 13
Dark Days Doubled

Synopsis:

- **Caregiver:** Beth, 52
- **Loved ones:** Father & Mother
- **Relationship:** Daughter / Father / Mother
- **Dementia type:** Father / Alzheimers. Mother / Vascular Dementia
- **Duration of care:** 5 years
- **Living situation:** Parents moved in with Beth
- **Support system:** Beth, neighbor helps occasionally

Story:

Dear Caregiver,

Where to even begin?

My story isn't just about caring for one person with dementia, which is a struggle in and of itself — it's about the domino effect that turned my life upside down.

It started with Dad. He was diagnosed with Alzheimer's, I think about eight years ago. Mom, the pillar of strength, took on the role of his caregiver without hesitation. I watched from the sidelines. I helped where I could, but mostly in awe of Mom's steadfast dedication.

For three years, Mom took care of Dad with grace and patience I didn't know a person could possess. She learned to navigate his mood swings, his forgetfulness, his gradual decline. I'd visit on weekends, giving her brief respites, but the bulk of the care fell on her shoulders.

Then, four years ago, the other shoe dropped. Mom started getting confused about dates and appointments. At first, we chalked it up to stress and exhaustion, but as her symptoms worsened, we couldn't ignore the truth. Mom was eventually diagnosed with vascular dementia.

Just like that, I found myself thrust into the role of caregiver for both my parents. I was 44, single, with a demanding career I loved. But none of that mattered anymore. My parents needed me, and I stepped up.

I don't even recall the first few years. I imagine they were a blur of doctor's appointments, medication schedules, and sleepless nights. Definitely sleepless nights. Dad's Alzheimer's had progressed to the point where he needed constant supervision. Mom, in the early stages of her own dementia, bless her heart, would still try to care for Dad, only to get frustrated and confused when she couldn't remember what to do.

I felt like I was drowning. Balancing their different needs, managing their medications, ensuring they were both safe and cared for. It was overwhelming. I had to leave my job, move back in with Mom and Dad and put my life on hold. The isolation was crushing. Friends stopped calling because I never had time to go out. I've always struggled with dating. Now it was an impossibility.

There were moments of tenderness amidst the chaos. Like when Dad, deep in the fog of Alzheimer's, would reach for Mom's hand and hold it tight. Or when

Mom would have a good day and we'd sit together, looking through old photo albums, sharing memories.

But there were also dark days. Days when Dad would get aggressive, not recognizing any of us. Days when Mom would cry in frustration at her own forgetfulness. Days when I'd close myself in the bathroom and cry. I used to do that a lot.

Three years ago, Dad passed away. The grief was immense, but I'd be lying if I said there wasn't also a sense of relief. Caring for one parent with dementia was still incredibly challenging, but it felt manageable in a way that caring for both hadn't.

Now, it's just Mom and me. Her dementia has progressed, but we've found a rhythm. I've learned to cherish the good moments — when she remembers a detail from my childhood, or laughs at a shared joke. I've also learned to be patient during the hard times — the repetitive questions, the mood swings, the nights when the sundowning keeps us both awake.

This has been the hardest thing I've ever done. Hopefully, the hardest things I'll ever have to do. Not sure if I can handle much more.

I've found support in unexpected places. The local dementia support group has become a lifeline. There's a part-time home health aide who gives me a few hours break each week. I've even started dating again, though explaining my situation is always a challenge.

Looking back, I'm in awe of how Mom cared for Dad, and I strive to show that same level of love and patience in caring for her.

This isn't the life I envisioned for myself, but it's the life I have. And in its own weird way, it's beautiful. Challenging, exhausting, and frustrating, but beautiful.

Making it work,

Beth

Key Advice:

I know it sounds cliche, but start a journal. Not some fancy "dear diary" thing, just a place to dump your thoughts. Bad days, good days, weird stuff Mom said, moments that made you laugh, cry, etc. It helps. Plus, one day you might look back and realize how far you've come. Trust me on this one.

Words of Encouragement:

It's messy and hard and some days it feels impossible. But you're showing up, and that counts for everything. So what if the house is a mess or you can't remember the last time you washed your hair? You're loving hard and under the toughest circumstances. Cut yourself some slack.

Chapter 14
3 AM Air Violin

Synopsis:

- **Caregiver:** Jasper, 48
- **Loved one:** Maurice, 82
- **Relationship:** Son / Father
- **Dementia type:** Lewy Body
- **Duration of care:** 4 years
- **Living situation:** Father lives with Jasper
- **Support system:** Jasper, his wife Amelia, part-time home health aid

Story:

You wanted a story? Our's is downright absurd, but I guess that's life, isn't it?

I'm Jasper, 48, former wannabe rock star turned classical violinist (yeah, I know). Four years ago, my dad, Maurice - the great conductor, the maestro, the guy who could make an entire orchestra quake with just a raised eyebrow — was diagnosed with Lewy Body Dementia. Now he struggles to remember which end of a fork to use. Heartbreaking doesn't even begin to cover it.

Our relationship? Let's just say it was... complicated. Growing up, I was more Nirvana than Beethoven, if you know what I mean. While Dad was busy conducting symphonies, I was in the garage, trying to make my guitar feedback sound "artistic." We were like two instruments perpetually out of tune with each other. There were shouting matches, silent treatments, and disappointments aplenty.

The years go by and then BAM! Suddenly I'm in charge of making sure he doesn't wander off to conduct traffic at the intersection. Talk about a role reversal. I was not prepared for this.

The first year? Holy crap. Dad would wake up at 3 AM, totally convinced he had a concert to conduct. There I'd be, bleary-eyed and cranky, finding him in the living room waving his arms like a madman at invisible musicians. My wife Amelia (saint that she is) suggested we just roll with it. So picture this: me, in my ratty old t-shirt and boxers, playing air violin while Dad conducts. At 3 in the freaking morning. If that's not love, I don't know what is.

But it wasn't always that... whimsical, I guess you could say. There were nights when Dad would get agitated, convinced that the "musicians" weren't following his lead. He'd shout and stomp, his face red with frustration. In those moments, I'd see flashes of the intimidating maestro he used to be, and I'd feel like that scared kid again, waiting for the critique that would inevitably come. But then I'd remember - I'm not that kid anymore, and he's not that man.

As things got worse, we had to get creative. Dad started falling all over the place, so we turned the house into something between a pillow fort and an insane asylum. Yoga mats everywhere, couch cushions strategically placed. Our home looked like it had been decorated by a toddler. I joked to Amelia that we should start a new home decor trend: "Dementia Chic." She didn't laugh.

There were moments that hit me like a ton of bricks. One night, as I'm helping Dad to bed (and trying not to think about how weird it is to be tucking in the guy who used to chase me to bed with threats of extra piano practice), he grabs my arm and says, "You know, Jasper, I always envied how easily music came to you." I nearly fell over. All those years of feeling like a disappointment, and now this? Wild. I stood there, frozen, not sure how to respond. Dad just looked at me with these clear eyes — clearer than they'd been in months — and smiled. And then, just like that, the moment was gone. But those words? They're etched into my heart now. I'll never forget.

But man, there are days when it's just... hard. Days when Dad looks at me like I'm a stranger. Days when I hide in the bathroom for a bit more time to myself. It's embarrassing to admit that, actually. It's not pretty, it's not noble, it's just... the way it is. There was this one time, about two years in, when Dad had a particularly bad day. He was confused, angry, scared. He looked at me and said, "Who are you? Where's my son?" And I just... broke. I yelled back, "I AM YOUR SON!" Not my proudest moment.

On those days, I try to remember something my old violin teacher used to say: "Music is not in the notes, but in the silence between." Turns out, caregiving is kind of the same. It's not about the big dramatic moments. It's about all the small, quiet ones. Weird stuff.

The magic is definitely in the little things. Like how I've learned to make Dad's favorite breakfast — eggs over easy, toast burnt just a little, because that's how he likes it. It's in the patience I've somehow found when I have to explain for the hundredth time that no, we can't go to the concert hall, because he's not conducting anymore. It's in the late nights spent researching new treatments, new approaches — anything that might make his life (and mine) a little easier.

So here we are, four years in. Still playing our weird duet. Sometimes we're in tune, usually we're so far off it's not even funny. But we keep at it, figuring it out as we go along. I've learned to find harmony in the chaos.

To all you other caregivers out there: We're all just making this up as we go along. We're not perfect, we're not saints, we're just people trying our best to take care of the ones we love.

This journey has changed me in ways I never expected. I've found patience I never knew I had, strength I didn't know I could muster, and a depth of love I never thought possible. Don't get me wrong — I still have days when I want to run away, when the weight of it all feels too heavy. But then I look at Dad, and I remember: this is the greatest gift I can give him.

Thanks for listening to my rambling, Ben.

Hope it wasn't too much of a downer.

Catch you on the flip side,

Jasper

Key Advice:

When all else fails, make it a game. Seriously. You'd be amazed what you can turn into a weird, laugh-or-you'll-cry kind of fun. And don't forget to find the music in the everyday moments - it's there, even when life seems out of tune.

Words of Encouragement:

You're doing great, even when it feels like you're just barely keeping it together. You've got this. Sort of. And that's okay. Remember, even the greatest symphonies have moments of dissonance - it's all part of the beautiful, chaotic composition of caregiving.

Chapter 15
Not Done Yet

Synopsis:

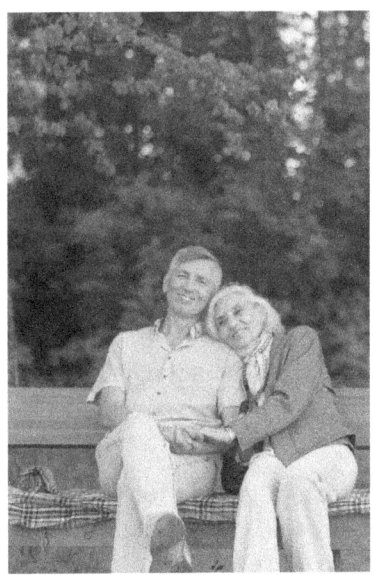

- **Caregiver:** Charlie, 67
- **Loved one:** Gloria, 69
- **Relationship:** Wife / Husband
- **Dementia type:** Frontotemporal dementia (FTD)
- **Duration of care:** Unspecified
- **Living situation:** At home with husband
- **Support system:** Husband, children, local FTD support group

Story:

[This story was submitted not by a caregiver, but by Gloria herself, who was diagnosed with Frontotemporal dementia. She is cared for by her Husband, Charlie.]

Dear Caregiver,

Gloria here. I know you are looking for caregiver stories. I'd like to share mine for your book if you'll have it.

Five years ago, I was running my own business. Then one day, I was staring at a spreadsheet, completely baffled. I couldn't read the words. The best I can describe it is that the letters and numbers looked like hieroglyphics.

After several rounds of doctors, they finally slapped a label on it: Frontotemporal dementia, also known as FTD.

I sold my business, but I didn't give up on life.

Now, don't get me wrong. It's no walk in the park. There are days when I feel like I'm trapped in a fog so thick I can't see my own hands. It's scary stuff. Some days when I look in the mirror and think, "Who's that old lady, and what's she doing in my bathroom?"

No magic wand will make this disappear. But you know what? I'm okay with that. I've had a good life, and I'm not done yet. As long as I can still string a few words together (most days), I'm going to keep trying, keep laughing, keep living.

It can be terrifying at times. There are nights when I lie awake, my mind racing with fears about the future. Will I recognize my grandchildren next year? I feel like I'm already a burden to Charlie, but how much worse will it get? The thought of losing more of myself is a tough notion to grapple with.

Each new day is a miracle. If there one silver lining to my diagnosis, it's that every single day is a miracle. The good days, the bad days — I thank God for each and every one of them.

Charlie, my rock, my everything. I don't have words to express my gratitude. He's learned to read my moods, to anticipate my needs, often before I even realize them myself. His patience seems endless. I worry about him, too. Is he taking care of himself? Does he resent this new role? But then he'll look at me with those kind eyes, and I know we're in this together.

There are unexpected positives in this new life of ours. I've developed a boldness I never had before. Worrying about social niceties seems trivial now, so I speak my mind freely. It's liberating! And the support we've found in our FTD group is invaluable. There's a special bond that forms when you're all in the same storm.

I've also found a new appreciation for the present moment. When your future is uncertain and your past is slipping away, the now becomes incredibly precious. The warmth of the sun on my face, the taste of a strawberry, the sound of my grandchildren's laughter — I soak it in with an intensity I never knew before.

To anyone out there facing a similar diagnosis: it's not the end of your story. It's a new chapter. But there's still joy to be found, purpose to be fulfilled, life to be lived.

And to the caregivers — thank you, thank you, thank you. Even when we forget to say it, even when we can't find the words, we're so grateful.

So that's my story.

With deepest gratitude,

Gloria

[The sections below were written by Gloria as advice and encouragement, not for caregivers, but instead for people who themselves are living with dementia]

Key Advice:

Write it down, folks. Not just the important stuff, but the silly things too. What makes you laugh, what ticks you off, your favorite color. It's like leaving a message in a bottle for your future self. You might not remember writing it, but reading it later it is like discovering a treasure.

Words of Encouragement:

This disease may blur our memories, jumble our thoughts, and shake our sense of self, but it cannot erase who we are at our core.

Yes, we're changing, but we're still here.

Still feeling. Still loving. Still living.

So stand tall. Face each day with whatever strength you have.

Keep going. Keep loving. Keep being you.

Your story matters. And it's not over yet.

Chapter 16

Love Is Always There, Isn't It?

Synopsis:

- **Caregiver:** Emily, 42
- **Loved one:** Mother (Claire), 68
- **Relationship:** Mother / Daughter
- **Dementia type:** Lewy Body
- **Duration of care:** 5 years
- **Living situation:** Mother moved from independent living to care facility to hospice
- **Support system:** Emily, her sister Sarah, and brother Michael

Story:

Dear Caregiver,

Mom was a piano teacher for over 40 years. Music wasn't just her profession; it was the language of our family. Our childhood was filled with the sounds of her gentle corrections guiding young fingers across ivory keys.

The first signs of trouble were subtle. She was faltering more often in her playing. We chalked it up to natural aging, but eventually the day came when she sat to play Für Elise, a piece she'd taught to hundreds of students over the years, and was unable to bring the notes together.

That's when we all knew something was wrong.

The diagnosis came soon after: Lewy Body Dementia. It was like someone had taken Mom's beautiful life and started randomly erasing parts of it, leaving gaps that grew larger with each day.

Mom moved from her home to an assisted living facility. We tried to make her new space feel like home, but it wasn't the same. The piano stood silent more often than not.

On good days, she'd sit at the piano and muscle memory would take over. In those moments, she was herself again. Claire the piano teacher, Mom, the woman who filled our lives with love and music.

On bad days, when words failed and confusion reigned, we'd sit with her, hold her hand, and reminisce about old times. The effect was almost magical. The agitation would fade, replaced by a calm smile, sometimes even a few hummed notes.

The end came too soon. As Mom lay in hospice, we surrounded her with love. We shared stories, sang softly, and held her close. And in her final moments, she opened her eyes, smiled, and took her final breath.

I'll never forget that.

Now, in the aftermath, we're left to interpret this complex story that was Mom's life. There were moments of discord sharp enough to make you wince. Arguments with doctors who seemed to misunderstand our concerns, battles with a healthcare system that often felt indifferent to our needs.

But there were also moments of such exquisite tenderness that they still bring tears to my eyes. Like when Mom, deep in her confusion, still managed to recognize Michael's twins. Or the day she looked at me and said, "Love is always there, isn't it?"

Those words will resonate in my heart forever.

To anyone else navigating this arduous path, I say this: Listen closely. Even when memories fade, love remains. In a touch, in a smile, in a moment of clarity. Those moments are worth every struggle, every heartache.

So here we are. Her story is over, but the echoes linger. We're left with memories both bitter and sweet. A legacy of love that no disease could ever truly silence.

Thank you for allowing me to contribute our Mother's story.

Emily

Key Advice:

Always be adaptable. Even the most prepared people have to adjust their plans. Expect and anticipate change. There are very few elements to caregiving that are predictable.

Words of Encouragement:

Keep going, keep loving, keep showing up. In this grand journey of life, your perseverance in caring for the person who needs you most is the most beautiful expression of all.

Chapter 17
The Power Of Presence

Synopsis:

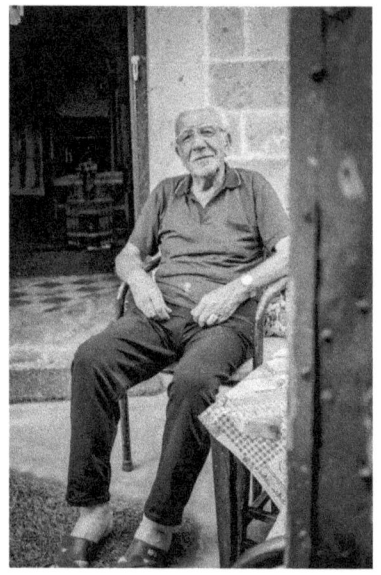

- **Caregiver:** Maggie, 48
- **Loved one:** Jim, 76
- **Relationship:** Father / Daughter
- **Dementia type:** Alzheimer's
- **Duration of care:** 5 years
- **Living situation:** Father in skilled nursing facility
- **Support system:** Maggie, her mother Helen, and her brother Nathan

Story:

You asked for a caregiving story, and I've been pondering how to share ours. It's a tale of love, loss, and the unexpected ways we find to communicate when words begin to fail.

Five years ago, my dad (Jim) was diagnosed with Alzheimer's. It's been a journey of continuous adjustments, heartaches, and surprising moments of joy. Let me share a few snapshots from our experience.

I remember when my brother Nathan flew in from D.C., excited to see Dad. But when he arrived, Dad thought Nathan was a nurse, there to help him shave. The disappointment on Nathan's face was crushing. The social worker gently explained that it's common for people with dementia to forget faces they haven't seen in a while, even family members.

Mom and I fell into a routine of visiting Dad together. She taught me the importance of keeping my voice cheerful, even when seeing Dad's decline broke my heart. Mom was a pillar of strength, never letting her sadness show in front of him.

In the early days, Dad would stand to greet Mom with a hug and a smile. I'd often tag along, and Mom would reintroduce me. As time went on, Dad began to enjoy activities similar to what I use in my kindergarten class - wooden puzzles, Play-Doh, finger paints. It was a bittersweet shift, but we learned to find joy in these simple activities.

Mom brought family photo albums to their visits. She never asked Dad if he remembered the people or events in the pictures. Instead, she'd simply share the stories behind them, bringing the memories to him, should he be able to recall them. Once, a photo of our old dog Rusty brought tears to Dad's eyes. It was a powerful reminder that even as memories faded, emotions remained strong.

For a long time, the highlight of Dad's day was greeting Mom with a delighted "Helen!" But then came the day when even that slipped away. The next morning, Mom called me in tears, saying she wasn't going to visit. "Why bother? He doesn't even know my name anymore." That was a low point, for sure.

I suggested we visit together that Saturday. When we arrived, I dropped Mom at the door and went to park the car. As I walked into the community room behind her, I witnessed something remarkable. Dad looked up, saw Mom, and started clapping. He couldn't say her name, but his joy at seeing her was unmistakable.

That moment taught us all an important lesson. Love doesn't always need words. Sometimes, it's expressed in a smile, a tear, or even a spontaneous round of applause.

Mom continued her daily visits until Dad passed away. Each visit mattered, each moment counted, even when words failed.

This journey has been challenging, but it's also shown us the enduring power of love and the importance of simply being present. Just being there.

Thank you for letting me share our story.

Warmly,

Maggie

Key Advice:

Never underestimate the power of your presence. Even when your loved one can't express it, your visits matter. Keep showing up, keep connecting, in whatever way you can.

Words of Encouragement:

To all caregivers navigating the confusing world of dementia: Your love and dedication speak volumes, even when words fail. The time you spend, the care you give, the patience you show - it all matters. You're doing important work, not just in caring for your loved one's physical needs, but in honoring their dignity and preserving their connection to the world. It's okay to feel frustrated or sad, but never doubt the value of your presence.

Chapter 18
Dementia-Powered Houdini

Synopsis:

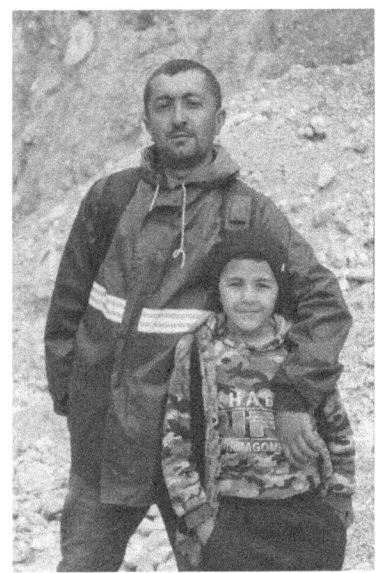

- **Caregiver:** Derek, 57
- **Loved one:** Frank, 79
- **Relationship:** Son / Father
- **Dementia type:** Mixed Dementia
- **Duration of care:** 4 years
- **Living situation:** Frank lives with Derek
- **Support system:** Derek, his sister Lisa (who lives out of state)

Story:

Dear Caregiver,

I'm convinced that I live in a sitcom. Not one of those warm, fuzzy family ones, mind you — more like a slapstick comedy where everything that can go wrong, does. That's my life.

I'm Derek, 57, reluctant star of "*My Dad, the Escape Artist.*" My co-star? Frank, my 79-year-old father, proud owner of a mixed dementia diagnosis and an uncanny ability to disappear faster than my patience.

Dad's always been a wanderer. Even before the dementia, he'd go on long walks, exploring every nook and cranny of our town. He knew every shortcut, every hidden park, every quirky little shop. It was charming then. Now? Now it's a recipe for disaster.

It started innocently enough He'd go out for the newspaper and come back a full hour later. Then he started forgetting how to get home from his favorite diner. The final straw was when he ended up halfway between our town and the next, convinced he was on his way to visit his long-deceased mother.

Last month, he managed to get three blocks away before a kindly neighbor recognized him and brought him home. Mrs. Peterson, bless her heart, found him trying to help prune her rosebushes.

My sister Lisa tries to help, but she lives three states away, so the assistance she can render is limited. Her solution to everything is to put Dad in a home. Easy for her to say when she's not the one looking into his confused eyes every day, seeing flashes of the vibrant man he used to be.

So, being the tech-savvy, problem-solving kind of guy I am, I came up with a brilliant solution: a tracking device. One of those nifty little gadgets you can slip into a pocket or attach to a keychain. I spent hours researching, reading reviews, and comparing features. I felt like I was cracking the Da Vinci Code of dementia care.

Problem solved, right?

For a while, it worked like a charm. I even started to relax a little. I could take a shower without worrying Dad would be halfway to Canada by the time I got out. I could sleep through the night without jolting awake every hour to check if he was still in bed. It was bliss.

Then came *The Great Uber Incident.*

We had a doctor's appointment across town. Usually, I drive, but my car was in the shop. Transmission trouble, because why not add car problems to the mix? So, I called an Uber.

The ride was uneventful. Dad even charmed the driver with stories about his days as a radio DJ (all mostly true, surprisingly). He had the driver in stitches with tales of celebrity interviews gone wrong and on-air bloopers. For a moment, I saw a glimpse of the charismatic man he used to be, the one who could light up a room with his stories.

It wasn't until we got home that evening that I realized something was wrong. The house was too quiet. No TV blaring old westerns. No off-key humming from the kitchen. No Dad shuffling around in his slippers, asking me for the hundredth time what we were having for breakfast.

Panic set in. I checked every room, calling Dad's name with increasing desperation.

With shaking hands, I pulled out my phone and fired up the tracking app — and there it was — the little blue dot that represented my father's location. The only trouble was that he was clear on the other side of town, *and moving at 40 miles per hour!*

My heart nearly stopped. Had he somehow gotten into a car? Was he being kidnapped? Should I call the police? Alert the National Guard? Post on Facebook?

I had just dialed 911 and was waiting on an answer, when I hear it.... a faint humming coming from... the bathroom?

I burst in, nearly taking the door off its hinges. And there was Dad, calm as you please, sitting on the toilet and working on a crossword puzzle.

"Hey, son," he said, looking up with a smile.

I stared at him, my mouth opening and closing, but no words were coming out.

"Dad," I finally managed to croak, "where's your tracker?"

He looked at me blankly. "My what?"

As it turns out, the tracker was enjoying a tour of the city courtesy of our Uber driver. Dad had left it in the car when we got out. It was probably having the time of its little electronic life, seeing parts of the city it had never seen before.

So there I was, simultaneously relieved that Dad was safe and mad enough to spit nails. I didn't know whether to hug him or lecture him. In the end, I did both.

We've since upgraded to a more secure tracking solution. Now, we're using a slick little device that lives in the sole of his shoe. He doesn't even know it's there, so it's less likely to be left behind, assuming his shoes stay on.

I've learned my lesson. No technology is Dad-proof. He's like a dementia-powered Houdini, always one step ahead of my best-laid plans.

So here's to all of us out there, trying to outsmart a disease that rewrites the rules every day. May our tracking devices stay put, our senses of humor remain intact, and our love for our wandering loved ones never waver.

Derek

Key Advice:

Always have a backup plan. Technology can (and probably will) fail, but a support network of neighbors, local businesses, and community members can be invaluable in keeping your loved one safe. And never underestimate the power of a good laugh — sometimes, it's the only thing that will get you through the day.

Words of Encouragement:

To all the caregivers out there playing eternal games of hide-and-seek: You are amazing. Your creativity, your resilience, your ability to laugh in the face of chaos — these are superpowers. On the days when you feel outsmarted, outmaneuvered, and just plain out of ideas, remember this: you're doing incredibly important work.

Your love and care are the constants in a world that's become confusing and scary for your loved one. Keep problem-solving, keep loving, and don't forget to find the humor in the absurd moments. You've got this, even when it feels like your tracking device is on the other side of town.

Chapter 19
A Moment Of Your Time

Dear Reader,

If you've found value in these pages thus far, I ask for your help in reaching other caregivers who may be struggling.

Every day, individuals are thrust into caregiving roles, feeling overwhelmed and unsure where to turn.

Your review could be the beacon that guides them to this book and the community of understanding within these stories.

If these shared experiences have touched you, if you've gained insights for your own journey, or if you simply believe these stories should reach others, please consider leaving a review.

A simple, honest reflection on what this book has meant to you could make all the difference to someone at the beginning of their caregiving path.

Thank you for considering this request. Your contribution has the power to make a significant difference in the lives of others.

With gratitude,

Ben Clardy

Chapter 20

Love In Rocky Soil

Synopsis:

- **Caregiver:** Olivia, 55
- **Loved one:** Beatrice, 96
- **Relationship:** Daughter-In-Law / Mother-In-Law
- **Dementia type:** Unspecified
- **Duration of care:** 3 months during Covid-19
- **Living situation:** Mother-in-law temporarily moved in with Olivia and her husband
- **Support system:** Olivia, her husband Ethan, home health services

Story:

Dear Caregiver,

While a global pandemic raged outside, inside our modest suburban home, a 96-year-old force of nature named Beatrice, my mother-in-law, was suddenly thrust into our care. Oh, and did I mention she was recovering from eye surgery and couldn't see a blessed thing? Welcome to my spring of 2020.

Beatrice's assisted living facility wouldn't take her back after her surgery. Something about COVID risks. So there we were, Ethan and I, transforming our living room into a makeshift bedroom faster than you can say "What the heck are we doing?"

Now, Beatrice isn't your average nonagenarian. This is a woman who treats aging like an extreme sport, complete with yearly catch-phrases. At 94, she was "Waltzing past walker territory!" When she landed on our doorstep at 96, her rallying cry was "Nine decades down, three more to go!" Each birthday, she'd come up with a new one, more outrageous than the last.

But let me tell you, the situation was far less "Golden Girls" and more "Survivor." Nights blurred into days. I catnapped on a pile of camping foam pads, jolting awake to Beatrice's confused calls. "Who's there?" Her voice often sounded so small and scared. I'd stumble over, repeating, "It's Olivia, Beatrice. You're safe. You're with us." And every time, she'd hug me like I was a life raft in a storm.

Sleep deprivation is a sneaky beast. I found myself putting the milk in the pantry and losing cups of tea in my own kitchen. Ethan wasn't faring much better. One time he mashed an extra zero on the microwave when heating a frozen dinner. We caught it before the microwave burst into flames, but that didn't stop every smoke detector in the house from going off. We were a hot mess.

But here's the thing about caregiving – it forces you to get creative. We started tag-teaming. Ethan would take Beatrice for her daily "adventure walks" (read: slow shuffles around the block) while I'd tidy up Hurricane Beatrice's wake. I'd engage her in epic domino battles while Ethan taught his sixth-graders online. It wasn't pretty, but we made it work.

And then there was the garden. That garden became our saving grace. Beatrice mourned her lost plot at the facility, so we went container crazy. Our patio transformed into a jungle of herbs and veggies. I'd bring her sprigs of rosemary or mint leaves, and watching her close her eyes and inhale deeply, lost in memories of gardens past – those moments made it all worthwhile.

After three months of this beautiful chaos, a spot opened up at a memory care facility. As we packed up Beatrice's things, I felt a mix of relief and sadness.

You know what stuck with me most? The day before she left, Beatrice asked how old she was. When we told her 96, she grinned and said, "Hah! Still young!" In that moment, I saw flashes of the firecracker she'd always been, still shining through.

Caregiving is messy, exhausting, and at times soul-crushingly hard. But it's also filled with unexpected moments of grace, laughter, and profound connection. It's a crash course in patience, creativity, and finding joy in the smallest victories.

So here's to Beatrice, still a sassy ball of fire at 96.

Key Advice:

Embrace the absurd. When life hands you a 96-year-old roommate and a pandemic, plant a garden.

Words of Encouragement:

Your efforts matter, even when progress is invisible.

Chapter 21
Stomping Tractors

Synopsis:

- **Caregiver:** Sarah, 42
- **Loved one:** Paul, 72, Sarah's Father
- **Relationship:** Daughter / Father
- **Dementia type:** Mixed. Alzheimer's & Lewy Body
- **Duration of care:** 2 years
- **Living situation:** Paul lives at home with Ellen, Sarah nearby
- **Support system:** Sarah and Ellen (her Mother)

Ben Clardy

Story:

Dear Caregiver,

I have a tale of love, loss, and little tractors.

Dad — Paul to most — was always a man of the land. He'd be up at dawn, checking the fields, fiddling with farm equipment. "The work's never done," he'd say, before Mom would coax him in for dinner.

It began subtly. He'd misplace his tools, call the neighbors by the wrong names. We brushed it off at first. Then came the day I found him in the living room, stomping around like he was crushing grapes.

"Dad?" I said. "What are you doing?"

He looked at me, eyes wide. "The little tractors! They're all over the floor!"

I didn't know how to respond. At first, I thought it was a joke. I actually recall laughing initially at the ridiculous scene. That notion passed quickly, followed by disbelief, followed by shock.

A week later, we had a diagnosis. Mixed dementia. Alzheimer's disease and Lewy Body.

Now our days are... unpredictable. Many mornings, Dad insists he needs to milk the cows, we haven't had cows in 15 years. Mom distracts him with pancakes — his favorite.

It's the little tractors that appear most often. They show up at the oddest times. During meals, in the middle of his favorite TV show. It's strange how they appear when he seems most distracted. It's not like he's thinking of tractors when he sees them.

Initially, we tried explaining they weren't real. Big mistake. He'd get more agitated, insisting we were the ones not seeing clearly. So we adapted our approach.

Now, when the "little tractors" appear, we grab brooms. It's a bit less violent than stomping, although Dad remains a fan of the stomping technique. "Time to sweep them away, Dad. We spend the next few minutes sweeping up imaginary tractors into equally imaginary dustpans. God, the more I tell of this story the more ridiculous it seems, but bear with me.

One day, after a particularly vigorous "tractor-stomping" session, Dad sat down heavily in his armchair. He looked at me, a clarity in his eyes I hadn't seen in months.

"Sarah," he said softly, "I know they're not real."

I felt my heart skip a beat. "You do?"

He nodded, a sad smile on his face. "Most of the time, anyway. But... it's nice, you know? Having you and your mom play along. It helps me feel..." He trailed off, searching for the word.

"Less alone?" I offered.

"Yes," he said. "Less alone." He reached out and squeezed my hand. "Thanks for stomping tractors with me."

I had to excuse myself after that. Spent a good ten minutes crying outside. It was a moment of connection I'll cherish forever.

Mom's been incredibly patient through all this. Sometimes, I catch her gazing out of the window, lost in thought. I know she's remembering the man Dad used to be. But then he'll approach her, put his arm around her, and say, "Ellen, have I told you today that you're more beautiful than ever?" And then he's himself again.

It's not all challenging. There are moments of joy. We've learned to treasure these moments, to capture them in our hearts like fireflies in a jar.

Our community has been supportive. They drop by with meals, help with chores Dad can't manage anymore. Our neighbor even brought his grandson's old toy tractor over. "For Paul," he said with a knowing smile. It's touching to see how people rally around in times of need.

We've had to make adjustments to our home. Locks on cabinets. Labels on doors and drawers to help him navigate. A GPS tracker disguised as a watch, for those days when his wandering feet take him further than they should.

Some days are tougher than others. Days when Dad doesn't recognize me, when he's convinced Mom's trying to harm him. But we persevere. Because that's what you do for family. We weather the hard times, cherish the good moments, and hope for better days.

It's a strange kind of grief, mourning someone who's still here. We've lost the man Dad used to be, or at least a big part of him, but we're learning to love the man he is now.

That's all we can do, right?

Sarah

Key Advice:

Sometimes, the kindest approach is to enter their reality. The truth can wait.

Words of Encouragement:

It's not always easy, but it is always worth it.

Chapter 22
Enduring Love & Leaks

Synopsis:

- **Caregiver:** Harold, 81
- **Loved one:** Mildred, 83
- **Relationship:** Husband / Wife
- **Dementia type:** Vascular
- **Duration of care:** 4 years
- **Living situation:** Couple lives in their home
- **Support system:** Harold, their daughter Linda, home health aide twice a week

Story:

Dear Caregiver,

I feel compelled to share our story, but I find myself searching for how to share this particular chapter of our lives. It's not the sort of thing one discusses in polite company, you see. But then again, dementia cares little for social niceties. Our daughter has encouraged us to share our story, despite its somewhat embarrassing nature, so I suppose I'll get on with it.

Mildred and I have been married for 58 years. We've weathered storms and basked in sunshine. We've raised a family, and grown old together.

It started with little accidents. A damp nightgown here, a wet chair there. Mildred was mortified, of course. "Must've spilled my tea," she'd say. I'd smile and fetch a towel, of course, pretending not to notice the distinct lack of tea in the vicinity.

As her dementia progressed, so did the, shall we say, personal care issues. Our laundry pile grew, and I found myself becoming quite the expert in stain removal. Who knew denture tablets could be so versatile? Old dogs, new tricks, I suppose.

The challenges, they do keep coming. But we face them together, with as much grace and humor as we can muster. Our daughter Linda has been a godsend through all this. She brings supplies, helps with housework, and gives me a much-needed respite now and then. "Dad," she said to me one day, "you're allowed to find this difficult. You're allowed to be frustrated." I just patted her hand. "My dear," I replied, "when you've been married as long as your mother and I have, you learn to roll with the punches." We always have — and we'll continue to do so.

We have our system now. Protective bedding, extra linens always at the ready, and a healthy sense of humor. I've learned to see the absurdity in our situation. After all, what's a little mishap between lovers?

There are moments, in the quiet of the night, when I allow myself to grieve for the woman Mildred used to be. The sharp wit, the impeccable manners, the fierce independence. But then she'll reach for my hand in her sleep, and I'm reminded that she's still here. Different, yes, but still my Mildred.

I won't pretend it's easy. There are days when I feel overwhelmed, when the constant care threatens to exhaust me. But then Mildred will look at me, really look at me, and say, "Harold, dear, whatever would I do without you?" And I know, in my heart, that I'll keep doing this for as long as I'm able.

So here we are, my dear Mildred and I, navigating this new phase of our lives. We may face challenges, but we're still together. And as long as we have each other, that's all that matters.

To all the other devoted partners out there, facing similar struggles: Take heart. You're not alone in this journey. And remember, a little patience and a lot of love can overcome the most daunting of obstacles.

Thank you for listening. I hope this letter finds you well, and in good spirits.

Yours in solidarity,

Harold

Key Advice:

When dignity and necessity clash, choose kindness over correctness. And always keep an extra set of linens handy.

Words of Encouragement:

To my fellow travelers on this challenging journey: You are doing a remarkable thing, even when it feels thankless. Your patience, your love, your ability to find grace in difficult moments - these are true acts of heroism. Remember to be kind to yourself. And if you find yourself smiling at the absurdity of it all, well, that's okay too. A sense of humor, like love, can carry us through the toughest of times.

Chapter 23
Elephants Eating The Roses

Synopsis:

- **Caregiver:** Evelyn, 69
- **Loved one:** George, 68
- **Relationship:** Wife / Husband
- **Dementia type:** Lewy Body
- **Duration of care:** 3 years
- **Living situation:** Couple lives in their home
- **Support system:** Evelyn, their son Michael, weekly support group

Story:

Dear Caregiver,

I find myself drawn to write about our evenings. They say the night brings rest, but for us, it often brings anything but.

George and I have been married for 40 years. He was always the night owl to my early bird, but these days, as the sun begins to set, I find myself wishing for morning.

Things started very gradually. Subtly. Almost imperceptibly, but it gradually worsened to the point of being problematic. The most noteworthy occurrence is what is referred to as "sundowning".

George would become restless as evening approached, pacing the living room, checking the locks over and over. Some nights, he sees shadowy figures lurking in the corners. Other nights, he's convinced we're on a sinking ship, frantically trying to bail water.

I've learned to prepare for our almost nightly adventures. I keep a "sundown kit" ready - his favorite sweater, a photo album, some calming lavender oil. I've become quite the actress, playing along with his realities while gently steering us back to reality. It's a process for sure, and skill that I never thought I'd have a need for.

One particularly memorable evening, George was adamant that a circus had set up in our backyard. "The elephants are eating all your roses!" he exclaimed. So, out we went in our slippers, to shoo away imaginary elephants. Thankfully, that particular hallucination has not repeated itself, but I'll never forget it.

Our son Michael has been a tremendous help. He installed blackout curtains and a light therapy lamp, hoping to trick George's confused circadian rhythm. It helps, some days more than others. Michael also set up cameras, so I can keep an eye on George from any room in the house. Modern technology — a blessing and a curse, as it highlights just how drastically our lives have changed in only a few short years.

The support group I attend has been a lifeline. There's comfort in knowing we're not alone in our struggles. We trade tips like battle-worn soldiers. Which foods to avoid in the evening, the merits of various calming techniques. One lady swears by puppet shows to distract her husband from his hallucinations. I haven't entirely worked up the courage to try that one yet. Hopefully, we can avoid that level of theatrics.

The nights are long, and sometimes I find myself longing for the peaceful evenings we used to share. But then George will say something unexpectedly funny or sweet, and I'm reminded that even in this odd twilight of our lives, there's still light to be found.

So we navigate our nights, George and I, sometimes adrift in his hallucinations, sometimes anchored in brief moments of clarity. It's not the retirement we planned, but here we are.

Thank you for listening. I hope this letter finds you well, and that your own evenings are more peaceful.

One night at a time,

Evelyn

Key Advice:

Routine is your friend. Establish a calming evening ritual and stick to it as much as possible. And remember, sometimes it's kinder to step into their reality than to force them into ours.

Words of Encouragement:

To my fellow travelers through the long nights: Your steadfast love is a beacon in the darkness. On the nights when confusion reigns and sleep seems a distant memory, remember that your presence brings comfort, even if it's not always apparent. Take care of yourself, find moments of rest where you can, and know that dawn always comes, even after the longest night.

Chapter 24
Viv, the Tornado

Synopsis:

- **Caregiver:** Claire, 50
- **Loved one:** Vivian (Viv), 75
- **Relationship:** Daughter / Mother
- **Dementia type:** Frontotemporal (FTD)
- **Duration of care:** 2 years
- **Living situation:** Vivian lives with Claire
- **Support system:** Claire, her husband Tom, therapist, online support group

Story:

Dear Caregiver,

My mother, Vivian, was never what you'd call warm and fuzzy. She was more... let's say, a force of nature. Brilliant, accomplished, and utterly convinced of her own superiority. Growing up, her approval was as rare and precious as desert rain. And about as nurturing.

Several years ago, Momma was diagnosed with frontotemporal dementia. The doctors explained how it could affect her emotions — in particular that of *empathy*. I remember nodding along, thinking to myself, "Well, she never had that to begin with."

Oh, how naive I was.

Imagine a tornado. Now imagine that tornado gains sentience and decides it doesn't like you very much. That's my mother now. The filter she once had, however thin, is gone. The casual cruelty has become constant. Every perceived slight is met with a barrage of insults that would make a sailor blush.

"Claire," she'll say, eyeing my outfit, "I see you've given up." Or when I bring her meals: "I guess this is why Tom is losing weight." Tom is my saint of a husband, who endures her barbs with a patience I can only envy. The man is an absolute saint.

Sometimes, I see the old Momma Viv. The woman who, for all her faults, could command a room with her wit and charm. But those moments are fleeting, quickly swallowed by the rage and confusion that seem to be her near-constant companions now.

I've had to develop a thick skin and a dark sense of humor. It's painful to admit that, but it's the armor I have. When Momma launched into a tirade about my "incompetence" in front of the home health aide, I simply smiled and said, "Yes, mother, I learned from the best." The aide looked horrified. Momma looked... I don't know... proud, maybe? It's hard to tell these days.

My therapist tells me it's okay to grieve for the mother I never really had, even as I care for the mother I have now. Most days, that's easier said than done. Especially when she decides 3 AM is the perfect time to rearrange the living room while loudly critiquing every decision I've ever made.

The online support group has been a lifeline. There's grim comfort in knowing I'm not alone in dealing with a problematic parent made more difficult by dementia. We trade war stories and coping strategies, celebrating small victories and commiserating over the bad days.

I won't lie - there are days when I want to walk out the door and never come back. Days when the weight of her words and actions feels too heavy to bear. I hope this isn't too much, but there are days that I feel like I might be the one to end her. She pushes me to have those dark thoughts. That's how bad it can be — but then I remember the times she showed me kindness. The day she taught me to ride a bike. The proud smile when I graduated college. When Tam and I got married. I hold onto those bright memories like a lifeline.

Caring for Momma is teaching me things about myself I never knew. I'm stronger than I thought. More patient. And capable of a love that doesn't depend on being loved in return. It's a hard lesson, learned through many tears and many sleepless nights, but a valuable one nonetheless.

So here I am, tending my thorny rose of a mother. My hands are scratched and bleeding, but I keep at it. Because underneath all the barbs and bitter words, she's still my mom. And even the prickliest roses need care.

Wish me luck,

Claire

Key Advice:

Set boundaries where you can, and don't take the cruel words personally (even when they're intensely personal). Remember, it's the disease talking, even if it's using a voice you've known all your life.

Words of Encouragement:

To my fellow caretakers of thorny souls: Your strength is remarkable. On the days when the barbs seem sharper and the insults cut deeper, remember that your care makes a difference, even if you can't see it. Take care of yourself - tend to your own garden too. And know that even in the harshest soil, compassion can grow. Keep nurturing, keep loving, and don't forget to wear your emotional gloves. Your hands - and your heart - will thank you.

Chapter 25
The Final 15 Days

Synopsis:

- **Caregiver:** Sarah and Michael, both 58
- **Loved one:** Eleanor, 84
- **Relationship:** Sarah's Mother-In-Law
- **Dementia type:** Alzheimer's
- **Duration of care:** 6 Years
- **Living situation:** Eleanor lived with Michael and Sarah
- **Support system:** Michael, Sarah, their children, local church community

Story:

Dear Caregiver,

I don't mean for this to be depressing, only real.

There's not much you can do to prepare for the silence afterwards.

The house is quiet now. Just far too quiet.

For six years, our lives revolved around Eleanor. The woman who taught Michael to tie his shoes, who welcomed me into the family with open arms. The woman we slowly lost, piece by piece, to Alzheimer's.

A week ago, she left us. Fifteen days without food or water. Fifteen. It was a peaceful transition, they said. I'm thankful for that, but peace feels foreign now.

The initial signs started small, as these things often do. Forgotten keys seem to be a common one. Missed appointments. The occasional repeated story. Forgetting names. You know how it goes. We laughed it off at first. "Mom's getting forgetful in her old age," Michael would say.

But then came the day she got lost driving to the supermarket she'd visited weekly for 30 years. The day she forgot to turn off the stove, nearly setting the kitchen on fire. The day she looked at her grandchildren and asked, "Just who are these lovely kids?"

The diagnosis hit us like a thunderbolt. Alzheimer's. We expected it, but it still shocked us.

We made so many changes. Child-proofing the house, but for an adult. Labeling drawers and cabinets. Setting up routines and reminders. Our lives bent and shifted to accommodate this new reality.

I quit my job. Michael started working from home. Our world narrowed to the confines of our house, expanding only for doctor's appointments and support group meetings.

The early days were hard, but there were moments of lightness too. Mom would have periods of clear-headedness where she was almost her old self. We'd sit on the porch, drinking lemonade, and she'd regale us with stories from her youth. In those moments, we could almost forget what was coming.

But it came, relentless as the tide. The good days became fewer. The bad days, more frequent. We watched as she struggled to remember how to use a fork. How to button her shirt. How to recognize her own reflection.

Ben Clardy

Remember when she got lost in the grocery store? We panicked, searching every aisle. Found her in the flower section, rearranging bouquets, happy as can be. We laughed then, relief making us giddy. The memory brings tears now.

Or the time she insisted on baking cookies at 3 AM? The kitchen was a disaster, flour everywhere, eggs cracked on the floor. But her smile... God, her smile as she offered us misshapen, half-raw cookies. We'd give anything to see it again.

The struggle was real. The sleepless nights, the endless doctor's appointments, the moments of frustration when she couldn't remember our names. The heartbreak and frustration of having to remind her, again and again, that her own parents had passed decades ago. Watching her relive that grief each time was like twisting a knife in our hearts.

But there was love too. So much love. In the gentle way Michael would brush her hair. In the songs I'd sing to soothe her when sundowning hit and confusion reigned. In the way our children would hold her hand and tell her stories, even when she couldn't follow the plot.

We learned to find joy in small victories. The days she remembered to use the bathroom. The meals she managed to eat without help. The rare moments when she'd look at us with recognition and say our names.

We became experts in things we never wanted to know. The stages of Alzheimer's. The best incontinence products. How to prevent bedsores. How to communicate when words fail.

Our friends drifted away, unable to handle the reality of our new life. But we found a new community in support groups and online forums. People who understood our struggles, our fears, our small triumphs.

The last few months were the hardest. Watching her fade away, her body forgetting even the most basic functions. The woman who once ran marathons, now bedridden. The voice that sang lullabies, now silent.

Those final fifteen days were an eternity and a blink of an eye. She just stopped eating and drinking. We sat vigil, holding her hand, telling her it was okay to let go. Remembering. Grieving. Loving.

And then... silence.

We recently returned to work. Routine. Normalcy. But what is normal anymore? The empty chair at the breakfast table mocks us. The silence in the living room, where her favorite TV shows once played, is deafening.

Dear Caregiver

We move through the day like ghosts. Muscle memory carries us through meetings, phone calls, lunch breaks. But our minds are elsewhere. With her.

Now, we're adrift. Our purpose, gone. The routine that anchored our days, vanished. We look at each other across the dinner table, lost. What now?

Friends offer condolences. "At least she's at peace," they say. But what about us? Where's our peace?

Yet, in the depths of our grief, a realization surfaces. *We would do it all again.* Every exhausting, heartbreaking, beautiful moment. For her. Always for her.

The sacrifices, the sleepless nights, the tears — they pale in comparison to the love we shared. The lessons we learned about patience, about resilience, about the depth of human connection.

We learned to live in the moment, because with Alzheimer's, moments are all you have. We learned to find humor in the absurd, joy in the smallest victories. We learned that love transcends memory, that connection goes deeper than words.

Yes, we lost so much. Our careers, our social life, our plans for the future. But we gained too. A deeper understanding of what truly matters. A stronger bond with each other, forged in the fires of adversity. A profound appreciation for the fragility and preciousness of life and memory.

The house may be quiet, but our hearts are full. Full of memories, of love, of gratitude for the time we had. For the woman she was, and the woman she remained, even as the disease took its toll.

We'll find our way. Slowly. Together. Just as we did through the journey of caregiving. We'll learn to live in this new silence, to find purpose beyond caregiving.

For now, we grieve. We remember. We love.

And in the silence, we listen for echoes of her laughter. We look for signs of her in the blooming flowers she loved, in the recipes she taught us, in the values she instilled.

Mom may be gone, but her legacy lives on. In us. In our children. In the countless lives she touched.

So we'll keep going. We'll honor her memory by living fully, by loving deeply, by finding joy even in the darkest times. Just as she taught us.

And maybe, in time, we'll find that the silence isn't empty at all — but full of love, of memories, of a life well-lived and well-loved.

Sarah

Key Advice:

Grief is not linear. Allow yourself to feel it all — the sadness, the anger, the relief, the love. There's no right way to mourn. Your journey was unique, and so is your healing. Remember, it's okay to laugh, to find moments of joy even in grief. It doesn't diminish your love or your loss.

Words of Encouragement:

To those still on the caregiving path, and to those who've reached its end: Your love makes a difference. In the hardest moments, remember the good ones. They're there, shining like stars in the darkness. The sleepless nights, the endless worries, the moments of frustration - they're all part of a love story. A difficult, beautiful, heart-wrenching love story.

And to those feeling lost in the aftermath, know this: The love you gave, the care you provided, it mattered. It still matters. You carried your loved one home. Now, carry their memory with you as you find your way forward. The journey doesn't end here. It just changes. And you have the strength to walk this new path, one step at a time.

You are stronger than you know, more resilient than you can imagine. You've climbed mountains, weathered storms. This new challenge? You can face it too. One day at a time. One memory at a time. One act of love at a time.

Remember, it's okay to not be okay. It's okay to need help. Reach out. To friends, to support groups, to therapists. You carried this burden for so long. You don't have to carry it alone anymore.

Your story, your love, your journey - they have power. They can light the way for others. So when you're ready, share. Your experience might be the lifeline someone else needs.

For now, be gentle with yourself. Rest. Remember. Love. And know that somewhere, somehow, the love you shared lives on. Always.

Chapter 26
The Abused Caregiver

Synopsis:

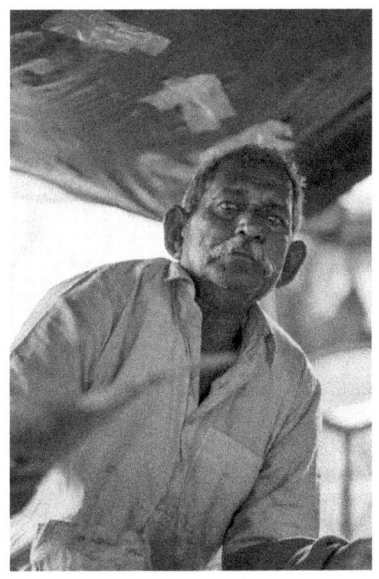

- **Caregiver:** Rosa, 55
- **Loved one:** Carlos, 92
- **Relationship:** Daughter / Father
- **Dementia type:** Alzheimer's
- **Duration of care:** 7 years
- **Living situation:** Carlos lives with Rosa
- **Support system:** Minimal, ten siblings who don't help

Story:

Dear Caregiver,

I've been staring at this blank page on and off for days. Trying to find the words. How do you put so much pain, resentment, and exhaustion into a letter? But here goes.

I'm Rosa, 55. The youngest of eleven children. For seven years, with rare exception, I've been the sole caregiver for my father, Carlos. He's 92, with atypical Alzheimer's and retinitis pigmentosa. Oh, and he's also a narcissist who abused me physically and emotionally throughout my childhood.

Ironic, isn't it? The one he hurt most is now responsible for him.

It's been anything and everything except easy. "Spread to thin" is a generalized way to describe my current state, but even that doesn't really do it justice. I've been at this for more than 7 years now, to various degrees. It's been getting harder and harder as his condition progresses.

I did have a nice long break. My brother took Dad to Mexico for a few months. Those months were... I can't even describe it. I breathed easier. I slept without nightmares. I remembered what it was like to live for myself. People get used to what "normal" feels like. They take it for granted. Feeling normal feels so out of reach and I want it back so badly.

He's back now. My respite is over, and it's like a storm cloud has settled over my life once again.

He's lost weight. His skin is dirty, his breath is foul. He refuses to bathe, claiming back pain. He won't even wash his hands after using the bathroom. The man who once prided himself on his appearance now looks like a shadow of himself.

And yet, his mind is still sharp enough to manipulate. He's lucid for everything except the bad things he's done. He treats me like trash while playing the saint for everyone else. It's maddening.

My siblings? They're ghosts. With the rare exception of my older brother, they're always too busy, never having time to help. But they're quick to criticize, quick to say he can't go to a nursing home. Easy for them to say when they're not the ones dealing with him day in and day out.

I'm falling apart. At 55, I have degenerative disk disease, osteoporosis, arthritis, and neurofibromatosis type one. I had a tumor removed in May. Some days, I think he's healthier than I am.

People tell me, "I don't know how you do it." The truth is, I don't either. I'm running on fumes, fueled by duty and guilt and a lifetime of conditioning to put everyone else's needs before my own. It feels like his disease is slowly killing us both.

I dream of escape. Of moving far away and starting a new life. But then reality crashes in. Where would I go? How would I support myself? And as much as I hate to admit it, there's a part of me that can't bear the thought of abandoning him, despite everything he's done.

The worst part? My mom was recently diagnosed with dementia. She's always been loving and kind — the complete opposite of my father. It feels like a cruel joke from the universe. The parent I love is slipping away, while the one who hurt me soldiers on.

I question God daily. Why me? Haven't I been through enough? When will it end?

I feel like a terrible person for even thinking these thoughts. But I'm so tired. Tired of caring for someone who never cared for me. Tired of sacrificing my health, my happiness, my life for someone who sees me as nothing more than a servant.

I don't know how much longer I can do this. I feel like I'm dying inside, a little more each day. Happiness seems like a foreign concept, something for other people but not for me.

I know I need help. I know this situation isn't sustainable. But I feel trapped, with no way out.

So here I am, pouring my heart out, because sometimes, that's easier than facing the people who should care but don't.

I don't know what tomorrow will bring. But for now, I'll keep going, because that's what I've always done. Keep going, keep surviving.

Thank you for letting me vent. For giving me a space to be honest about the ugliness of this situation. I hope this helps someone.

Rosa

Key Advice:

Burnout is real. I'm there.

Sorry, but I don't feel qualified to give advice.

Words of Encouragement:

[None given]

[NOTE FROM THE AUTHOR]: I've been in correspondence with Rosa since receiving her story. After reading what she wrote, I was very concerned for her well-being. It's impossible to imagine the difficulty of her situation after what she's been through. I'm pleased to share that her situation has improved. Carlos has been relocated to an assisted living facility that specializes in dementia care. Her ten siblings, who had not been offering help directly, have since pooled their resources to cover the cost of their Father's care. Divided 11 ways, the associated costs are quite manageable. Rosa is doing much better now.

Chapter 27
Reverse Burglary

Synopsis:

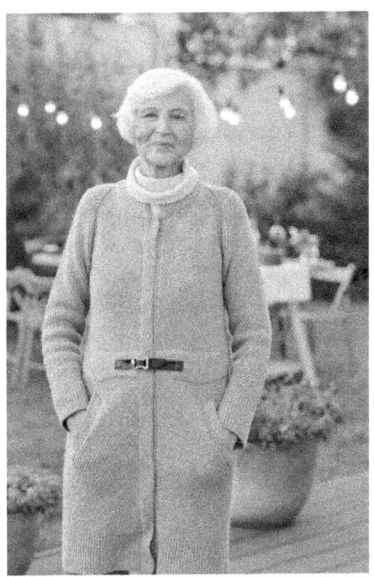

- **Caregiver:** Lori, 48
- **Loved one:** Doris, 76
- **Relationship:** Daughter / Mother
- **Dementia type:** Early Alzheimer's
- **Duration of care:** 2 years
- **Living situation:** Doris lives independently, Lori nearby
- **Support system:** Lori, limited family support

Ben Clardy

Story:

Dear Caregiver,

I'm Lori. My mom, Doris, is 76 and in the mid-stages of Alzheimer's. She's still fiercely independent. Getting her to accept help is like trying to bathe a cat.

The latest episode in our ongoing saga? The Mystery of the Disappearing Check. Mom gets three checks a month — two direct deposits and one by mail. Simple enough, right? Oh, if only.

Last month, the mailed check pulled a Houdini. When I asked Mom about it, she looked at me like I'd suggested the moon was made of cheese.

This month, same story, different excuse. "Oh, I'm not depositing that," she declared, as if turning down an invitation to a boring party. "They need to direct deposit it." Never mind that it's never been direct deposited anytime prior.

I tried to explain, to reason, to plead. Mom just smiled that smile that says, "Isn't it cute how my daughter thinks she knows things?" and assured me she had it all under control.

Under control. Right.

The kicker? Her doctor thinks she's doing great. I'm beginning to suspect this doctor got their medical degree from a cereal box.

So here I am, playing financial Sherlock Holmes. I've considered getting a P.O. box, having her mail redirected, setting up mobile deposits. But without power of attorney, my hands are tied.

And power of attorney? Ha! Mom would sooner tap dance on the moon than grant that. She trusts no one, least of all the daughter who's been managing her affairs for the past two years.

Meanwhile, bills pile up. I'm sneaking money into her account like some reverse burglar. "No, Mom, I'm sure the electric company just made a mistake. Your bill must have been paid already." I'm not proud of the lies, but I'm less proud of the idea of Mom and I sitting in the dark.

I know it's the disease talking. I know Mom isn't being difficult on purpose. But some days, oh boy.

There are moments of lightness, though. Like when Mom insisted she'd "taken care of" the missing check. I had visions of her burying it in the backyard like a squirrel with an acorn. For all I know, that's exactly what happened.

Ben Clardy

Story:

Dear Caregiver,

I'm Lori. My mom, Doris, is 76 and in the mid-stages of Alzheimer's. She's still fiercely independent. Getting her to accept help is like trying to bathe a cat.

The latest episode in our ongoing saga? The Mystery of the Disappearing Check. Mom gets three checks a month — two direct deposits and one by mail. Simple enough, right? Oh, if only.

Last month, the mailed check pulled a Houdini. When I asked Mom about it, she looked at me like I'd suggested the moon was made of cheese.

This month, same story, different excuse. "Oh, I'm not depositing that," she declared, as if turning down an invitation to a boring party. "They need to direct deposit it." Never mind that it's never been direct deposited anytime prior.

I tried to explain, to reason, to plead. Mom just smiled that smile that says, "Isn't it cute how my daughter thinks she knows things?" and assured me she had it all under control.

Under control. Right.

The kicker? Her doctor thinks she's doing great. I'm beginning to suspect this doctor got their medical degree from a cereal box.

So here I am, playing financial Sherlock Holmes. I've considered getting a P.O. box, having her mail redirected, setting up mobile deposits. But without power of attorney, my hands are tied.

And power of attorney? Ha! Mom would sooner tap dance on the moon than grant that. She trusts no one, least of all the daughter who's been managing her affairs for the past two years.

Meanwhile, bills pile up. I'm sneaking money into her account like some reverse burglar. "No, Mom, I'm sure the electric company just made a mistake. Your bill must have been paid already." I'm not proud of the lies, but I'm less proud of the idea of Mom and I sitting in the dark.

I know it's the disease talking. I know Mom isn't being difficult on purpose. But some days, oh boy.

There are moments of lightness, though. Like when Mom insisted she'd "taken care of" the missing check. I had visions of her burying it in the backyard like a squirrel with an acorn. For all I know, that's exactly what happened.

284

Or the time she decided her wallet was "safer" hidden in the freezer. Because nothing says "secure" like nestling your ID between the frozen peas and the ice cream.

In all seriousness, I'm at my wit's end. I'm trying to respect Mom's independence while also making sure she doesn't accidentally donate her life savings to a nonexistent charity. It's a tightrope walk.

If you've got any magical solutions up your sleeve, I'm all ears. Heck, I'd settle for a semi-functional one at this point.

Until then, I'll be here, playing Easter-egg-hunt with paper checks and praying for a miracle.

In questionable sanity,

Lori

Key Advice:

Document everything. Keep a record of missing checks, conversations with your mom, and any financial discrepancies. This could be crucial if you need to demonstrate the need for more oversight in the future. Also, consider consulting with an elder law attorney to explore your options for financial management without full power of attorney.

Words of Encouragement:

To all the unofficial detectives out there, piecing together the puzzles of your loved ones' lives: You're doing important work, even when it feels futile. Your persistence matters. Your care matters. It's okay to feel frustrated, to want to throw in the towel sometimes. But remember, you're not just managing finances - you're protecting your loved one's dignity and independence for as long as possible. That's no small feat.

Chapter 28
The Comfort of Discomfort

Synopsis:

- **Caregiver:** Rachel, 43
- **Loved one:** Her Mother
- **Relationship:** Daughter / Mother
- **Dementia type:** Alzheimer's
- **Duration of care:** 2 years
- **Living situation:** Parents living with Rachel
- **Support system:** Minimal family support

Story:

I don't really want to get into it. It's been a rough couple of years.

Mom's got awful Alzheimer's. Dad's not far behind. I gave up my career, moved back to my hometown, and now I'm their full-time caregiver at 43. My life plans? Out the window. Things are bad and I can't see them doing anything other than getting worse as time goes on.

When Ben asked if I'd like to share my story for this book, my first thought was "fuck, no", but then I realized maybe it could help someone else. So here I am. Rather than tell a sad story, I'll just share what might be helpful.

Key Advice:

Get savvy about finances and legal stuff. I learned this the hard way. The system's a maze, and it's designed to confuse you. Start educating yourself now about elder law, Medicaid, power of attorney, all that shit. Find an elder law attorney if you can afford it. If not, hit the internet hard. Knowledge is power, and you're going to need all of it you can get.

You're going to feel guilty. About everything. Taking time for yourself, getting frustrated, not doing enough, doing too much. It's part of the package. But here's the thing: guilt doesn't help anyone. Not you, not your folks. Recognize it, then tell it to fuck off.

Find something that's just for you. That has nothing to do with Alzheimer's. Maybe it's kickboxing. Maybe it's painting. Maybe it's just sitting in your car and screaming. Whatever it is, make it yours.

Get comfortable being uncomfortable. This shit is gonna push you way out of your comfort zone. You'll be dealing with things you never thought you'd have to. Personal shit, financial decisions, medical emergencies. It's scary and it's hard. But the sooner you accept that discomfort is part of the deal, the easier it gets to handle.

Your old goals and aspirations? They might not fit anymore. I'd be surprised if they do. "Success" might look like getting through the day without a meltdown. Or finding a new food your mom will eat. Or managing to take a shower.

Plan for the worst, hope for the best. It sounds grim, but having a plan for worst-case scenarios can actually be freeing. It lets you stop worrying about "what if" and focus on "what now". Just don't let the planning consume you.

287

Words of Encouragement:

This gig sucks. Let's just be real about that. It's unfair, it's hard, and some days it feels impossible. But you know what? You're doing it anyway. That takes guts.

You're allowed to be angry. You're allowed to grieve for the life you thought you'd have. You're allowed to love your parents and sometimes hate your parents and still resent the situation. It's fucked up, but that's the new normal.

Remember, you're not just a caregiver. You're still you. With dreams and needs and a life of your own. Don't lose sight of that.

You're figuring out stuff you never thought you'd have to deal with. And you're doing it. Maybe not perfectly, but you're doing it.

Ultimately, I think the thing to keep in mind is this: it's temporary. Eventually, this will end. All things do. I know I'm going to miss them like crazy when that day comes.

I don't know if hearing this stuff helps, but it's what I've got.

Chapter 29
Mother Of 4 + 1

Synopsis:

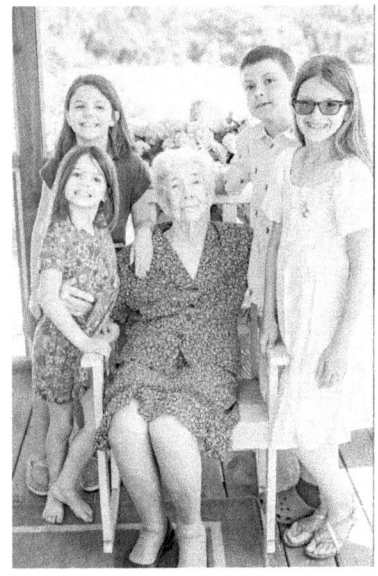

- **Caregiver:** Amanda, 36
- **Loved one:** Evelyn, 76
- **Relationship:** Daughter / Mother
- **Dementia type:** Advanced Alzheimer's (stage 4/5)
- **Duration of care:** 6 years
- **Living situation:** Evelyn lives with Amanda and her family
- **Support system:** Amanda and her husband, Mark

Story:

Dear Caregiver,

Have you ever tried to juggle while riding a unicycle on a tightrope? No? Well, welcome to my world. I'm Amanda, 36 years old, and I'm pretty sure I'm living in a circus.

My mother, Evelyn, is 76 and in the advanced stages of Alzheimer's. She lives with us, needing round-the-clock care. Did I mention I have four kids? Yeah, four. Because apparently, I looked at my life and thought, "You know what this needs? More chaos."

It wasn't always like this. Three years ago, Mom was living independently in the house I grew up in. She was forgetful, sure, but we chalked it up to normal aging. Then came the day she left the stove on and nearly burned down the kitchen. That was our wake-up call.

After the diagnosis, we tried in-home care. But as Mom's condition worsened, it became clear she needed more support. That's when we made the decision to move her in with us. I thought, "We can handle this." Oh, sweet summer child that I was.

My husband, Mark, is amazing, but he works long hours as a construction foreman. He leaves before dawn and often doesn't get home until after the kids are in bed. On weekends, he's Super Dad, taking the kids on adventures so I can focus on Mom. But during the week? It's mostly me, juggling more balls than I can keep track of.

Most days, I feel like I'm failing at everything. I'm not fully present for my kids, I'm not giving Mom the attention she needs, and I'm pretty sure I haven't had a full night's sleep since... well, I can't even remember.

Imagine this: I'm trying to cook dinner for six while my youngest is using the walls as his personal art canvas. Meanwhile, Mom wanders in, confused about where she is, and my 8-year-old is having a meltdown because her favorite shirt is in the laundry. Oh, and the 9-year-old? He's decided now is the perfect time to practice his harmonica. it might sound crazy, but this is a fairly "normal" level of chaos for us.

I worry constantly. Am I neglecting my kids? Will they resent me for not being able to attend every school event? Am I shortchanging Mom on the care she deserves? And let's not even talk about my marriage. Mark and I are like ships passing in the night, exchanging quick kisses and status updates on the kids and Mom.

I've tried setting up schedules, dividing my time, creating systems. But the thing about kids and Alzheimer's? They don't care about your carefully crafted plans. They operate on their own timelines, usually conflicting ones.

We've looked into other options. A nursing home for Mom, maybe. But the guilt of even considering it eats me alive. Plus, have you seen the cost of nursing homes lately? On a single income (because let's face it, I can't work outside the home right now), it's just not feasible.

I feel guilty all the time. Guilty when I'm focusing on the kids and Mom needs me. Guilty when I'm caring for Mom and missing out on precious moments with my children. Guilty when I take five minutes for myself and the house descends into chaos.

Don't get me wrong, I love my mom and my kids fiercely. But some days, the weight of responsibility feels crushing. I find myself daydreaming about running away to a deserted island. Just me, a hammock, and sweet, blessed silence.

I know I'm not alone in this. There must be countless other caregivers out there juggling elderly parents and young kids. But in the trenches of daily life, it sure feels lonely.

So here I am, reaching out into the void. Hoping for... what? Advice? Commiseration? A magic wand to add more hours to the day? I'm not even sure anymore.

All I know is that I'm tired. Bone-deep, soul-weary tired. And tomorrow, I'll wake up and do it all over again. Because that's what we do, right? We keep trying our best even when our best feels woefully inadequate.

If you've got any wisdom to share, I'm all ears. Or even just a virtual hug. Those are good too.

I appreciate the opportunity to share. It helps to know that someone else out there may find some peace, or some form of benefit from my story.

Sincerely,

Amanda

Key Advice:

Prioritize self-care. It's not selfish; it's necessary. Even if it's just 15 minutes a day, find time for yourself. You can't pour from an empty cup. Also, don't be afraid to ask for help. Look into respite care options, even if it's just for a few hours a week. It can make a world of difference.

Words of Encouragement:

To all the superhero caregivers out there, juggling multiple generations: Remember, you don't have to be perfect. Good enough is good enough. Your children will remember the love and the lessons in compassion they're learning, not the missed school plays. Your mother is receiving care from the person who loves her most. You're teaching your children invaluable lessons about family, love, and sacrifice. On the days when you feel like you're failing, remember this: you're not. You're showing up, you're loving hard, and you're doing the best you can. That's more than enough. It's messy, it's hard, it's ugly — it's also somehow beautiful.

Chapter 30
Pain She Wouldn't Trade

Synopsis:

- **Caregiver:** Margaret, 72
- **Loved one:** Paul, 75
- **Relationship:** Wife / Husband
- **Dementia type:** Lewy Body
- **Duration of care:** 8 years
- **Living situation:** Paul lived at home with Margaret
- **Support system:** Margaret and her children

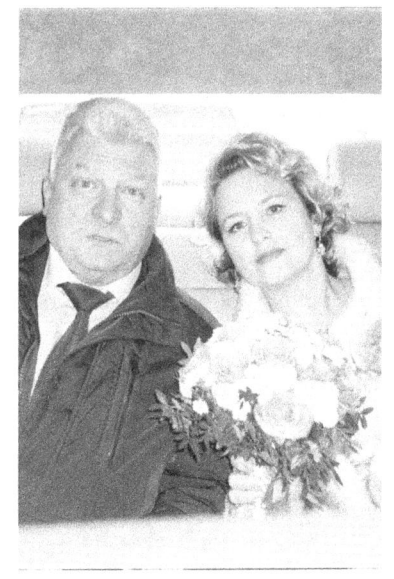

Story:

Dear Caregiver,

My house is quiet now. The medical equipment has been cleared away, the prescriptions returned to the pharmacy. All that remains are memories and the faint scent of Paul's aftershave.

My name is Margaret. For 52 years, I was Paul's wife. For the last 8 years, I was also his caregiver as we lived with Paul's Lewy Body Dementia. And now, I find myself adrift, trying to redefine who I am without him by my side.

Paul left us in the early hours of Monday, August 19th. It was peaceful, they tell me. He simply slipped away, like he was stepping out of a room. Knowing Paul, he probably didn't want to make a fuss.

The pain is indescribable. It's a physical ache, like someone has hollowed out my chest with a dull spoon. But you know what? I wouldn't trade this pain for anything, because it's a testament to the joy Paul brought into my life.

Paul was... everything. Kind doesn't begin to cover it. He was the type of man who would shovel the neighbor's driveway without being asked, who always had a joke ready to lighten the mood, who could fix anything with a bit of duct tape and determination.

Even as the dementia took hold, that essential Paul-ness remained. He might not remember what year it was, but he never forgot to tell me I was beautiful. He could get lost in our own backyard, but he always found his way back to my side, drawn by some invisible thread of love that even Lewy Body couldn't sever.

The last few years were beyond difficult. Harder than anything I've ever faced. There were days when I didn't recognize the man in front of me, days when I wondered how much more either of us could take. But there were also moments of pure, transcendent love that I'll carry with me always.

Like the time Paul, deep in the fog of dementia, suddenly looked at me with clear eyes and said, "Maggie, my love, thank you for dancing with me all these years." Or the day he couldn't remember how to tie his shoes but insisted on helping me plant the garden, because he knew how much I loved fresh tomatoes.

To those of you still in the thick of it: just keep going. That's all. What you're doing matters more than you know. On the days when it feels like too much, remember that love persists, even when memories fade.

And to those who, like me, find themselves on the other side of this journey: it's okay to grieve. It's okay to feel lost. The love you shared, the care you provided, it made a difference. It mattered. It still matters.

Paul may be gone, but the love we shared lives on. In the memories we created, in the lives we touched, in the family we built. And always in me.

So here's to my Paul, the love of my life, my partner in all things. Our dance may have ended, but the music plays on.

Unwavering,

Margaret

Key Advice:

In grief, be gentle with yourself. There's no right way to mourn, no timeline for healing. Honor your loved one by living fully, loving deeply, and finding moments of joy, even in the midst of sorrow.

Words of Encouragement:

To the unsung heroes of love's last chapter: Your devotion paints masterpieces in the twilight of life. In the blur of sleepless nights and endless days, you're crafting a legacy of love that defies the ravages of time and illness. Your patience in repetition, your grace in indignity, your strength in weakness — these are the brushstrokes of your own, one-of-a-kind love story.

When doubt creeps in, remember: every act of care is an act of rebellion against the darkness of disease. You're not just managing symptoms; you're preserving dignity, nurturing connection, and honoring a lifetime of love.

In the aftermath, as you navigate the strange terrain of 'after', know this: The love you've poured out hasn't evaporated. It's soaked into the very fabric of your being, transforming you in ways you may not yet recognize. Your capacity for compassion, your reservoir of strength, your ability to find beauty in the smallest moments — these are the gifts your loved one has left for you. Take hold of that and never forget it.

Chapter 31
Greta Undercover

Synopsis:

- **Caregiver:** Amelia, 43
- **Loved one:** Greta, 76
- **Relationship:** Daughter / Mother
- **Dementia type:** Vascular Dementia
- **Duration of care:** 5 years
- **Living situation:** Greta lives with Amelia
- **Support system:** Amelia, limited external support

Story:

Dear Caregiver,

Seven days on a cruise ship in the middle of the ocean with my 76-year-old mother. She has vascular dementia and refuses to wear her hearing aids. What could possibly go wrong?

I should preface by mentioning that Mom's always been a huge fan of old spy movies. James Bond, Mission: Impossible, you name it. She used to joke that she missed her calling as a secret agent. Her dementia causes her to be quite paranoid at times, and quite imaginative at others. So with that said...

The trip was a mix of frustrating, hilarious, and occasionally heartwarming moments. Mom spent most of the first day convinced we were on some sort of covert operation. She kept whispering to me about "being undercover" whenever a crew member walked by. I tried explaining we were just on vacation, but she'd wink and say, "Of course", as if I was playing my part in maintaining our cover.

The casino, in particular, was a constant source of fascination. All of the flashing lights, buzzers, and bells must have made her feel like she'd stumbled onto a secret base of operations. When we would walk past, she'd casually take a seat outside and "surveil" the scene from afar. She never left that area on her own accord and always required a bit of coaxing before we could move on.

Formal night was... memorable. Mom refused to wear the dress we'd packed, insisting it was "too flashy." I assume this was because it would attract too much attention. After a great deal of compromise and negotiation, she settled on wearing her flannel jammies. Yes. Flannel jammies to formal night. Of course, by this point, I feel like a good portion of the guests and crew knew Mom well enough to understand the situation. There she sat, happy as a clam, enjoying her lobster dinner — in her jammies.

Mom loved watching the sunset from our balcony every evening. For those few minutes, she was deeply at peace, much more like her old self. One night, she even called me by my childhood nickname, *Millie*. It caught me off guard and nearly made me cry.

By the end of the trip, I was exhausted but so grateful for the experience. It wasn't the relaxing vacation I'd imagined, but it gave me some precious moments with Mom that I'll always cherish.

I'm considering booking another trip. Just a short hotel stay this time, nothing too ambitious. Am I crazy for even thinking about it? Maybe. But part of me hopes we might catch another one of those sunset moments.

Thanks for allowing me to share.

Amelia

Key Advice:

Try to find joy in the small moments, and don't be afraid to play along with your loved one's reality sometimes. It can lead to unexpected connections and even a few laughs.

Words of Encouragement:

You're not just a caregiver; you're a co-star in your loved one's story, as crazy as that story might be. And that role, with all its weird challenges and surprises, is absolutely invaluable.

Chapter 32
Frontotemporal Cassanova

Synopsis:

- **Caregiver:** Linda, 61
- **Loved one:** Harold, 81
- **Relationship:** Daughter / Father
- **Dementia type:** Frontotemporal
- **Duration of care:** 3 years
- **Living situation:** Harold lives with Linda
- **Support system:** Linda, her brother Tom, limited external support

Story:

Dear Caregiver,

I never thought I'd be writing about my father's sudden transformation into a geriatric Casanova, but here we are. Life sure has a way of throwing curveballs, doesn't it?

Dad — Harold, to everyone else — is 81 and has frontotemporal dementia. For most of my life, he was the epitome of a proper gentleman. Now? Let's just say he's developed a penchant for making sailors blush.

It started innocently enough. A wink here, a slightly off-color joke there. We brushed it off as Dad just "lightening up" in his old age. But then came The Incident. It occurred at our church's bake sale, of all places.

I should also mention that he has a set of expensive hearing aids that he's supposed to wear everyday, but unless he'd forced to, he'll avoid wearing them — which causes him to speak at an unnaturally high level.

So there's my Dad, surrounded by sweet little old ladies selling pies, and he suddenly decides to loudly share his thoughts on the, ahem, "assets" of the woman running the event. In graphic detail — complete with enthusiastic hand gestures. The collective group of octogenarians instantly turned silent. We may be asked to leave the church.

It's not just words, though. Last week, we were getting Frosties at Wendy's, and Dad decided to discretely pinch the bottom of the woman in line in front of us. I had no idea he did it until the woman whipped around and assailed him. I've never apologized so profusely in my life. The poor woman was understanding once I explained, but I wanted to melt into the floor.

The thing is, when he's not around women, Dad is as docile as a lamb. He'll sit and watch his old black and white TV shows, comment on the weather, reminisce about his days as a teacher. But the moment a woman enters his line of sight? It's like someone flipped a switch, and suddenly we're dealing with a randy teenager with no filter.

My brother tries to help, but he finds the whole situation more amusing than anything. "At least Dad's still got some spark," he'll say, chuckling. Easy for him to laugh — he's not the one having to apologize for him.

I've tried distractions, redirections, even sort of a "swear jar" system. Nothing seems to work. The neurologist says it's not uncommon with his type of dementia, but that doesn't make it any easier to handle.

The worst part? Sometimes, in the middle of one of his... episodes, I'll catch a glimpse of the old Dad. He'll look confused, almost scared, like he knows something's not right but can't figure out what. Those moments break my heart more than any embarrassing comment ever could.

We've had to limit our outings. The local grocery store has become our main adventure, and even that can be a minefield. Last time, Dad loudly commented on the "perky melons" in the produce section. He was talking about actual melons, but the context and his tone made it sound much, much worse. Two women nearby overheard and gave us looks that could curdle milk. I wanted to explain, but how do you even begin that conversation?

So here we are, navigating this bizarre new reality. I've become an expert at scanning rooms for potential targets, steering Dad clear of unsuspecting women, and coming up with creative excuses.

I miss the old Dad. The one who always had a kind word for everyone. But I'm learning to love this new version too, inappropriate comments and all. Because underneath it all, he's still my dad.

So that's my story.

Hanging in there,

Linda

Key Advice:

Remember that the behavior is the disease, not the person. It's okay to laugh sometimes — humor can be a powerful coping mechanism. And always, always have a quick exit strategy planned.

Words of Encouragement:

If your loved one has lost their filter, it's okay to be embarrassed. You're choosing love over convenience, patience over frustration, and dignity over despair. That's no small feat, but you're doing it anyways because you're honoring the person beneath the changes.

Chapter 33
Worthless Siblings

Synopsis:

- **Caregiver:** Rachel, 52
- **Loved one:** Martha, 78
- **Relationship:** Daughter / Mother
- **Dementia type:** Alzheimer's
- **Duration of care:** 4 years
- **Living situation:** Martha lives with Rachel
- **Support system:** Rachel, minimal external support

Story:

You asked for an honest story. Here it is — in all it's shitty glory. Know why? Because my so-called "family" is a bunch of selfish, useless cowards.

Four fucking years I've been taking care of Mom alone. Where are my siblings? Living their perfect little lives. They can't be bothered to be a part of this.

Sarah, my older sister, the big-shot exec? Too busy counting her money to pick up a damn phone. Can't spare five minutes to ask how Mom is. How we are.

Mike? My brother who lives 20 minutes away might as well be on another planet. He's got time for golf, for vacations, for every-fucking-thing except us. Can't even be bothered to sit with her for an hour so I can catch my breath.

You know what kills me? They have the absolute gall to criticize. That she's not eating enough, that she's no getting enough exercise. Well, why don't you come help, you useless shits?

They don't see the sleepless nights. The doctor visits. The endless medications. The accidents. The tears. The confusion. They don't hear Mom crying in the night, forgetting where she is, who she is.

They don't know that I can't remember the last time I had a full night's sleep, a day off, a moment to myself. My life has disappeared into a black hole, and they're too self-absorbed to even notice.

I'm drowning here. Drowning in responsibility, in resentment, in a life I never asked for. And where are they?

Sometimes I fantasize about walking away. Let them deal with it. Let them see what it's like to have your life erased, to become nothing but a caregiver. But I can't. If I did, I truly think Mom would die.

I hate myself for thinking it, but it almost seems like an easy way out. But I'm better than that. I wouldn't do that. Mom deserves better than that and better than what I can manage to give as it is.

I'm not asking for a medal. I'm asking for a fucking phone call. A grocery run. An hour - just one fucking hour - of respite. Is that really too much to ask?

They'll show up at the funeral, I'm sure. All tears and "we'll miss her so much." Miss her? You've been missing her for years, you hypocrites.

I hope they remember this. When they're old, when they need help, I hope they remember every missed call, every declined invitation to help, every criticism thrown from the safety of their uninvolved lives.

Because karma's a bitch. And right now, so am I.

I'm tired. I'm angry. I'm bitter. This isn't who I wanted to be. But this is who I've become.

Sorry for the rage.

Actually, no. I'm not sorry. This is real.

Still fighting.

Rachel

Key Advice:

I'm supposed to offer some pearls of wisdom here, but honestly? I'm too pissed off to play nice. So here's my advice: Don't be a doormat. If your family won't help, stop expecting them to. It's less disappointing that way. And for God's sake, take care of yourself, because no one else will.

Words of Encouragement:

I'm not in the mood to offer warm, fuzzy platitudes. But if you're in the same boat as me, dealing with useless siblings and shouldering this burden alone, here's what I've got:

You're not crazy for being angry. You're not a bad person for resenting this situation. Your feelings are valid, and don't let anyone tell you otherwise. What you're doing is fucking hard, and you're doing it anyway. That takes guts.

To everyone out there screaming silently while smiling for the world: I get it. I'm you. We're in this shitshow together, even if we're apart. And if all you did today was make it through without losing your damn mind, that's enough.

Chapter 34
Sisters in the Shadows

Synopsis:

- **Caregiver:** Nancy, 73
- **Loved one:** Alana, 75
- **Relationship:** Sister / Sister
- **Dementia type:** Lewy Body Dementia
- **Duration of care:** 7 years
- **Living situation:** Alana lives with Nancy
- **Support system:** Nancy and her neighbor, Rachel

Dear Caregiver,

I'm Nancy, 73, caring for my older sister, Alana. She is 75 and has Lewy Body dementia. We've always been close, living just a few streets apart in our hometown of Bend, Oregon. Now, we're closer than ever, but in ways neither of us could have imagined.

About four years ago, Alana began having vivid hallucinations. I'll never forget the fear in her voice when she called me late one night, whispering that there were strangers in her house. I rushed over, heart pounding, only to find her alone, curled-up in a corner of her bedroom.

The diagnosis came soon after that: Lewy Body dementia. The doctor explained it was a progressive brain disorder that would affect her thinking, movement, behavior, and mood. I remember Alana's face when we got the news — a mix of fear and determination. "Well," she said, trying to smile, "at least we're in this together, sis."

And together we've been. I moved Alana in with me and my husband, Bob. He's been a saint through all of this, picking up the slack when I'm overwhelmed and always ready with a cup of tea and a listening ear. Our house has transformed. We've installed grab bars in the bathroom, removed throw rugs to prevent falls, and labeled drawers and cabinets to help Alana navigate on her good days.

The first year was a blur of doctor's appointments, medication adjustments, and learning to navigate this new reality. We've become experts in things we never wanted to know, such as the best incontinence products, how to prevent bedsores, the intricacies of power of attorney and related paperwork.

Alana's symptoms were erratic. Some days she was almost her old self, cracking jokes and reminiscing about our childhood adventures. She'd regale Bob with stories of our mischief-filled youth, like the time we "borrowed" Dad's car for a joyride and ended up stuck in a muddy field. Other days, she'd be lost in a fog of confusion, unable to recognize me or Bob. Those days are the hardest.

The hallucinations have been the most difficult part to deal with. Alana often sees people who aren't there, sometimes friendly figures, other times more sinister. I've learned to validate her experiences without feeding into the delusions. "I know you see them, Alana," I'll say, "but I promise you're safe here with me." Sometimes, she sees our late parents, and those moments are bittersweet. She finds comfort in their presence, even if it's not real.

Sleep has become a precious commodity. Alana's sleep patterns are completely off-kilter. She'll be up at 3 AM, convinced it's time to go to work (she's been retired for 10 years). I've lost count of the nights I've spent sitting with her, gently reminding her where and when she is, until exhaustion finally takes over and she drifts off. The constant vigilance is exhausting, but I'm terrified of what might happen if I sleep too deeply.

There are moments of joy amidst the challenges. Like when we sit on the porch on good days, watching the sun set over the Cascade Mountains, and she'll suddenly remember a detail from our childhood that I'd long forgotten. Or when she has a streak of lucidity and tells me how much she appreciates everything I'm doing. Those moments make it all worthwhile.

We still try to maintain some semblance of normalcy. Every Saturday, weather permitting, we take a short drive to Pilot Butte. Alana always loved the view from up there, and even on her bad days, the familiar landscape seems to calm her. Sometimes, we'll get ice cream afterwards, just like we used to do with our kids when they were little.

But I won't give you the wrong idea — this journey has been incredibly difficult. There are days when I feel like I'm drowning in responsibility, barely keeping my head above water. My own health has taken a hit. The stress and lack of sleep have left me feeling decades older than my 73 years. I've had to cancel my own doctor's appointments more times than I can count because Alana was having a bad day.

Our neighbor, Rachel, has been a godsend. She comes over a few times a week to sit with Alana, giving me a chance to run errands or just take a breather. Those moments of respite are like coming up for air after being underwater for too long. Rachel's kindness reminds me that there's still goodness in the world, even when our days feel dark.

The hardest part is watching my vibrant, intelligent sister slowly slip away. Alana was always the life of the party, quick with a joke and full of energy. She was the one who taught me to stand up for myself, who cheered the loudest at my college graduation, who held my hand through my divorce years ago. Now, there are days when that spark is barely visible. But then she'll say something, or give me a certain look, and I'll see a glimmer of the sister I've known and loved all my life.

I find myself grieving for the future we'll never have. The trips we planned to take in our retirement, the grandchildren we hoped to spoil together. We always talked about taking an Alaskan cruise, but now that dream seems as distant as the stars. But I'm also deeply grateful for this time we have, as challenging as it is. Caring for her has taught me depths of patience and love I never knew I possessed.

Alana and I are writing the final chapter of our story together. It's not the one we would have chosen, but we're facing it the way we've faced everything in life — side by side, hand in hand. In the quiet moments, when the sun is setting and Alana is peaceful, I can almost believe that love is stronger than any disease. And maybe, in its own way, it is.

With love,

Nancy

Key Advice:

Write down funny moments, cherished memories, and even frustrations. It can serve as both an emotional outlet and a precious keepsake of your final journey together. Lastly, don't underestimate the therapeutic power of nature. Even if it's just sitting on the porch or a short drive to a scenic spot, connecting with nature can provide calming moments for both of you.

Words of Encouragement:

To those caring for a sibling with dementia: You're rewriting the script of your relationship in the most profound way. The roles you've known all your life are shifting, but the love remains constant.

Remember, every time you explain a hallucination away, every time you guide them back to bed, you're not just caregiving — you're continuing a lifetime of shared experiences and inside jokes that only siblings can have. It's messy, it's hard, but it's also beautiful in its own bittersweet way.

Chapter 35
Reunited After Decades

Synopsis:

- **Caregiver:** Joseph, 72
- **Loved one:** Valarie, 71
- **Relationship:** Partners
- **Dementia type:** Vascular Dementia
- **Duration of care:** 1.5 years
- **Living situation:** Couple lives together
- **Support system:** None mentioned

Ben Clardy

Dear Caregiver,

Life has a way of surprising us, doesn't it? I'm Joseph, 72 years old, and I never imagined I'd be caring for my once-fiancée and now partner of five years, as she battles vascular dementia. But here we are in Kissimmee, Florida, writing an unexpected chapter in our love story.

Valarie and I first met in our senior year of college in Boston. It was 1973, and we were two starry-eyed kids with big dreams. I was studying engineering, and Valarie was pursuing her passion for art history. We fell hard and fast, getting engaged just before graduation. We had it all planned out. I'd work as an engineer, she'd teach art, and we'd build our life together.

But life had other plans. I got an offer for a prestigious internship in California, and Valarie was accepted into a graduate program in New York. We tried long-distance for a while, but eventually, the strain became too much. With heavy hearts, we decided to part ways, promising to remain friends but losing touch as the years went by.

For decades, we lived separate lives. I built a career in Silicon Valley, got married, had two kids, and eventually divorced. Valarie, I later learned, had a successful career curating for museums across Europe, never marrying but living a full life with art and lots of travel.

Then, seven years ago, fate intervened. We both attended a college reunion in Boston. The moment I saw her across the room, it was like no time had passed. Her laugh was just as infectious, her eyes just as bright. We spent the whole evening catching up, and by the end of the night, we both knew we'd been given a second chance.

We started dating long-distance again, me in California and Valarie in London. After two years of frequent flyer miles and long video calls, we decided to retire and start our new life together. We chose Kissimmee, Florida — close enough to the theme parks to feel the magic, but far enough to enjoy peace and quiet.

For three years, life was everything we'd dreamed of back in college. We'd explore local art galleries, arguing playfully about brushstrokes and color theory. We'd take long walks around Lake Tohopekaliga, planning trips to the places Valarie had lived in Europe. We even started volunteering at Give Kids The World Village, a nonprofit resort for children with critical illnesses. Valarie would lead art workshops for the kids, her face lighting up as she helped them create masterpieces.

Things were beyond great — but things also rarely stay the same for long. I started noticing changes in Valarie. She'd forget the names of artists she'd studied for years. She'd get lost on our walks around the lake. Sometimes, she'd stare at a blank canvas for hours, unable to start a painting. At first, we both dismissed it as normal aging, but deep down, I was becoming more concerned.

The diagnosis came a year and a half ago: vascular dementia. The neurologist explained how reduced blood flow to Valarie's brain was causing cognitive decline. I felt like the world stopped spinning. Valarie, ever the optimist, squeezed my hand and said, "Well, Joseph, looks like we'll have to make the most of the time we have left."

Since then, our golden years have taken a different shape than we'd planned. Instead of European adventures and lazy days by the lake, we're navigating a maze of doctor's appointments, medication schedules, and cognitive exercises. I've become an expert in things I never thought I'd need to know, like how to prevent falls, how to manage mood swings, and even how to gently remind Valarie of who I am on her worst days.

The hardest part is watching my brilliant, vibrant Valarie struggle with tasks that used to bring her so much joy. The woman who could once discuss the nuances of Renaissance art for hours now has trouble remembering the names of colors. The adventurer who fearlessly explored the streets of Paris and Rome now gets anxious about leaving our house.

But it's not all darkness. We still have our moments of light and laughter. Like when Valarie insists on wearing her favorite beret to bed because she's convinced it helps her "think more French." Or when we sit on the porch during Florida's spectacular thunderstorms, and she'll suddenly recite a poem she learned in college, the words flowing as if no time has passed.

Our volunteer work has taken on new meaning. On Valarie's good days, we still go to Give Kids The World Village. She can't lead workshops anymore, but she sits with the children, encouraging them as they create. The kids don't mind if she sometimes mixes up their names or repeats herself. They just love her gentle guidance and kind smile. Seeing her connect with the children, art bridging the gaps in her memory, is a beautiful reminder of the woman I've always loved.

There are challenges, of course. Valarie's sleep patterns are erratic, and she often gets confused and agitated in the evenings — a symptom I've learned is common and is called "sundowning." I've learned to be patient, to validate her feelings even when I don't understand them. I've also learned to ask for help when I need it. Our neighbors have been incredibly supportive, and I've joined a local caregiver support group that's been very helpful and encouraging.

Some days are harder than others. There are times when Valarie doesn't recognize me, and that cuts deep. But then she'll look at me with sudden clarity and say, "Joseph, my love," and I know that our connection still runs deep.

There are certainly many moments when I feel overwhelmed, when the weight of responsibility feels crushing. I've had to learn to take care of myself too, stealing moments for a phone call with my daughter or even a nap when I get the chance. It's a balancing act, but one I'm committed to mastering.

In our younger days, Valarie was always the free spirit, the one who encouraged me to see the beauty in the world. Now, our roles have reversed in many ways. But in caring for her, I feel like I'm finally able to return the gift she's given me throughout our relationship.

Every time I help Valarie navigate a confused moment or remind her of a cherished memory, I'm not just being a caregiver, I'm honoring the promises we made to each other, both in our youth and in our reunion. It's a different kind of love story now, but no less beautiful for its challenges.

To anyone out there caring for a partner with dementia, especially if you've found love later in life: it's a special kind of challenge, isn't it? We're navigating the joy of rekindled love alongside the heartbreak of cognitive decline. It's hard, but it's also a profound expression of love.

Valarie and I may not be creating new memories the way we once did, but we're still on this journey together. And really, isn't that what love is all about? Being there for each other, come what may.

As the sun sets over Lake Tohopekaliga, casting a golden glow on our little corner of Kissimmee, I'm grateful for this unexpected chapter in our love story. It may not be the retirement we planned, but it's ours. We face each day the same way we faced our reunion — with open hearts, ready for whatever life brings our way.

A fellow traveler on this journey,

Joseph

Key Advice:

Embrace routine, but stay flexible. Don't underestimate the therapeutic power of art and creativity. Even if your loved one can no longer create as they once did, engaging in simple artistic activities can be soothing and spark moments of connection. Lastly, create a memory book together while you still can. Fill it with photos, ticket stubs, and mementos from your past. It can serve as a powerful tool for reminiscence therapy and a treasure trove of memories for both of you.

Words of Encouragement:

To those who have found love again later in life, only to face the challenge of dementia: Remember that your love story isn't ending; it's evolving. Every act of care is a testament to the depth of your connection. Keep holding on to those moments of connection, no matter how fleeting. They are the glimmers of gold in this chapter of your story.

Chapter 36

The Common Thread

As we draw near the conclusion of this book, we're left with a tapestry of experiences, each thread a story of love, struggle, and resilience.

What can we learn collectively from all of these diverse stories?

My first observation is a simple one:

Caregiving is hard as hell.

The sleepless nights, the constant worry, the physical and emotional toll — it's a journey that pushes human endurance to its limits. It's a role that no one chooses, but one that many of us find ourselves thrust into, often without warning or preparation.

Yet, paradoxically, it's also one of the deepest, if not the deepest, expressions of human connection I've ever encountered. In these stories, we've witnessed love that transcends the boundaries of what we typically consider possible. We've seen spouses, children, friends, and even strangers step up to provide care that is nothing short of heroic in its dedication and selflessness.

One of the cruelest aspects of caregiving, particularly for those dealing with degenerative conditions like dementia, is the difficulty in seeing how your care is helping while you're providing it. You pour your heart and soul into caring for someone, only to watch them continue to decline. It's a twisted kind of heartbreak, a unique form of grief that caregivers carry with them day in and day out.

But here's what else I've learned from these stories:

Dear Caregiver

It's worth it.

It's worth it in ways that might not be immediately apparent. It's worth it in the moments of connection, fleeting though they may be. It's worth it in the dignity preserved, in the comfort provided, in the love expressed through acts of service. It's worth it because it changes us, the caregivers, in profound and often unexpected ways.

These stories have shown us that caregiving is a crucible, painfully burning away our preconceptions about love, about human resilience, about what really matters in life. It reveals strengths we never knew we had, teaches us patience we never thought possible, and, yes — pushes us to limits we never desired to reach.

To those of you in the trenches of caregiving right now: *what you're doing matters*. It matters more than you can possibly know in the moment — but trust the words of the many countless caregivers who have been where you stand now. The care you provide, even on the days when it feels futile, is creating ripples of love and compassion that extend far beyond your immediate situation.

To those who have been through this journey and are now looking back: *your experience has value*. Your story, with all its pain and triumph, all its mundane details and profound revelations, has the power to light the way for others.

And to those who haven't yet experienced caregiving but have read these stories: *remember them*. Let them open your heart to the struggles and triumphs of the caregivers around you. Let them prepare you for the day when you might be called upon to provide care.

In the end, what these stories teach us is this:

Caregiving is a profound expression of our shared humanity. It's a reminder that we are all connected, all vulnerable, and all in need of compassion. It's a challenging journey, yes, but one that has the power to transform us, to deepen our capacity for love, and to show us what really matters most in life.

Chapter 37
Thank You

To all the brave caregivers who shared their stories,

Words cannot fully express my gratitude for your willingness to open your hearts and lives to the readers of this book. Your raw, honest accounts of the joys and struggles of caregiving will touch countless lives.

Each of you took the time to revisit moments of profound challenge, heartbreak, and unexpected beauty. You shared the sleepless nights, the small victories, the painful losses, and the moments of connection that define the caregiving journey — and all for the benefit of your fellow caregivers.

To those who shared moments of humor amidst the challenges — like impromptu dance parties, misplaced items in odd locations, and creative problem-solving — thank you for reminding us all of the healing power of laughter. Your ability to find light in dark moments is genuinely inspiring.

To those who bared their souls and shared their darkest moments — the feelings of resentment, exhaustion, and hopelessness — your honesty will help others feel less alone in their struggles. Your courage in facing these difficult emotions head-on is commendable.

To those who offered practical advice born from years of experience — your wisdom will be a lifeline to those just beginning this journey. The tips, tricks, and hard-won insights you've shared will make a real difference in the lives of your fellow caregivers.

Dear Caregiver

And to those who shared stories of loss and grief — thank you for allowing us to witness the depth of your love and the power of your dedication. Your reflections on life after caregiving will help prepare and comfort others facing similar transitions.

Your stories collectively paint a picture of caregiving that is complex, challenging, and ultimately deeply meaningful. You've shown that while this path is often difficult, it is also rich with opportunities for growth, connection, and profound expressions of love.

This book would not exist without your willingness to be vulnerable and share your experiences. Your words will reach people in their moments of greatest need, offering comfort, guidance, and hope.

From the bottom of my heart, thank you for trusting me with your stories. Your courage and compassion will touch more lives than you can imagine.

With deepest gratitude,

Ben Clardy

Chapter 38
Before You Go

Dear Reader,

I hope these experiences have touched you, offered comfort, or provided insights for your own journey.

Now that you've absorbed these powerful narratives, I have a small but important request:

Please consider leaving your review for this book.

There are many people in the world who have recently found themselves thrust into the role of caregiving, and sharing your thoughts can help them find this book. Your review doesn't need to be long or eloquent - just honest.

By taking a few moments to share your perspective, you're extending the impact of these stories beyond these pages, potentially reaching someone at their moment of greatest need.

Thank you for considering this request.

With heartfelt appreciation,

Ben Clardy

www.ingramcontent.com/pod-product-compliance
Lightning Source LLC
Chambersburg PA
CBHW071710120626
46550CB00001B/168